WHEATON PUBLIC LIBRARY
796.35764 FLE
Fleming, Gordon H.,   1984
The dizziest season :the Gashouse Gang c

3 5143 00111092 8

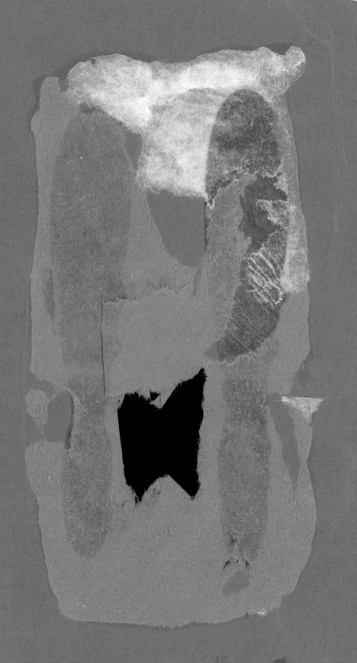

··· THE ···
DIZZIEST SEASON

BY THE SAME AUTHOR

George Alfred and the Victorian Sensation Novel

Rossetti and the Pre-Raphaelite Brotherhood

That Ne'er Shall Meet Again:
Rossetti, Millais, Hunt

The Young Whistler.

The Unforgettable Season

THE DIZZIEST SEASON

The Gashouse Gang Chases the Pennant

G. H. FLEMING

WILLIAM MORROW AND COMPANY, INC.

NEW YORK   1984

All entries in this book come from newspapers of 1933 and 1934. In no instance did I change the wording of a passage, but sometimes, for the sake of readability, I deleted words, phrases, and sentences that I regarded as irrelevant, nonessential, or repetitious. G.H.F.

Copyright © 1984 by G.H. Fleming

Grateful acknowledgment is made for permission to reprint portions of the works of the following:

John Kieran: © 1934 The New York Times. Reprinted by permission.
Damon Runyon: © 1962 Mary Runyon McCann and Damon Runyon, Jr., as children of the author
Paul Gallico: Reprinted by permission: Tribune Company Syndicate, Inc.
Grantland Rice: © 1934 North American Newspaper Alliance, Inc.

All rights reserved. No part of this book may be reproduced or utilized in any form or by any means, electronic or mechanical, including photocopying, recording or by any information storage and retrieval system, without permission in writing from the Publisher. Inquiries should be addressed to William Morrow and Company, Inc., 105 Madison Avenue, New York, N.Y. 10016.

Library of Congress Catalog Card Number: 84-60213

ISBN: 0-688-03097-1

Printed in the United States of America

First Edition

1 2 3 4 5 6 7 8 9 10

BOOK DESIGN BY ANN GOLD

FOR
Gus Flattmann, Jay Gauthreaux, Jim La Rocca,
Arthur Schott, and Tony Tortorich,
with thanks for many provocative and
stimulating comments on baseball.

∘ *Preface* ∘

As years go, 1934 was not exactly dull—the Great Depression—Hitler—the New Deal—Bruno Hauptmann's indictment in the Lindbergh case—the killing of John Dillinger—the sinking of the *Morro Castle*—the San Francisco general strike—Max Baer's knockout of Primo Carnera—the repeal of Prohibition.

And 1934 was the year of the most colorful team in the history of American sports, the baseball Cardinals of St. Louis. (They came to be known as "The Gashouse Gang," an ex post facto term coined in 1935 by Tom Meany, of the New York *World-Telegram*.)

The Cardinals of 1934 fascinated almost everyone with even a remote interest in baseball. Naturally they provided a field day for the sportswriters. Here, for example, is how they appeared to a prominent New York writer, Frank Graham of the *Sun:*

> They may not be the greatest team that ever played—these Cardinals—although surely they are one of the best—but whether you are for them or not they capture your imagination and inspire your respect. They don't look like a major league ball club—or as major league ball clubs are supposed to look in this era of the well-dressed athlete. Their uniforms are stained and dirty and patched and ill fitting. They don't shave before a game, and most of them chew tobacco. They have thick necks and knotty muscles, and they spit out of the sides of their mouths and rub the backs of their hands across their mouths and then wipe the backs of their hands across their shirt fronts. They fight among themselves and use quaint and picturesque oaths. They are not afraid of anybody—enemy ball players, fans, umpires, club owners, league officials, not even the august [*baseball commissioner*] Judge Landis himself. They don't make much money, and they work hard for it. They will risk arms, legs, and necks—their own or the other fellow's—to get it. But they also have a lot of fun playing baseball.

The star of stars among these Cardinals of 1934 was Jay Hanna "Dizzy" Dean, who was second only to Babe Ruth on the roster of baseball's colorful personalities. In 1934, Dean had his best season, and also his goofiest season, prompting Bill Corum, sports editor of the New York *Evening Journal,* to observe, late in the year, "This has been the dizziest season in twenty years . . . and through it all Dizzy Dean has held his place at the top." But neither in athletic talent nor in craziness were the Cardinals a one-man team. Dizzy Dean was surrounded by an able supporting cast: his brother Paul, Pepper Martin, Joe "Ducky" Medwick, Lippy Leo Durocher, Ripper Collins, Tex Carleton, Wild Bill Hallahan, and the great second baseman who was known everywhere as "the Fordham Flash," Frank Francis Frisch, the team's manager.

They were a good team, a fun team, a colorful team, the Cardinals of 1934, and they were a principal participant in one of the most exciting of all baseball seasons. As Martin J. Haley, of the St. Louis *Globe-Democrat,* wrote immediately after the last regular season game, "This year's race was the hottest right down to the wire since 1908."

The National League season of 1934 was indeed strikingly similar to that of 1908. In both years the pennant was won on the last day of the season. In both years the Giants were an involved party, battling against the Cubs and Pirates in 1908 and against the Cardinals in 1934. In both years a contending team was managed by a "McGraw." In 1908, it was the real McGraw, John J. himself, of the Giants. In 1934, it was "John McGraw, Jr.," the name often given to Frankie Frisch, one of McGraw's star players and his best pupil. Finally, in both years a Giant first baseman committed a notorious, never-to-be-forgotten blunder, one occurring on the field late in the season, the other off the field before the beginning of spring training.

My interest in these two years is more than that of a fan.

A while back I put together a book entitled *The Unforgettable Season,* which is a reconstruction of the National League pennant race of 1908. In the preface to that book I noted that the story would come not from me but from those who had seen and heard all that had happened, as related in contemporary newspapers. In the present volume I have retained the modus operandi of my earlier book. I have read all of the relevant newspapers, those published in 1934 in National League cities—St. Louis, Boston, Brooklyn, Chicago, Cincinnati, New York, Philadelphia, and Pittsburgh—and I have selected and edited those materials which in my opinion provide the best first-hand, eye-witness account of another unforgettable season.

Linking the two volumes are several writers who were active in both years: John E. Wray, of the *St. Louis Post-Dispatch*; Jack Ryder, of the Cincinatti *Enquirer*; Irving Vaughan of the Chicago *Tribune*; and Joe Vila, of *The Sporting News* and the New York *Sun*. They are now joined by a new generation of journalists who became part of what has been called the Golden Age of Sportswriting: Grantland Rice, Paul Gallico, Damon Runyon, Westbrook Pegler, John Lardner, Dan Parker, Dan Daniel, Frank Graham, John Kieran, Joe Williams, Bill Corum, Tom Meany, Jimmy Powers, John Drebinger, and others. All of them will be encountered in this book, along with the St. Louis regulars, men like Sid Keener and J. Roy Stockton.

The Cardinals of 1934 had fun playing baseball. And the nation, in the midst of the century's worst depression, had fun watching and reading about them. Now, retrospectively, let us share some of their fun.

Once again it is time to call out, "Play ball!"

° *Acknowledgments* °

Katy Feeney was most gracious in providing me with the opportunity to examine various materials in the offices of the National League in New York. The staff members of the newspaper division of the New York Public Library and librarians at the Brooklyn Public Library were accommodating and courteous. James L. Toomey, vice-president and director of public relations for the St. Louis Cardinals, patiently answered numerous questions. Ned Colletti, assistant director of public relations for the Chicago Cubs, and Jim Ferguson, publicity director for the Cincinnati Reds, promptly answered letters of inquiry. The noted baseball historian Arthur Schott never failed when I needed him. Evelyn Chandler and Gregory Spano, interlibrary loan librarian and microfilm librarian at the University of New Orleans, were consistently helpful. My extraordinarily efficient research assistant, Paula Caruso, helped me almost every single day that I worked on this book. To all of these persons I extend thanks.

THE ST. LOUIS CARDINALS OF 1934

CATCHERS

	Birth Date	B	T	Pos.	G	AB	R	H	HR	RBI	BA
Davis (Spud)	12-20-04	R	R	C	107	347	45	104	9	65	.300
DeLancey (Bill)	11-28-11	R	L	C	93	253	41	80	13	40	.316
Healey (Francis)	6-29-10	R	R	C	15	13	1	4	0	1	.308

FIELDERS

	Birth Date	B	T	Pos.	G	AB	R	H	HR	RBI	BA
Collins (Ripper)	3-30-04	B	L	1B	154	600	116	200	35	128	.333
Crawford (Pat)	1-28-02	L	R	IF	61	70	3	19	0	16	.271
Durocher (Leo)	7-27-05	R	R	SS	146	500	62	130	3	70	.260
Frisch (Frankie)	9-9-98	B	R	2B	140	550	74	168	3	75	.305
Fullis (Chick)	2-27-04	R	R	OF	97	301	29	75	0	38	.249
Martin (Pepper)	2-29-04	R	R	3B	110	454	76	131	5	49	.289
Medwick (Joe)	11-24-11	R	R	OF	149	620	110	198	18	106	.319
Orsatti (Ernie)	9-8-03	L	L	OF	105	337	39	101	0	31	.300
Rothrock (Jack)	3-13-05	B	R	OF	154	647	106	184	11	72	.284
Whitehead (Burgess)	6-29-10	R	R	IF	100	332	55	92	1	24	.277

PITCHERS

	Birth Date	T	G	IP	SO	BB	W	L	ERA
Carleton (Tex)	8-19-06	R	40	241	103	52	16	11	4.26
J. Dean (Dizzy)	1-16-11	R	50	312	195	75	30	7	2.66
P. Dean (Paul)	8-14-13	R	39	233	150	52	19	11	3.43
Haines (Jesse)	7-22-93	R	37	90	17	19	4	4	3.50
Hallahan (Bill)	8-4-02	L	32	163	70	66	8	12	4.26
Mooney (Jim)	9-4-06	L	32	82	27	49	2	4	5.47
Vance (Dazzy)	3-4-91	R	25	77	42	25	1	3	4.56
Walker (Bill)	10-7-03	L	24	153	76	66	12	4	3.12

1933

∘ *Tuesday, October 10* ∘

[*Three days earlier, on October 7, the New York Giants had defeated the Washington Senators, 4–3, to win the World Series four games to one.*]
Congratulations to the new World Champions—the Giants! Rated by the experts as a hopeless contender, this amazing team fought through one of the hardest National League races in years, and, again the underdog, went on to win the World Series.

It takes healthy nerves to win day after day. It means something when you discover that 21 out of 23 Giants smoke Camel cigarettes.

Carl Hubbell says, "I can't risk getting ruffled nerves, so I smoke Camels."

Mel Ott says, "Jumpy nerves and home runs don't go together, so I stick to Camels." [*In the World Series of 1933, Hubbell was the only pitcher to win two games, and Ott was the only player to hit two home runs.*]

From a newspaper advertisement

∘ *Saturday, November 4* ∘

"Dizzy" Dean's culinary efforts at the *Globe-Democrat* Cooking School at the Washington University Field House last night attracted 9,500 spectators and brought them to their feet. "Just separate those eggs, Dizzy," said Miss Jessie DeBoth, the teacher.

"Dizzy" slowly and precisely went to work. Then he twirled one in his famous right, and let it go into the gallery. And another and another. The eggs proved to be rubber and carried the house.

St. Louis *Globe-Democrat*

○ *Monday, November 6* ○

It is reported that Dizzy Dean signed a contract calling for a salary of $12,000. That's a lot of scratch, but he's worth every penny of it. Dizzy puts in the cash customers. [*As later entries make clear, Dean's salary, in fact, would be considerably less than $12,000.*]

Sid Keener, St. Louis *Star-Times*

○ *Tuesday, November 7* ○

Whether or not Sunday baseball shall be legal in Pennsylvania will be decided at today's election.

The Keystone State's three big league clubs are required to be idle at home on Sundays while all other teams are free to play. No club has been harder hit by blue laws than the Pirates, who have had to make numerous one-day jumps to Brooklyn, Chicago, and Cincinnati for Sunday games. If such contests become legal in Pennsylvania, schedule-makers can eliminate these trips, costing many thousands of dollars, and this will be welcomed by club owners in these days of depression.

Edward F. Balinger, Pittsburgh *Post-Gazette*

○ *Wednesday, November 8* ○

Philadelphia will have baseball and football on Sunday afternoons in the future.

In the first referendum on the Sabbath Observance law, which has stood since 1794, Sunday sports advocates carried this city by an overwhelming majority, 370,858 to 57,740. Voters in Pittsburgh and other populous centers throughout the state also authorized local officials to license Sunday games. [*The act provided that baseball and football might be played between two and six P.M. on Sundays. Other states with Sunday restrictions were Massachusetts and New York. In Boston games could be played between two o'clock and six-thirty. In New York and Brooklyn, games could be played until darkness if necessary, but could not begin until two o'clock.*]

Philadelphia *Evening Bulletin*

◦ *Thursday, November 9* ◦

John A. Heydler, president of the National League, hailed the victory for Sunday baseball in Philadelphia and Pittsburgh.

"It will assure an equalized schedule for the first time in the 59-year history of the league," declared Heydler.

Philadelphia *Public Ledger*

◦ *Tuesday, November 14* ◦

Kenesaw Mountain Landis, commissioner of baseball, believes nothing is wrong with the game except "depression."

"Steel, factories, railroads, newspapers, agriculture, baseball—we rode down together, and we'll ride back together," he said today.

"A man can't go to a baseball game when he hasn't any money," Landis went on. "He won't have money as long as he doesn't have a job. The American people love baseball. Many of them now peer over the fence or through it, and they will return as paying customers as soon as they have money."

St. Louis *Globe-Democrat*

◦ *Thursday, November 16* ◦

Only a short time ago "Dizzy" Dean came from Houston as a freshman to take a big league baseball course on the Cardinals' bench. [*In 1930, Dean was with the Cardinals briefly and pitched in one game. After spending the 1931 season with Houston, in the Texas League, he became a permanent member of the St. Louis pitching staff in 1932.*]

Today he's a full professor in Ray Doan's baseball college at Hot Springs, a member of the 1934 faculty. [*Doan, who had never been a major league player, operated a school in Hot Springs, Arkansas, for boys and young men who wished to enter professional baseball.*]

Prof. Dean will no doubt lecture on pitching. But perhaps another aspect of the national game which Dizzy might even more consistently present is the spirit which players put into their efforts.

At times Dizzy's antics have not commended themselves to fans. But two particulars in which he has excelled and won over the fans are willingness to work and intense earnestness while playing.

These are virtues all too frequently absent from the professional baseball player's mind. Wrapped up in himself, many a player eases up on the diamond, but Dean always does his best, intensely interested in winning.

If the rising young player could learn to "shoot the works" in every game, to put heart as well as hands and legs into the game, it might salvage many a baseball investment. And none is better fitted to set laggards an example than Prof. Dean himself.

John E. Wray, *St. Louis Post-Dispatch*

∘ *Sunday, November 19* ∘

Baseball men expect to hear long-winded arguments on the question of broadcasting when major league club owners meet in Chicago next month.

Opponents of broadcasting will ask the others to consider banning the radio as an experiment in the campaign for bigger crowds and less red ink on the ledgers.

Last year the opponents tried vigorously to get the leagues to ban the radio, but several clubs, notably the Chicago Cubs, threatened to broadcast in any event, and the other clubs felt they were forced to continue broadcasting in self-defense.

J. Roy Stockton, *St. Louis Post-Dispatch*

∘ *Friday, December 1* ∘

The All-Star game, played for the first time last summer in Chicago, was a tremendous success from every angle. It is obvious that the contest should be an annual feature. Its benefits to the game are so manifest that to turn a blind eye and a deaf ear to them would be incredible stupidity. And yet the retention of this remarkable impetus to baseball interest is in serious doubt!

The American League is lukewarm about an All-Star game. In the National League there is strong opposition. Why? Because there is no financial gain in it for the major leagues!

The profits go to charity. In the Chicago game they went to an organization which cares for indigent ball players. It is a disgrace that the major leagues should have to be urged to stage a publicity benefit for themselves, which also would help old, broken-down members of the diamond fraternity.

Dan Daniel, New York *World-Telegram*

∘ *Wednesday, December 6* ∘

Now that liquor is legal again, there may be a fresh crop of such colorful characters as Rube Waddell, the outstanding refreshment seeker of the prewar era. It would do the magnates no harm at the box office to have one or two stout elbow benders on the pay roll. Babe Ruth was never so popular as in the period before his salvation, when he used to put the city to bed with great regularity. [*The Eighteenth Amendment, prohibiting the consumption of alcoholic beverages, had just been repealed.*]

John Lardner, *New York Post*

∘ *Thursday, December 7* ∘

Somebody has started agitation for baseball to come under the NRA. [*The National Recovery Act (NRA) was part of the Roosevelt administration's New Deal program for dealing with the Depression. Businesses that came under the NRA had to conform to certain standards of wages and working conditions and were permitted to display the blue eagle NRA insignia on their place of business, on stationery, and on advertisements.*]

It is doubtful whether any benefit would accrue by having baseball submit a code [*to bring it under the jurisdiction of the NRA*]. No sweatshop conditions exist in the game, nor is it likely that any minimum wage requirement is violated.

True, no collective bargaining is provided for, but there is no way in which a uniform scale could be put into effect. The stars would resent any effort to put their pay on a common level with that of recruits; while the latter usually are hopeful of some day drawing as much as the stars.

Most men in baseball support the NRA, for they realize that provisions for more pay and leisure are certain to redound to the benefit of the game. But the game's leaders do not see how their submission of a code would help matters, except as a patriotic gesture.

The Sporting News

○ *Thursday, December 14* ○

Chicago—the battle of American and National League stars will become an annual feature, the club owners have decided. The 1934 game will probably be played in New York.

St. Louis *Globe-Democrat*

○ *Friday, December 15* ○

Chicago (AP)—The major leagues voted to adopt a uniform ball, livelier than the one used during the past few years in the National League and patterned along the specifications of the American League sphere. This decision was made by club owners of both leagues in their joint meeting.

Paul Mickelson, St. Louis *Globe-Democrat*

National Leaguers have finally surrendered. They have come out for inflation—of batting averages, to be accomplished by a return of the lively ball.

The new deal baseball would act like the New Deal dollar is supposed to—it would stimulate business. The "business" would be the manufacture of more and better base hits.

It is a theory that a lively ball would make all clubs look better. Weaker hitting clubs would increase the power of their entire team, and the discrepancy between teams which own the few super hitters and clubs which cannot afford to buy super pitchers to stop them would be reduced.

It is the prevailing belief that the public worships at the shrine of the Big Wallop and the High Batting Average. As regards the Knot Hole Gang attendance and the free ladies' day patronage, this is true. With many of these the climax of a game is not a steal of home but a knock over the wall. Whether the lively ball or the batter's prowess accomplishes this doesn't concern them. But the old "die hard" boys who like to see a run EARNED will never be reconciled to seeing a tally gained by intelligence and planning offset by a rubber-cored wallop over the roofs.

John E. Wray, *St. Louis Post-Dispatch*

◦ *Tuesday, December 19* ◦

Frank Francis Frisch, leader of the Cardinals, has started a personally conducted good will campaign among the athletes who will carry the St. Louis banner under his guidance.

Frank's first official visit was to Rochester, N.Y., hometown of James "Ripper" Collins, the Redbird first baseman. Frank spent the day with the "Ripper," attended a banquet at which Collins was guest of honor, and spoke a few kind words about Jim's value to the Cardinals.

Frank will contact other players and is confident that when the race starts he will have a squad of happy ball players, with a common purpose—to win the pennant.

It is no secret that there was considerable friction on the club last year, before and after Frisch was appointed to succeed Charles E. Street as manager, and the man on the street will tell you that the big question hangs on Frisch's ability to whip or cajole the Redbirds into a fighting unit with the necessary esprit de corps.

[*On July 24, 1933, Charles "Gabby" Street was discharged as the Cardinal manager and replaced by the team's thirty-four-year-old second baseman, Frisch. Some players were unhappy about the departure of the easygoing Street and did not react favorably to Frisch's strictness, and there were widespread reports of dissension on the team.*]

J. Roy Stockton, *St. Louis Post-Dispatch*

° Sunday, December 24 °

St. Louis (UP)—Dizzy Dean continues as an individual even in the Christ-mas season, sending two cards of greeting instead of one. One shows himself holding the medal he got for fanning 17 batsmen in one game last season; the other shows himself doing the trick. [*Dean struck out seventeen Cubs on July 30, 1933, in St. Louis.*]

Chicago *Tribune*

° Tuesday, December 26 °

Major league ball players are due for a sad awakening when they receive their 1934 contracts. Drastic salary reductions are on the way.

John J. McGraw [*who had retired as manager of the New York Giants in May 1932*] spoke on the subject last week: "Salaries must come down. The business is getting out of hand—owners are losing too much money. The highest salary for one of baseball's greatest pitchers, Christy Mathewson, was $10,000."

One of the game's most brilliant shortstops, Bobby Wallace, did not go above $6,500. Yet two years ago Ralph Kress spoofed at the Browns when they offered him $8,000, and Frankie Frisch moaned when the Cardinals sliced him from $20,000 to $18,500 in 1932.

Unless there is a sharp increase in patronage, most big leaguers will be paid about $7,500. That may be a comedown, but it is higher than was paid many of the stars years ago.

Sid Keener, St. Louis *Star-Times*

There appears to be a misconception among fans as to the rights of a player with ten years of service in the majors. Many think that when a player has completed ten seasons he automatically is entitled to free agency, should he demand it. Such is not the case.

This is the rule governing the situation: "The contract of a player who has been in the major leagues for ten complete seasons shall not be as-signed except to another major league club, without his consent."

This means that a player cannot be sent to the minors without his con-sent. The ten-year player does not become a free agent if he is sent to another major league club. But if he does not desire to go to the minors and no major league club claims him, the ten-year man must be given his unconditional release.

As long as he is retained in the majors, however, the ten-year player has no more privileges than any other and is under the control of the club by which he is reserved.

The Sporting News

1934

∘ *Thursday, January 4* ∘

Sportsman's Park, home of the Browns and Cardinals, continues to operate without a public address system. When the gates are opened for the 1934 season, I hope that amplifiers will have been installed.

It is very bush-league nowadays to have an announcer strut around the park in a futile attempt to inform fans of the numerous changes through an old battered megaphone.

The game opens and Announcer Jim Kelley makes his appearance. "B-a-t-t-r-e-e-z-e fer t-u-h-d-a-y-'s g-a-m-e!!" shouts Kelley. After he has completed his task he returns to his stool close to the grandstand screen. He remains at that point unless a substitute batter or runner, or relief pitcher, makes his appearance. Then Kelley swings into action. However, often the change has been made and play is resumed before Mr. Announcer gains contact with bleacher patrons. [*Jim Kelley and his megaphone were a regular feature at Sportsman's Park from 1926 until 1936.*]

The loud speaker is no longer an experiment. It is a necessity at sports events, including major league baseball games. [*An electronic public address system was installed in Sportsman's Park in 1936, when Jim Kelley and his megaphone were succeeded by George Carson and a microphone.*]

Sid Keener, St. Louis *Star-Times*

∘ *Saturday, January 13* ∘

At 10:30 yesterday morning, Babe Ruth, a cigar in his mouth and cap in his hand, entered the office of his employer, Colonel Jacob Ruppert, in the Brewery on Third Avenue, to discuss his salary.

At 10:36 Ruth, the same cigar in his mouth and his cap on his head, was on his way out. Ruth had accepted terms. A record had been established. The salary discussion, which usually requires a month or more, was over in six minutes.

The conversation between them went something like this:

"Well, Babe," said the colonel, "what do you want?"

"Well, colonel," replied the Babe, "what do you say?"

"Twenty thousand dollars," snapped the colonel.

"No," said the Babe. "I couldn't sign for that."

"Well," said the colonel rapidly, "what do you want?"

"I'd like to get $35,000," said the Babe.

"Will you sign for $35,000?" asked the colonel.

"Yes," said the Babe.

"All right," said the colonel, "I'll give you $35,000."

And it was done.

By offering a comparatively small sum, $20,000, Ruppert made the Babe's demand seem large. The Babe slipped into the trap. [*Although Babe Ruth in fact had a business agent, Christie Walsh, who managed his financial affairs, no one, not even Ruth, was represented by an agent during the actual salary negotiations, which were carried out by the players and owners themselves.*]

Ruth will take a cut of $17,000. It is startling to think of a salary that can be cut $17,000 and still be the largest in a profession. It is even more impressive when one knows that the Babe's salary has been cut $45,000 in the last three years.

Rud Rennie, New York *Herald-Tribune*

∘ *Wednesday, January 17* ∘

New York (AP)—The nicely calculated maneuver of the New York Yankees in signing Babe Ruth early at a greatly reduced salary paves the way for club owners to effect further pay roll retrenchment.

Colonel Ruppert took a load off the minds of his associates. In past years the magnates' difficulties with star performers have never been made easier by the Babe's prolonged arguments in the realm of high finance.

At least eight major league clubs plan a general or partial reduction of salaries for the third straight year. It is estimated that big league pay rolls have been trimmed 25 percent in the last two years, and economy is still the watchword.

It now appears that only these nine players, including four player-managers, will be in the $20,000 class:

Babe Ruth, Yankees, $35,000
Bill Terry, Giants, $30,000
Al Simmons, White Sox, $27,500

Lou Gehrig, Yankees, $23,000
Chuck Klein, Cubs, $22,000
Mickey Cochrane, Tigers, $20,000
Joe Cronin, Senators, $20,000
Jimmie Foxx, Athletics, $20,000
Frank Frisch, Cardinals, $20,000

[*As implied in the article, these salary figures were not official, only specula-
tive. Gehrig and Foxx, indeed, had not yet signed their contracts. Player-
managers on this list are Terry, Cochrane, Cronin, and Frisch. In 1934 the
National League would have six player-managers: Terry, Frisch, Charley
Grimm of the Cubs, Jimmy Wilson of the Phillies, and for part of the season,
Bob O'Farrell of the Reds and Pie Traynor of the Pirates. One reason for the
large number of player-managers in this Depression year was financial, since
these men received one salary for performing two jobs.*]

Alan Gould, St. Louis *Globe-Democrat*

∘ *Thursday, January 18* ∘

Bradenton, Fla.—Jerome Herman "Dizzy" Dean is sojourning in this
spring training site enjoying life to the utmost. Dizzy and his wife have
been here since December 22, and Dean has been hunting, fishing, playing golf, and otherwise living the life of a winter visitor.

Dizzy believes that he and his young pitching brother Paul, who is expected to become another ace on the Cardinal staff, will lead the team to
the National League pennant.

"How are they going to stop us?" he snapped. "Paul's going to be a
sensation. He'll win 18 or 20 games. I'll count 20 to 25 for myself. I won
20 last season, and I know I'll pass that figure."

St. Louis *Star-Times*

We will not go into the justice of the color line, but we know that there is a
color line which is adhered to most strictly. The color line was thrown to
the magnates at the baseball writers' dinner in New York last year by
Heywood Broun, the famous columnist. He asked why Negroes were not
permitted to play in the big leagues, and he is still asking.

Dan Daniel, *The Sporting News*

° *Sunday, January 21* °

Chicago baseball fans will be able to hear the Cubs and White Sox games broadcast as heretofore.

The arrangement was not effected without some dickering, however. The result of the dickering will be radio ballyhooing of games during the morning and early afternoons.

Under terms of the agreement, the radio fellows at 10 o'clock will loose the first of five baseball announcements, the last of which is to be sung at 2:30, a half hour before game time. No announcement is to be less than 25 words.

Edward Burns, Chicago *Tribune*

° *Thursday, January 25* °

Bill Terry, manager of the world champion Giants, breezed into town to chat with the writers.

"I'll start with the same team that won the pennant," he said.

"You mean," he was asked, "the team we picked for sixth place last year?"

Terry laughed. "The same team," he said. "Anybody want to bet a hat that we don't win again?"

No one wanted to bet.

"Pittsburgh, St. Louis, and Chicago will be the teams to beat," Terry said.

"Do you fear Brooklyn?" he was asked.

"Is Brooklyn still in the league?" he replied.

Rud Rennie, New York *Herald-Tribune*

° *Friday, January 26* °

Because of his unkind cut at the Dodgers, William Harold Terry is in for a ride.

When those Brooklyn jockeys get through with Memphis Bill, he'll feel like a spavined nag that has hauled one load too many.

It is amusing how quickly a Brooklynite can be aroused by a slur against the Dodgers. And if Bill Terry is as thin-skinned as some say he is, he is due for a miserable season so far as Giant-Dodger games are concerned.

Harry Nash, *New York Post*

∘ *Monday, January 29* ∘

It doesn't take much to start a baseball war in Brooklyn. In so far as Flatbush, Red Hook, Gowanus, Brownsville, Bushwick, Coney Island, and Bath Beach are concerned, Bill Terry's remark the other day about the Dodgers was like the shot that rang out on the bridge at Concord.

Chagrined over the aftermath of what he regarded as an innocent interjection, Terry has headed for the wilds of Arkansas until the war blows over. But Bill will have to wait a long time for the fans of Brooklyn to forget. He will hear his exclamation thrown back at him many an afternoon during the 22 games between the Giants and Dodgers.

Dan Daniel, New York *World-Telegram*

Front offices of most baseball clubs never put more than two players' wives within ear shot of each other at ball parks. Pitchers' wives usually are carefully segregated from mates of the fielders. The infielders' little women blame poor pitching for misadventures, and the brides of the pitchers yell murder when an infielder boots one while papa is pitching.

You probably have guessed what this would lead to if all the wives were seated in a group. Not that they aren't fine gals, but you can't blame 'em for being prejudiced.

Arch Ward, Chicago *Tribune*

∘ *Saturday, February 3* ∘

There will be no radio broadcast of baseball games from Sportsman's Park this year, according to an announcement this morning after a conference between President Sam Breadon of the Cardinals and President Louis B. von Weise of the Browns.

Broadcasts have continued at Sportsman's Park since 1926. Originally three stations broadcast games daily, including Sundays and holidays, and the stations operated free of charge. In the last two years the broadcast was paid for by the two stations operating, and their privilege confined to week-days.

St. Louis Post-Dispatch

The question of radio broadcasting, one of major league baseball's most vexing problems, continues to furnish heat for Hot Stove League fans.

A poll of cities conducted by the United Press reveals a sharp difference of opinion on radio broadcasting.

The New York Yankees and Giants, continuing a policy adopted in 1933, will not allow games to be broadcast, nor will the Pittsburgh Pirates, who have always opposed the plan. Both Philadelphia clubs have barred radio from their parks.

Detroit and Cleveland probably will continue to permit broadcasting. In Cleveland, however, the plan hinges on the willingness of radio stations to meet the price demanded for the privilege, $15,000.

The Brooklyn club, which permitted the broadcast of some games last season, has made no definite plans for 1934.

Chicago *Daily News*

° *Sunday, February 4* °

Another milestone set up by the NRA:

From now on athletes whose names are cited in advertising athletic goods must actually use them or have designed the equipment. Otherwise the advertiser is a "chiseler" liable to have his Blue Eagle taken away, and be fined in the bargain.

St. Louis *Globe-Democrat*

° *Wednesday, February 7* °

Frankie Frisch settled into a comfortable chair in the Waldorf and lighted a cigarette.

How does he like being a manager?

"Fine. But it isn't easy," he said. "One of the things I'm learning is how to handle men. Maybe you've heard I'm tough. It isn't so, but it could be. If anybody should get tough, I can get tough, too."

What are his ideas on discipline?

"Few, simple, and reasonable. The players must be in bed by midnight. They can get up any time they choose so long as they get to the park at noon when we're in St. Louis and in time to take hitting practice when we're on the road. They can eat what they can digest and drink within reason. I won't try to regulate their personal habits."

What are his notions about training?

"I got most of them from John McGraw [*for whom Frisch played during his first eight years in professional baseball, from 1919 through 1926, when he was a member of the New York Giants.*]. We'll work out twice a day, from 10 until 11:30 and from 2 until 4."

How much latitude will pitchers and catchers have in deciding how to pitch to batters?

"We'll meet every day before a game and go over the opposing hitters. We'll decide how to pitch to each man and how to play for him. We'll stick to the plan—unless it goes wrong."

What is the recipe for success as a manager?

"It isn't original with me. The secret of success lies in knowing your men—and when to take out your pitcher."

Frank Graham, New York *Sun*

◦ *Thursday, February 8* ◦

The spring baseball tide rises in Florida next month, there being a decided shift to the Palmetto State for pre-season prepping.

Here is the line-up of spring training camps:

NATIONAL LEAGUE		*AMERICAN LEAGUE*	
Boston	St. Petersburg, Fla.	Boston	Sarasota, Fla.
Brooklyn	Orlando, Fla.	Chicago	Pasadena, Cal.
Chicago	Catalina Island, Cal.	Cleveland	New Orleans, La.
Cincinnati	Tampa, Fla.	Detroit	Lakeland, Fla.
New York	Miami Beach, Fla.	New York	St. Petersburg, Fla.
Philadelphia	Winter Haven, Fla.	Philadelphia	Fort Myers, Fla.
Pittsburgh	Paso Robles, Cal.	St. Louis	West Palm Beach, Fla.
St. Louis	Bradenton, Fla.	Washington	Biloxi, Miss.

The Sporting News

Will there be taps for night baseball this year? [*Night baseball had been played only in the minor leagues.*] There will not be so many after-the-sun-goes-down games. When the nocturnal play craze was at its height, several major league magnates seriously considered the possibility of inaugurating it in their parks. If any club owner still cherishes the idea, he is keeping notably silent.

The pendulum is swinging the other way in the minors, too, for it never seemed natural to play baseball after dark. Whatever excuse might have existed for the night game, other than climate, no longer holds. The New Deal has assured people more leisure with money to spend in enjoying it. This means that lack of time to get away from work cannot be an excuse for failure to draw crowds to ball parks.

An emergency may have justified night games, but that period appears to have passed. It seems that night baseball is now definitely on the way out. The mourners probably will be few. It was a noble experiment, but, like so many others, it didn't live up to the expectations of its supporters. [*The first night game in the major leagues would be played in Cincinnati on May 24, 1935.*]

The Sporting News

∘ *Friday, February 9* ∘

New York (AP)—Major league baseball is due for some brisk action on the diamonds this year if the athletes carry out the conviction of club owners that the game needs more aggressive playing spirit and less fraternizing.

Players will be urged to adopt the attitude that no favors are to be asked or comradeship manifested, on or off the field.

Specifically, here are some things which club owners classify as objectionable:

1. Fraternizing between rival players around the batting cage during pre-game practice.

2. Visits of players to the opposing team's bench to discuss engagements for the evening, inquire about the health of one's family, or debate the merits of their golf games.

3. Manifestations of "old pal" stuff between base runners and infielders.

4. Public or private beer drinking among players of rival teams, before or after games.

The aim and object is to revive "old time spirit" which seems to have yielded too much to the softening influences of high salaries and social activities during boom times.

St. Louis Post-Dispatch

Leo Durocher, Cardinal shortstop, is in St. Louis to settle his contract dispute. He's been asked to take a slice of $3,500, and he said that "such a request is most unfair."

"I realize that conditions require most of us to accept smaller salaries," Leo explained. "But when you ask a man to take $5,000 instead of $8,500—that's too much. But I'm sure we'll get together. I don't think the Cardinals can be serious in asking me to accept that kind of a salary."

St. Louis *Star-Times*

∘ *Friday, February 10* ∘

Cardinal President Sam Breadon said that most of his players have come to terms. One of the unsigned is Lippy Leo Durocher, in town with a wardrobe that stamps him as one of the fashion plates of baseball.

Martin J. Haley, St. Louis *Globe-Democrat*

∘ *Tuesday, February 13* ∘

The report that Mr. Casey Stengel may replace Mr. Max Carey as manager of the Brooklyn Dodgers is too good to be true.

Mr. Stengel is so pre-eminently the man for this delicate and delicious assignment it just isn't in the cards for him to be named.

Just as there is no limit to the obtuseness of a baseball magnate, I have my doubts that there is any beginning to his astuteness, and thus I am not optimistic that plain logic will prevail.

Brooklyn is the last frontier of baseball fiction, the lone surviving outpost of big league romance. Across the bridge baseball is still an Olympian game, and the men who play it still gods.

Only in Flatbush has baseball retained its original qualities of emotion, its neighborly intimacy, its passionate kinship. A defeat plunges the borough into black despair, a victory lifts it to a purple tinte d'horizon.

This has been so for a great number of years, and it is to be hoped it will be so for a great number of years to come. This sort of enthusiasm is too precious to lose. [*This enthusiasm came to an end in 1957, when Charles O'Malley, lured by the gold of Southern California, moved the Dodgers to Los Angeles.*].

Joe Williams, New York *World-Telegram*

° *Wednesday, February 14* °

Leo Durocher would lead the National League in hitting if he could handle a bat with as much skill as he does a billiard cue.

Reputed to be the major leagues' outstanding pocket billiard player, Durocher will meet Frank Taberski, a former pocket billiard champion, in an exhibition match Friday night.

St. Louis Post-Dispatch

° *Thursday, February 15* °

Boston, Chicago, Detroit, and Cincinnati are four major league cities assured of broadcasting games this season. Whether there will be others has not been determined.

Advertisers consider play-by-play accounts of games a good medium. Prices for broadcasts in Chicago, particularly, are rising rapidly, and Walgreen is paying Station WGN $45,000 for the season. The Goodrich Tire Company is considering taking advantage of broadcasts in cities where they are available, and contracts are being negotiated in several such locations.

The Sporting News

Protests continue to trickle in against the decision of local clubs to abandon radio broadcasts.

The ball clubs defend their action with reasonable explanations. They believe that the radio has taken away more business than it has created. They believe that on threatening or cold days hundreds of fans will remain at home when, without radio, they would attend the games.

Another argument lies in the return of the saloon, beg pardon, tavern. With a radio in every restaurant, beer shop, tavern, handbook, and cigar store, many fans might prefer to remain in the cool of the thirst parlor hearing the game at ease with a Gambrinus special handy and plenty of conversation—all without the price of admission.

John E. Wray, *St. Louis Post-Dispatch*

(INS)—Jerome H. "Dizzy" Dean admits he was good with the old ball. But now, aided by the new ball—but let "Dizzy" speak for himself. He does this right well.

"Watch the fast ball pitchers make that white apple sail this season," Dean predicted. "I have averaged 20 victories a season with the old ball. With the new ball I feel certain I will win 25 games."

"Dizzy" believes the new ball will bring joy to fast ball pitchers and curves to curve ball artists. The reason, he says, is the changed seam. It won't be raised as much this season as it was last, which allowed curve ball pitchers to get a good grip and make it do tricks.

St. Louis *Star-Times*

∘ *Tuesday, February 20* ∘

The Cardinals can proceed with their unfinished business—John Leonard Martin, the "Pepper Box Kid," has signed his contract.

After scribbling his signature yesterday, Martin was asked to comment on the financial terms.

"Shucks, no one's interested in what they're paying me," said the Pepper Kid. "All the fans want to know about me is what kind-a year I'm going to give 'em. You can say that Pep'll be hustling, giving his best and trying all the time."

That's Pepper Martin—plain as an old boot, but all to the jerry with his baseball philosophy. Martin is my type of player. No one ever saw him snooping around the clubhouse trying to create dissension. He's too busy trying to win ball games to enter into petty uprisings.

Few players would accept a major transfer in position without voicing a loud complaint. Yet here was Pepper moving from the outfield to third base last season and turning in a swell job on the far corner. Pepper doesn't care where he plays—any position suits him.

Pepper Martin is an unusual character in the profession. Yes, sir, that boy's all wool and two miles wide. [*The star of the Cardinals' 1931 World Series triumph over the Philadelphia Athletics, Martin gained his nickname in 1925, when he played on the Cardinals farm team in Fort Smith, Arkansas, and his manager, Blake Harper, saw similarities between the aggressive young ballplayer and a scrappy boxer from Brooklyn named Pepper Martin.*]

Sid Keener, St. Louis *Star-Times*

∘ *Friday, February 23* ∘

"It's going to be a good baseball season," said the old bleacherite. "This will be the first season since the repeal of the 18th Amendment, and business should be better at all the parks. Guys knock over a couple of shots and the talk gets around to baseball, and if it's a nice day someone will suggest they go to the ball park, and they all pile uptown. That will be happening all over town this summer."

But might not some decide it's more comfortable to listen on the radio?

"It used to be great fun in saloons where they had a scoreboard and the bartender chalked up the runs as they came in, inning by inning. There was suspense and excitement in that. I got more of a kick out of it than I ever have listening to baseball over the radio, which bombards you with so many words. The simple listing inning by inning gave a chance for thought and speculation and a little serious attention to one's drinking. Now we're victims to a couple of broadcasters gabbing away when we might better be dipping our beaks reflectively in something silent and soothing."

Will Wedge, New York *Sun*

∘ *Saturday, February 24* ∘

Charles Dillon "Casey" Stengel sprawled in a chair in the Hotel New Yorker yesterday and announced that he had signed a contract to manage the Brooklyn Dodgers for 1934 and 1935.

"The first thing I want to say," said Stengel, "is that the Dodgers are still in the National League. Tell that to Bill Terry. And I don't care what you fellows call my club—the Daffiness Boys, the Screwy Scrubs, or anything, so long as they hustle."

Caswell Adams, New York *Herald-Tribune*

∘ *Sunday, February 25* ∘

Around the National League players are calling Frankie Frisch John J. McGraw, Jr. They say he is more like the popular conception of McGraw than McGraw himself.

Frisch learned his baseball under McGraw on the New York Giants. He learned a lot of things that aren't in the rule books. [*Upon graduating from Fordham University in 1919, Frisch went to the Giants, without playing even one game in the minor leagues.*]

McGraw's fiery temper and pugnacious aggressiveness have become a tradition in baseball. Frisch, players say, gives every promise of carrying on from where the "Little Napoleon" left off. His men insist that in his toughest days McGraw was no tougher, no more sarcastic, no more intolerant of failure, than Frank Francis Frisch, the Fordham Flash. [*Frisch became "the Fordham Flash" in his first year with the Giants, when he replaced the injured regular second baseman, Larry Doyle, and played spectacularly.*]

Yet, he has the unqualified loyalty of his players. They say he is fair and considerate and that his baseball is fundamentally sound. He is inspired by the burning desire to win.

His scathing speech in the privacy of the clubhouse after a particularly distressing defeat makes McGraw, to those who knew him, seem like a piker. He is not intolerant of mistakes due to inexperience, but he detests the player who doesn't try.

New York *Daily News*

∘ *Friday, March 3* ∘

Because he now weighs almost 200 pounds, Dizzy Dean expects to break the major league record for strikeouts this year. [*The record was then held by Rube Waddell, who, pitching for the Philadelphia Athletics in 1904, registered 349 strikeouts.*]

When Dizzy joined the Cardinals two years ago he worked so hard that in midsummer he weighed about 165 pounds. Branch Rickey [*the Cardinals' vice-president and general manager, who was more actively involved in the affairs of the club than was the president, Sam Breadon*] promptly advised him to ease up and take on some flesh. He was heavier last summer but still under 190. With more avoirdupois, Rickey contended, he could develop a greater fast ball.

Last summer Dean struck out 17 Cubs in one game, his speed fairly blinding batters. Now, as he shapes up as a 200-pounder, six feet three inches tall, Rickey says that Dizzy's smoke will surpass that of Walter Johnson and all other famous speed merchants. [*Many observers believe that the fast ball of Walter Johnson, a Washington Senator from 1907 through 1927, traveled at a speed greater than that of any other pitcher in baseball history.*]

Joe Vila, New York *Sun*

° *Monday, March 5* °

Albany, Ga.—Manager Frankie Frisch will put the Cardinals through their first paces of the training season at Bradenton, Fla., tomorrow. Frisch prefers two workouts a day, and he has ordered two practices for opening day.

"We'll be in Florida to get into condition, and we might as well hop to it right away," says Frisch.

Frisch has set midnight as curfew hour, and players may sleep until 7:30. Frisch has placed no restrictions on food, but he has banned beer and liquor drinking.

Although Frisch doesn't like golf for his players, he has placed no embargo against it yet. He feels that golf may be all right for pitchers who work only every fourth day, but he believes other players are busy enough on the diamond without adding extra exercise by playing golf. Fishing will be allowed so long as it does not interfere with baseball.

Martin J. Haley, St. Louis *Globe-Democrat*

Bradenton, Fla.—Paul Dean, who won 22 games and lost 7 for Columbus of the American Association, is holding out for $1,500 more than the Cardinals have offered and is prepared to work in a common mill if the Redbirds don't meet his terms, Paul and his brother Jerome Herman "the Great" Dean disclosed.

"Yes, sir, Paul has a job all lined up, and he's not going to pitch unless the Cardinals pay him," Jerome explained.

"The club offered him a raise over what he got at Columbus, but it wasn't enough for a man of his skill. It was the same salary the club offered other young pitchers, and Paul ain't an ordinary pitcher. He's a great pitcher. He's even greater than I am, if that's possible. And Paul is willing to gamble on his ability. He sent back his contract and Mr. Rickey sent him another exactly the same, and threatened to make Paul pay for the postage if he sent that one back. But that didn't scare brother Paul. He shot it back, too. But he told Mr. Rickey he'd pitch for nothing until he won a certain number of games, say 15, and then let the Cardinals pay him $500 for each victory. And the club turned that offer down! You can't tell what a club's going to do nowadays."

J. Roy Stockton, *St. Louis Post-Dispatch*

◦ *Thursday, March 8* ◦

Casey Stengel has a grave duty to perform. He must give Brooklyn a ball club that is both efficient and screwy. Brooklyn fans enjoy victory, but they enjoy it most with a large dose of what scientists call Flatbush folly, or red hook raving, or dementia greenpointensia, or plain, ordinary phrenitis.

John Lardner, *New York Post*

◦ *Friday, March 9* ◦

Bradenton, Fla.—Leo Durocher made a flying trip from St. Louis in his automobile. He left St. Louis on Wednesday morning at 7:15 and arrived yesterday at 4 P.M. And this through one day of rain and an hour's layover in Chattanooga, where Leo was pinched for driving too fast.

St. Louis *Star-Times*

○ *Saturday, March 10* ○

Less than a week has been spent by the Cardinals in training, but already it is clear that Frank Frisch is one of the hardest taskmasters in the big leagues. The tongues of the players are hanging out.

St. Louis *Star-Times*

Miami Beach—With the signing of Jimmy Foxx by Connie Mack, the last holdout siege is ended.

How much Foxx signed for is open to conjecture. Some friends say $18,000. Others whisper through the corner of their mouths, "Twenty grand, but he was warned by Mack not to talk."

One veteran of the game insists that Foxx is a sucker, for Jimmy had Mack where he wanted him—with the support of the fans. But, as is so often the case with ball players, Foxx lacks financial finesse and is crazy about baseball. He kept looking at the baseball panorama out of the corner of his eye. And Mack knew it. Ergo, Foxx's $18,000 instead of $25,000. [*In 1933, Foxx had led the American League in batting (.356), in home runs (48), and in runs batted in (163). In 1980, the San Francisco Giants paid Rennie Stennett $600,000, in exchange for which Stennett batted .244, hit 2 home runs, and drove in 37 runs. In 1982, George Foster, who received about two million dollars from the New York Mets because of his reputation as a hitter and a slugger, batted .247, with 13 home runs and 70 runs batted in. And in 1983, Reggie Jackson was paid more than a million dollars by the California Angels for compiling a batting average that, literally, was less than his weight, .197.*]

Dan Daniel, New York *World-Telegram*

○ *Monday, March 12* ○

Bradenton, Fla., March 11—Paul "Harpo" Dean signed his 1934 contract today. [*During spring training, Paul Dean was sometimes called "Harpo" because of the contrast between him and his talkative brother.*] Branch Rickey was out of town, but the Deans sought out Sam Breadon. Dizzy had Paul in tow. They pitched camp in Breadon's hotel rooms, and he batted back contract adjectives as quickly as they were pitched. The game progressed for an hour or so before reaching a decision. Both sides declared they were satisfied.

Salary terms were not disclosed. Paul had been holding out for better than the $3,000 proffered. If he got any more, he's not saying. In fact, he doesn't go in much for words. He lets Dizzy pinch-hit for him, and you know Diz.

We tried out Harpo, but he wouldn't budge, save to nod his curly head up and down as the straight-haired Diz unwound.

"We're going to win between us 40 or 45 games this year," Dizzy said modestly.

"How many will Paul win?" we managed to break in.

"I don't know," was the comeback, "but I guess he'll win more than me. You know Paul's a great pitcher, got lots of stuff, haven't you, Paul?" (Harpo nodded.)

Paul, however, must work to win his job with the Birds. He'll train alongside other pitchers trying to hold down major league berths.

That's the way Breadon sized it up, even after hearing Dizzy shove in this final phrase: "If we don't win 40 or 45 games between us, we'll give the money back to you, Mr. Breadon. Won't we, Paul?"

Harpo was a bit slow on that nod. Of course, we're pulling for the Dean boys, but returning the money certainly would make a good piece for the paper.

Martin J. Haley, St. Louis Globe-Democrat

Practically all big leaguers are showing old-time interest in their profession this spring. Many of the big shots were bumped in the Florida real estate boom, and then the stock market. They realize that the only way to recoup their losses is to stick to their own game—to bat out their income with base hits.

Sid Keener, St. Louis Star-Times

∘ Wednesday, March 14 ∘

Bradenton, Fla.—I am not selling the Cardinals as a sure-shot for the National League pennant, but I am saying that the players are inspired by the dynamo supplied by Frankie Frisch.

I was impressed with the spirit of several of the boys. Pepper Martin came along with tobacco dribbling out of his mouth.

"It's a great ball club," said Pepper.

Dizzy Dean jogged along the base path. "Who's going to beat us?" asked Jerome Herman.

"My arm's in great condition," announced Jesse Haines, 41 years old [*and a Cardinal pitcher since 1920*].

"Who wouldn't throw his arm off for this bunch after getting away from the Phillies?" queried Catcher Virgil Davis. [*A member of the Phillies for six years, Davis had recently been traded to the Cardinals. In 1933, he batted .349.*]

I followed the maneuvers of the players. They were hustling at the command of Frankie Frisch. He's a hard driver. He preps them with the stinging whip of a Simon Legree. There is no play with the Redbirds. Frisch is leading them with one goal—the pennant!

Sid Keener, St. Louis *Star-Times*

Bradenton, Fla.—Coming from comparatively somnolent Fort Myers [*where the Philadelphia Athletics were training*], your correspondent landed in the thick of excitement in the Cardinal camp. The Dean Brothers were celebrating the winning of the pennant!

Dizzy Dean, much the dizzier and more adroit talker, announced that he had sat down with pencil and paper and doped the Giants right out of the race. When questioned as to the validity of his so-called reasoning Dizzy expounded, "It will require about 95 games to win the pennant, and the Giants can't take that many. That's why we will win."

Dizzy said his brother Paul and he would take from 45 to 50 contests between them. This would leave Bill Hallahan, Tex Carleton, and the others with the necessity of winning only 50. It is all very simple, but the Giants refuse to be intimidated.

The Giants cannot figure the Dean Brothers as even remotely connected with the next World Series. Fourth place is as high as any of them will rate the Cardinals. And not the least important reason is a feeling that all is not harmony on the St. Louis club. Frisch is a corking leader, but it is no secret that some of his men resent his having been promoted over the less fiery Jimmy Wilson. [*Wilson was the Cardinals' regular catcher in 1933, and when Gabby Street was dropped as manager, some players expected and hoped that he would be replaced by Wilson. After the season had ended, he was traded to the Phillies, and soon thereafter he was named manager of the team.*]

Dan Daniel, New York *World-Telegram*

Cardinal outfielder Ernie Orsatti talked of retiring from baseball and going into the movies out in Hollywood.

"I thought I was fair in my salary demands," said Orsatti, "but Mr. Rickey insisted that I accept a 25 percent cut. That's too much."

When questioned on the matter, Rickey said, "If Orsatti's prospects in the movies are as encouraging as he outlined to me, he would be foolish not to quit baseball." [*A thirty-year-old native of Los Angeles, Orsatti had worked for motion picture companies as a handyman, an assistant camera-man, and, most notably, as a stunt man. He had doubled for several actors, including Buster Keaton, when it was necessary for them to perform dangerous feats. He was now in his eighth season with the Cardinals.*]

St. Louis *Star-Times*

° *Thursday, March 15* °

Bradenton, Fla.—Frankie Frisch is a one-man manager. Other master-minds in baseball may feel it necessary to appoint a "Brain Trust" or a "Board of Strategy" to assist them, but the "Fordham Flash" will play a lone-hand in directing the Cardinals.

If he is successful, he will take the credit. If he fails, he will shoulder the blame.

Today Frisch outlined his program as manager.

"I'm the boss," he said. "I'll call all the shots. The boys will come to me for all instructions. No one will nod me off on a signal. I'm the yes-guy on this ball club."

Pausing a moment, Frankie stroked his thinning sandy hair. Then he jumped up and shouted, "Yes, sir, I'm going to run this club. I'm a one-man manager. If President Breadon and Branch Rickey wanted a staff of managers to run the team they would not have signed me. They seem willing to trust me to be the manager with no assistants or advisers."

Frisch noted that John McGraw operated the Giants on that basis. "And Mac was pretty successful," said Frisch.

"I consider myself fortunate," he went on, "to have been one of McGraw's pupils. I might never have become known as the 'Fordham Flash' but for the training I received from McGraw. I could have flopped as a ball player under any other teacher.

"No one was permitted to disagree with McGraw. He let us know that he did not care for suggestions from players. At the same time he impressed upon us the value of team play over individual play.

"It didn't matter with McGraw how we got the winning run or who got it, so long as we won. The player who scored the winning run wasn't permitted to brag. McGraw would come back with 'The Giants got it.'"

Sid Keener, St. Louis *Star-Times*

Lippy Leo, Speedy, the Jockey! Leo Durocher, Cardinal shortstop, will answer to any of them. He has nicknames galore, this New England laddybuck. He's one of those fellows at home anywhere—in a tough ball game, on a horse, at the billiard table, around the golf links. Nothing shy about him in conversation or on the dance floor, and if you crave a little serious bridge he's ready for it, as ready as his wardrobe, which includes all the changes for the various bids of the day or night. [*The twenty-eight-year-old Durocher was starting his seventh season in the major leagues, his second as a Cardinal.*]

Martin J. Haley, St. Louis *Globe-Democrat*

○ *Saturday, March 17* ○

Leo Durocher is a human megaphone, always jibbering and entering into numerous discussions and arguments. He likes to disagree with Frisch on all subjects. He fired this challenge at the boss: "Betcha fall suit of clothes I hit .285 this year. And if you hit .325 I'll buy you the best overcoat on the market." Frisch accepted both offers.

Pepper Martin drives Durocher goofy. The Pepper Kid is a bundle of nerves around third base. "See these short gray hairs around my ears," remarked Leo. "Martin put them there last summer. We'd get in a tight spot, with three on for the other fellow and one out with the score tied. Johnny takes himself a fresh chew, removes his glove, lodges it under his arm and starts gazing at the clouds. 'Hey, Johnny,' I shout to him. 'Come on, get on your toes, something's liable to happen—look, the pitcher's ready to go to work.' Martin looks over and groans, 'Aw, don't get excited—I'm ready for the fire department.' I never saw anyone like him. But a great fellow on a ball club. I wish I could tie him as a player."

Incidentally Martin isn't "Pepper" or the "Kid" to his pals. He's "Johnny" or "John." They never refer to him as "Pepper." He's a riot. Other big shots go in for expensive limousines. Pepper came over from Oklahoma in a Ford with a truck chassis. That's good enough for the

Pepper Kid. [*Martin was now thirty years old and beginning his fourth full season with the Cardinals. He was christened Johnny Leonard Roosevelt Martin—not John, but Johnny. He was born and lived all of his life in Oklahoma.*]

The real hot tip in camp is Paul Dean, and they say Paul will be a better pitcher than Dizzy in 1935. According to the inside dope, Paul will be another Walter Johnson, just as fast as the former smokeball king of the American League.

Paul idolizes Dizzy. They're like two peas from the same can. Whenever Diz strolls down Main Street, Paul is right at his heels. At the park when Diz starts warming up, Paul is at his shoulder. [*Paul Dean was now five months short of his twenty-first birthday, two years and seven months younger than Dizzy.*]

Sid Keener, St. Louis Star-Times

The Giants refer to the Cardinals as "coolie help" because Branch Rickey has them working for next to nothing.

Rud Rennie, New York Herald-Tribune

Los Angeles has been demanding a place in a major league for a long time, but nobody gave the idea serious consideration until a leading journal printed an editorial saying it was high time something was done about it. Airplanes would be used for the jumps, of course. [*As yet, no major league team had used air travel.*]

Arch Ward, Chicago Tribune

∘ *Monday, March 19* ∘

Miami Beach—The Cardinals had just beaten the Giants for the third straight time. Spring victories may not mean anything, but don't let anybody tell you that managers don't like them.

Frank Frisch looked very pleased as he sat in the lounge of his hotel and puffed on an after-dinner cigar. He is a little wider and thicker than he used to be. His hair is thinning and beginning to gray at the temples. But he is sunburned and vigorous looking, and the same twinkle is in his eye that must have been there when he came from Fordham to the Polo Grounds to show the Giants how second base should be played. [*Like most big league players who had been to college, Frisch played football as well as baseball. As a senior at Fordham, in 1918, Frisch was selected by Walter Camp to be one of the halfbacks on the second string of his all-American team. A genuine student, Frisch majored in chemistry and received a B.S. degree. He grew up on 206th Street in the Bronx, and his father, a wealthy lace-linen manufacturer, was not pleased that his son had chosen to become a professional baseball player.]*

He took over the management of the Cardinals last year when it was too late to do anything about them. This year he is starting out on his own, and while the general public may not have tumbled to the fact that the Cardinals constitute a real menace to the peace and security of the Giants, the ball players and other managers talk about them in that fashion.

So what does Frank think about them?

"I don't know yet," he said, "but these fellows have the best spirit I ever saw on a ball club, and that goes for the Giants of 1921, 1922, 1923, and 1924 [*winners of four consecutive National League pennants*]. One reason that we were good was that we were willing to hustle. Well, these players of mine are willing to hustle. They're more than willing. They're positively determined!

"And we've got some good ball players. You won't see a better outfielder than Joe Medwick. He can do everything—hit, run, throw, and think. He's another Pepper Martin. He even looks like him. He's always got his head up, always trying. [*In 1933, his rookie season, the twenty-one-year-old Joe Medwick had a batting average of .306, with 18 home runs and 98 runs batted in.*]

"Collins, at first base, has taken on polish, and the fans won't miss Jim Bottomley any more. [*One of the most popular of all Cardinals, Bottomley played first base for ten seasons until he was traded to Cincinnati after the 1932 season.*] I'm still holding up pretty well for an old man at second base. At shortstop, I'll back Durocher against anybody as a defensive player, and this spring the sucker has been powdering the ball at the plate. I hope he keeps it up, but he'd be a big help to any club if he couldn't hit a lick.

"At third base we have Martin. He's a swell ball player, and maybe some day he'll be a great one. He plays ball for all he's worth every day, and you can ride the devil out of him and he never gets mad.

"Most of the catching will be done by Virgil Davis, a first-rate catcher and a great hitter.

"Pennants are won, however, largely on pitching, and we have plenty of that.

"First, there is Dizzy Dean, and, second, there is Paul Dean. There is nothing dizzy about Dizzy Dean when he steps into the box. He has every-thing a pitcher ought to have and knows what to do with it. His only complaint is that he can't pitch often enough. What a man! [*According to a possibly apocryphal story coming from his father and repeated by J. Roy Stockton of the St. Louis* Post-Dispatch, *Dean gained his nickname when he pitched a spring training game for Houston against the Chicago White Sox in 1930. One White Sox player reportedly said, "I can't hit that dizzy pitcher," and the name stayed with him.*]

"The main difference between Dizzy and Paul is that Paul is quieter. Otherwise he's a dead ringer for his brother. He looks like him, walks like him, and has the same sharp baseball brain. He's as fast as Dean.

"Behind the Deans come Bill Hallahan, Bill Walker, Tex Carleton, and Jim Mooney."

And how does the pennant race look?

"Tight," Frisch said. "The Giants have the edge because they're the champions. The Cubs have been strengthened by the addition of Chuck Klein. The Pirates and also the Braves will be tough."

He puffed at his cigar again.

"And," he said, "we'll be in there, too."

Joe Williams, New York *World-Telegram*

∘ *Tuesday, March 20* ∘

Bradenton, Fla.—What kind of a fellow is Paul Dean? Is he anything like his brother? Will he be as good a pitcher?

Dizzy's fame, you recall, preceded him to the major leagues. He was a remarkable pitcher in his first minor league season, 1930. [*In 1930, after winning 17 games and losing 8 for St. Joseph, in the Western League, Dean advanced to Houston, in the Texas League, for whom he won 8 games and lost 2.*] He was also a "character," an eccentric recruit whose unconventional deeds and expressions made him a premier gate attraction.

Dizzy was a natural showman. People wanted to see this fellow who sprang up from nowhere to land in newspaper headlines. Now he's such a hero around Sportsman's Park he can't do anything wrong so far as the fans are concerned, even on days when he's "all wet."

Paul probably has a tougher row to hoe than Diz had at the outset of his Cardinal career. All Diz had to do was to act natural. Paul will probably be himself, too, but the fans will ever be comparing Paul with Dizzy. Will he measure up?

We've found Paul so different in certain characteristics from Dizzy that he brought to our mind "Harpo" of the Marx brothers. Paul says so little, in contrast to Dizzy, we hardly know he's around. He's a serious fellow who tends to his knitting, on the field and off.

It is in their pitching that Paul and Dizzy are alike. Physically they resemble each other also. Both are tall, rangy. Diz is almost four inches over six feet. Paul is about an inch shorter. They weigh about the same, between 190 and 200 pounds. Paul looks his age, 20½ years. Dizzy, 23, seems older. But if you look only at their pitching motions, their windup, their delivery, they are identical twins. How did it happen? To begin with, Paul says it's an accident that he's a pitcher.

"Dizzy and I played on the same semipro team when we were kids," Paul said, "but he was a pitcher and I played shortstop. I was still playing short when I went to high school for two years, but in 1930 I became a pitcher all of a sudden.

"I was playing a semi-pro game. Our regular pitcher was knocked out. The coach asked me to go in. I did, and have been pitching ever since. I was an overhand pitcher, but I'm side arm now, just like Dizzy. We were living in San Antonio after he came back from his first year in the minors, 1930, and he showed me how he pitched. So I took after him. It felt more natural to pitch the way Dizzy did than the way I had been pitching."

Dizzy says his fast ball is not as fast as Paul's, but that his curve is better. Paul says he doesn't know what the difference is.

"We both rely on our fast ball more than our curve," Paul said. "I didn't have much of a curve until last year, when it started to break well."

Last season was Paul's best in three years of minor league work. He won 22, lost 7, and paced the American Association with over 200 strikeouts. Dizzy won 20 games and lost 18 for the Cardinals. He was the major league strikeout king, fanning 199.

When Dizzy let the world know that "we'll win 40 to 45 games between us this season," he did not consult Paul. When Paul's opinion was sought, he said, "I wouldn't want to say how many we might win, but I've got confidence in Dizzy."

Martin J. Haley, St. Louis *Globe-Democrat*

◦ *Monday, March 26* ◦

Much is expected in St. Louis this year from Joe the Duck, known to official scorers as *Medwick, lf.* Joe the Duck broke in last season with a batting average of .306, very good for a freshman. He takes a good, square, robust cut at the ball like Paul Waner's swing from the other side of the plate. Joe the Duck should be quite a ball player in his sophomore year. [*When Medwick was playing for Houston in 1931, a young female fan said that he walked like a duck, from which remark he acquired the nickname "Ducky," sometimes extended to "Ducky Wucky." Before Medwick left Houston, late in the 1932 season, a candy bar had appeared in that city bearing the name Ducky Wucky. Asked about this nickname, Medwick once said, "It makes me want to fwow up."*]

A special word might also be said for the left wing of the infield, patrolled by that peculiar pair, Pepper Martin and loquacious Leo Durocher. Pepper is a transplanted outfielder whose awkward manner and bowlegs are reminiscent of Honus Wagner. [*Although in 1933 he moved from the outfield, where he had performed during the preceding five years in Houston and St. Louis, to third base, this was not a new position for Pepper Martin. He had spent his first three years in the minor leagues, 1924–26, playing third base.*] Loquacious Leo is a jockey who fields like Lajoie and hits like Lefty Gomez. [*One of baseball's legendary players, Napoleon Lajoie, a major leaguer from 1896 until 1916, is often called the greatest of all second basemen. Lefty Gomez, Yankee pitcher of the thirties and early forties, was a notoriously weak hitter, whose major league career included no home runs or triples and a batting average of .147.*] Between them they have more energy and fire than you'll find in the entire rosters of many clubs.

John Lardner, *New York Post*

◦ *Tuesday, March 27* ◦

Bradenton, Fla.—The Cardinals' playing is strongly tinged with opportunism. Frisch has taught them to be fast on their feet, alert in their minds, and ready to capitalize on the slightest boner. The Flash is still a good base runner himself, and he has a couple of agile lieutenants in Pepper Martin and Joe Medwick.

Frisch, of course, is not getting better with the passage of years. The

Fordham Flash is in danger of becoming an ex-Flash. But he has another couple of seasons of sound ball playing in his constitution, and his turn-around batting will help him hang on. [*Frisch was a switch-hitter, as were two others who would become members of the Cardinals' regular lineup, first baseman Ripper Collins and right fielder Jack Rothrock.*] Pitchers still glance about uneasily when Frisch advances to the dish.

John Lardner, *New York Post*

∘ *Wednesday, March 28* ∘

Bradenton, Fla.—It is a long time since any St. Louis training camp has been directed by as versatile a manager as Frank Francis Frisch, and this observer cannot remember any camp where the players had such a splendid opportunity to learn so much from one man.

No matter what the Cardinals are studying, Frisch can teach them. When the boys take to the sliding pits, Frank confesses that he is not a star at sliding, but he knows his faults and can tell the others how to do it. He stands in the pit and coaches them.

"You'll have to keep that arm up and that leg," he tells Medwick. "If you keep dropping on that knee you won't have any legs left after three years. There, that's better. The idea is to slide, not just sit down."

If the boys are batting, Frank quickly notes flaws. He knows that no two men bat alike. But there is a difference between individual style and flaws which will handicap any batter. If a man hits a ball solidly, like Joe Medwick, Frisch pays no attention to seeming faults. Joe "steps in the bucket," as the trade describes it—steps away from the plate, instead of into the pitch. But Joe can do that and hit the right field fence. Frank does not try to change a natural hitter like that. But he has advice for Medwick. Joe's great fault last year was that he hit at too many bad balls, especially at critical times. Over-eagerness causes a young man to do that, and Frank figures experience will curb the tendency.

Frank also can show the boys how to tag a runner, how to get set for a throw, how and when to cut off a throw from the outfield, how to shift for hitters and why; how to run the bases and how to get a lead on a pitcher. He coaches the base runners to watch pitchers carefully, for some little movement that tips off whether they will pitch to the plate or throw to the base.

Managers less versatile than Frisch, or who did not reach the peak as players, frequently find it difficult to command respect during instruction. But the Cardinals know that Frank has been and still is one of the best, and they take his instructions as words from a master. [*Unlike most of their modern counterparts, the major league managers of 1934 all had been, or were still, outstanding players. The playing credentials of seven of them were good enough for admission into baseball's Hall of Fame: Mickey Cochrane, Detroit; Joe Cronin, Washington; Frisch; Rogers Hornsby, St. Louis Browns; Walter Johnson, Cleveland; Bill Terry, New York Giants; and Pie Traynor, Pittsburgh. Traynor succeeded George Gibson shortly after the season had begun.*]

J. Roy Stockton, *St. Louis Post-Dispatch*

◦ *Sunday, April 1* ◦

Mr. Terry, the fellow who said, "Brooklyn? Are they still in the league?" still feels that way about Casey Stengel's kaleidoscopic Dodgers. When he saw two Brooklyn base runners fighting for possession of one base twice in one afternoon, he remarked, "How long have these fellows been down here? They're in midseason form already!"

John Kieran, *The New York Times*

A profit sharing system has been initiated by Larry MacPhail, vice-president of the Cincinnati Reds. The proposal provides that the players will benefit from any increased attendance at home.

MacPhail has set the home attendance goal at 275,000 paid admissions. If the Reds reach that goal, each player will receive a 5 percent increase in pay. If the attendance reaches 325,000 the increase will be 10 percent, and if it reaches 350,000 the players will receive 15 percent increases.

New York *Daily Mirror*

◦ *Thursday, April 5* ◦

Cincinnati fans will get a limited amount of broadcasting this season, 85 games, of which 72 will be away from home. Three stations will be on the air, and each will pay $2,000 for the privilege, the station gaining its own revenue from the sale of advertising time.

Walter "Red" Barber, formerly with Station WRUF, Gainesville, Fla., will do the broadcasting for WSAI. He was chief announcer for the Florida station for four years, in which he built up a large following. Red will do home and road game broadcasts and plans a resume every evening, together with interviews of National League players. [*Thus would begin the major league broadcasting career of the longtime voice of the Brooklyn Dodgers, one of the few members of his craft who are members of baseball's Hall of Fame.*]

The Sporting News

Babe Ruth will be on the air this summer with a series of programs sponsored by the Quaker Oats Company over the National Broadcasting Company's network. The Babe will give three 15-minute broadcasts a week and will be paid one grand per broadcast, $39,000 for 13 weeks. That is $4,000 more than he will collect from the Yankees for the season.

The Sporting News

Atlanta—Before today's game, half the Yankee ball club spent the morning in jail. They went over to the federal penitentiary and called on Al Capone. [*Kenesaw Mountain Landis, baseball's first commissioner, who would not permit Bing Crosby to become a part owner of the Pittsburgh Pirates because he owned racehorses, and who was adamantly opposed to blacks entering professional baseball, seems not to have objected to this visit. Landis and Capone had resided simultaneously for many years in the same city, Chicago. It is not at all clear why the players might have maintained a relationship with Al Capone; subsequent writers on the New York Yankees have been silent on this matter.*]

Richards Vidmer, New York *Herald-Tribune*

○ *Sunday, April 8* ○

Bradenton, Fla.—Frankie Frisch's Cardinals are through with Spring training and in splendid condition for the opening of the season. Hard work under a broiling Florida sun has made muscles firm and obedient and put excess avoirdupois to rout, and if the Redbirds do not fly high it will not be because of poor condition.

Everything inspires optimism, and it can be said without reservation that the Cardinals are good enough to win.

J. Roy Stockton, *St. Louis Post-Dispatch*

◦ *Monday, April 9* ◦

Fifteen thousand men and women poured into Shibe Park to see the first legal Sunday baseball game ever played in Philadelphia [*an exhibition between the Athletics and the Phillies*].

It was an orderly crowd, and not one untoward event marked the afternoon. Had they not been informed of the fact, persons living two blocks away would not have known a game was being played. The contention of baseball chiefs that baseball would not disturb the serenity of a Philadelphia Sabbath was justified by the discreet behavior of those who attended.

James C. Isaminger, Philadelphia *Inquirer*

◦ *Tuesday, April 10* ◦

Because salaries, reduced throughout the baseball world, will be slow to climb, Branch Rickey was asked if he thought the game will still attract ambitious college men and sand-lotters with fair business prospects.

"We have more young men than we can use," was Rickey's reply. "We are swamped with applications. We have organized the Nebraska State League and equipped every team with players, and no salary will be above $50 a month."

"But, Mr. Rickey, won't better educated men hesitate to go in for baseball with the drastic reduction of salaries?"

"No, indeed. We can get all the college graduates we want. Baseball still is attractive financially to young men."

Rickey was asked about the average salary and the average baseball life span.

"The average should be $6,500 for a star player. And he should be able to play for eight years."

"Well, Mr. Rickey, the player gives baseball the years in which, in other business, he would build up his earning capacity, with prospects of a steady income through his life. At $6,500 a year, would a man have much to show for his baseball labors?"

"The thrifty man should leave baseball with a snug savings account. Out of $6,500 a man should be able to save $5,000. Thus, after eight years, without interest on his money, a player should be able to retire with more than $40,000."

"Do you know any players who could save $5,000 out of $6,500?"

"Yes, we have many players who will save more than that."

"Mr. Rickey, do you save $5,000 out of each $6,500 you earn?"

"I do not."

"You have help at your house, your children go to the best schools, you eat well, travel, and have automobiles."

"Well, of course a player could not expect to save $5,000 if he lived like that."

J. Roy Stockton, *St. Louis Post-Dispatch*

∘ *Wednesday, April 11* ∘

(AP)—The New York Giants are the choice of the experts to win the National League pennant. Of 97 sports writers, 40 named the Giants and 34 picked the Cubs to land on top.

Here's the box score on the poll, showing the number of selections for each club for each position:

	1	*2*	*3*	*4*	*5*	*6*	*7*	*8*
New York	40	27	23	7				
Chicago	34	31	18	10	3	1		
Pittsburgh	9	20	36	25	4	3		
St. Louis	13	17	17	36	7	5	2	
Boston	1	1	2	12	61	9	7	4
Brooklyn			1	1	10	30	29	26
Philadelphia		1		5	7	20	31	33
Cincinnati				1	5	29	28	34

The New York Times

◦ *Friday, April 13* ◦

A divorce suit filed by Ruby Hartley Durocher, 27, wife of Leo Durocher, 28, crack shortstop of the St. Louis Cardinals, was begun yesterday before Judge Charles Hoffman in Domestic Relations Court. Durocher filed a cross-petition which referred to a divorce suit by Mrs. May McDonald against her husband, Charles, well known concessionaire at the ball park in Cincinnati, in which Mrs. McDonald alleged that McDonald had been too friendly with Mrs. Durocher.

Mrs. Durocher's counsel, Arthur Fricke, called her to the stand and had her identify several mushy love letters and telegrams, signed "Virginia," "Marie," and "Sis," and addressed to Durocher. Virginia, Marie, and Sis wrote or wired often. Marie evidently was on the stage with the Atlantic City Beauty Pageant at one time and later in a New York show chorus, according to her letters. One "Marie" letter told of being lonesome because her only chance to go out was with "old fossils" who were "not like my loving Leo." She closed "with all my love." The letters from the others were equally voluble in endearing expressions. Mrs. Durocher said she found the letters in her husband's room at a St. Louis hotel when she visited him last June. [*The Durochers had been separated for some time, and Mrs. Durocher lived in Cincinnati.*]

Last January, Mrs. Durocher said, her husband tied her up with a bed sheet and hit her on the jaw. She exhibited a photograph of herself with a badly distorted jaw.

Durocher's attorney, Frank C. Schroer, asked her, "Isn't it a fact that you were highly intoxicated and that was the only way your husband could subdue you?" She answered, "No."

Admitting that McDonald had called upon her at her apartments, she denied having received any presents or financial assistance from anyone except her relatives. Her husband gave her $100 a month of his $6,000 salary, and that was all, she said, but he bought her clothing and a fur coat.

Asked about "expensive perfume," she said she bought it with her own money, explaining that she had about $600 when they were married and had sold a diamond ring for $75 and pawned another for $150.

"You drink quite a bit, don't you, Mrs. Durocher?" asked Schroer. She replied, "I do, on occasions."

The case was continued until Monday.

Cincinnati *Enquirer*

∘ *Sunday, April 15* ∘

Frank Frisch believes that players are paid for doing the correct thing. No praise is necessary. To do the right thing is a matter of course, deserving no commendation or comment. He wastes no words except when a mistake is made. If a player makes a brilliant stop and a nonchalant throw, he overlooks the stop and chides the player for the throw.

It isn't that Frisch doesn't appreciate good plays. No, indeed. The other day there was a throw to third base and a return throw to second. That evening Frank mentioned [*right fielder Jack*] Rothrock's shift on the play.

"That throw to me at second was wild," he explained. "It almost got away. Looking over my shoulder I saw that Rothrock had shifted to back up the play."

Frisch didn't praise Rothrock. It was the big thing to do. He would have spoken if Rothrock had failed to do the proper thing. But Rothrock's position with the club was bolstered and his chances of remaining enhanced. [*The twenty-nine-year-old Rothrock had been with the Boston Red Sox from 1925 through 1932, during which time he performed at first base, second base, third base, shortstop, and in the outfield, and, in one game in 1928, played all nine positions. In 1933 he was with Columbus, in the American Association, where he batted .347. A good fielder and one of the fastest men in the game, Rothrock was the strongest candidate for the regular place in right field.*] What good would a word of praise do? McGraw never handed out bouquets, and Frisch is of the McGraw school.

J. Roy Stockton, *St. Louis Post-Dispatch*

If baseball leaders want J. Cash Customer at the ringside regularly, they will have to cut prices of admission, because the fundamental cause of the drop in receipts has been lack of spending money.

Young men and women are unable to pay the prices. When a youth escorts a girl to a baseball game, it costs him upwards of $2.50, including carfare. For this sum he could take his companion to a neighborhood picture show five times!

His choice is inevitable.

John E. Wray, *St. Louis Post-Dispatch*

◦ *Monday, April 16* ◦

Baseball means more than a few hundred or thousand players struggling for pennants and pay.

It means a new interest, an added thrill, in the lives of 20 or 30 million—from the major cities that see the play to the minor hamlets that sent most of the players on their way to fame.

It means a chance for many millions to lose and forget the drabness of their lives for two hours of an afternoon, in the speed, action, and skill of stars, surrounded by the vocal cataclysm of packed stands, watching not only the Hubbells, the Foxxes and the Kleins, but also the coming stars from the minor circuits who play their part in the drama that runs from April to October.

Baseball means clean, fresh, thrilling outdoor entertainment over a period of six months. Baseball's stage is set above green turf, beneath a blue sky, and there is no set or certain end to any act or scene.

Many millions haven't the time, money, or opportunity for games of their own. Baseball is their main substitute, their main mental and physical relaxation.

Grantland Rice, New York *Sun*

◦ *Tuesday, April 17* ◦

Despite denials by Mrs. Durocher that she was ever in rooms in the Netherland Plaza Hotel [*in Cincinnati*] with another man, direct evidence to the contrary was presented yesterday at the hearing of her contested suit for divorce from Leo Durocher.

Mrs. Durocher told of the ball player beating her up and denied that she had come home drunk or had told him that their child was not his. She added, "I had one black eye a month after I was married to that man."

She denied attending a "party of all blondes" at an apartment. Mrs. Durocher is a blonde.

Questioned by her husband's attorney, she denied ever being intimate with Charles McDonald or any other man, or of going out with other ball players.

Then Durocher took the stand and said, concerning the night he struck his wife, "I got home about 11 o'clock and went to bed. About 2 o'clock my wife came in. She turned on the light and took off her coat and hat, then snatched the covers off the bed. She seemed intoxicated, and I smelled liquor on her breath. I took the covers back and she snatched them a second time, cursing me.

"I tried to quiet her by telling her she would wake the baby, and out of a clear sky she said, 'The baby needn't concern you. It doesn't belong to you.' I said, 'What did you say?' She said, 'You heard me; the baby doesn't belong to you.' Then I struck her."

Most letters addressed to him and signed with girls' names were classed as "fan mail" by Durocher.

Mrs. Clara Durocher, Durocher's mother, who is a maid at the Netherland Plaza, told of how one night she heard the voice of her son's wife coming from Room 1706. She and another maid knocked on the door.

"A man came to the door and asked for some towels," she said. "He was in his shorts. I saw Mrs. Durocher in a dressing gown. When the room was cleaned up there were whisky bottles and face powder there, and lipstick on the pillow slips."

Asked if she could identify the man at the door, she replied, "Mr. McDonald."

[*The maid who had accompanied Mrs. Clara Durocher to the door took the stand and verified her story.*]

Judge Hoffman said that he would decide the case today.

Cincinnati Enquirer

∘ *Wednesday, April 18* ∘

[*On April 17, opening day, in St. Louis, the Cardinals beat Pittsburgh, 7–1. Winning pitcher, Dizzy Dean; losing pitcher, Heinie Meine.*]

(AP)—Before the largest opening day outpouring of fans in three years, baseball regained its place on the sports pages.

The eight games, four in each league, drew an aggregate attendance of better than 180,000.

Pittsburgh Post-Gazette

The Buccos yesterday took part in one of the dullest openers in the long history of Pittsburgh teams. The weather was fine, but aside from the spring zephyrs there wasn't a thing to give the Pirates a tinge of joy.

The Pirates didn't have any more life than a bunch of silent men, and to make matters worse the contest dragged almost two and one-half hours [*which today would be considered a rather short game*]. Heinie Meine and Dizzy Dean went through a lot of slow motion on the mound, the only difference being Dean had a lot of zip when he let go of the ball. Heinie didn't have enough stuff to fool a high school club.

To add to the drab picture, the 7,500 fans acted as if they came to court spring fever. Joe Medwick awakened the lethargic crowd in the third when he hit a home run, but the good home folks went back to sleep and slumbered until the band brought them to with the home waltz at the end of the ninth.

Speaking technically, Jerome the Dizzy hurled a fine game as he limited the Pirates to six hits. His fast ball was smacking like a pistol in Spud Davis' mitt in the closing rounds.

Charles J. Doyle, Pittsburgh Sun-Telegraph

Yesterday I was particularly interested by three members of the home varsity—Pepper Martin, Joe Medwick, and Dizzy Dean—and the manner in which the entire mob responded to Frankie Frisch's appeal to "keep hustling."

Martin hit whistling doubles far into the outfield on his first two trips to the plate. Medwick rifled two line singles to the meadows and then punched a powerful round-trip ticket with a mighty belt into the left field seats. Dean was bearing down to make good his boast that he'd "win at least 20 games this year."

Then I noted Frisch running at top speed on infield grounders and easy outfield flies. The Flash isn't going to give other members of the team an opportunity to coast—if they follow in his footsteps.

Sid Keener, St. Louis Star-Times

The baseball industry buys less and receives more advertising than any other industry in the country, but this spring, for the first time, it is in a position to repay, in public service, some of the favors it has enjoyed. The opening of the season not only marks the close of the toughest winter of the great American depression, but is a reminder that the country didn't quite get mad enough to sting itself to death when things were at their worst.

There were prophets who would have laid you no better than even money that the parks would reopen as usual in 1934, and the fact that this non-essential industry is resuming in its routine way gives proof in the dawn that the flag is still there. If the magnates had been unable to come up with their ground rent and the price of new suits and equipment, it would have been good political business for the administration to stake them to a loan.

The spiritual importance of this resumption is best appreciated if you consider how morose the citizens would have felt if told that the major leagues would be compelled to quit operations.

As a career baseball is much less attractive now than in other years, for wages have been revised sharply downward, and club owners have no players' union to contend with. The individual athlete, as always, is obliged to take it or leave it, except that this year he is obliged to take much less—or leave it.

He is one toiler who positively is not done right by being denied the right of collective bargaining and even forbidden to shop around for another job with a more liberal employer than the one to whom he finds himself rather agreeably enslaved. But the case of the baseball peon presents theoretical grievances not nearly as urgent as the practical problems of other workmen, and it has never reached the preferred docket.

Even on as little money as $2,500 for an eight-month year of four-hour days plus $2.50 a day for two meals when he is on the road, he lacks defenders who would try to shove his complaint ahead of that man's who is willing to grab a hoe, hod, or hammer and hire out to the CWA. [*The Civilian Works Administration, the first major program of the Roosevelt administration to relieve some of the unemployment, provided jobs for four million persons.*]

The magnate himself is a curious critter, for he seldom admits that he has made a dollar even when he has entertained a World Series on his premises, yet hangs onto his franchise until the bank sends the sheriff around to claim it.

And when that happens, some other man suddenly reveals himself as a magnate at heart and bids in the property by announcing that he will pour money into it with a hose and give loyal fans a ball club worthy of their devotion.

The fact is, of course, that the fans were not loyal, for if they had been the old owner would not have had to go through the wringer.

I have sometimes wondered why the owners, practical in most business dealings, have overlooked great advertising possibilities open to them. It would be worth something to a company manufacturing soup or hats or mousetraps to be represented in box scores in every American daily paper and across page one of most afternoon editions by a ball club bearing the name of its product. [*In 1934, late editions of afternoon newspapers, which outnumbered morning newspapers, contained progress reports of that day's baseball games on page 1.*]

But Jake Ruppert, who made his fortune on beer, never has identified with the stein on the table, and the late William Wrigley did nothing to remind citizens that the Cubs were a subsidiary of a man who made gum.

In many smaller cities, the local lunchroom king or automobile dealer subsidizes the semi-pro club for a few hundred dollars and keeps his concern in print all summer, but Mr. Ruppert and Mr. Wrigley, declining this advantage, called their clubs the Yankees and Cubs.

Westbrook Pegler, New York *World-Telegram*

Leo Durocher was granted a decree in Domestic Relations Court yesterday, divorcing him from Ruby Hartley Durocher.

Judge Hoffman granted the decree on the ground of gross neglect, but gave custody of their child, Barbara, three years old, to the wife. This had been agreed to by Durocher.

When asked by Judge Hoffman what he thought he should pay for support of the child, Durocher said he would pay any amount the Court thought proper. Judge Hoffman's decision says, "Mr. Durocher shall pay for the support and maintenance of the child $25 a week until October 1, 1934, after which he shall pay $10 a month until further order of this Court."

Cincinnati *Enquirer*

∘ *Thursday, April 19* ∘

[*On April 18, in St. Louis, the Cardinals lost to Pittsburgh, 7–6. Winning pitcher, Larry French; losing pitcher, Burleigh Grimes.*]

Of the 16 home runs in the major leagues yesterday, 4 were made at Sportsman's Park. Joe Medwick was the only Cardinal to hit for the circuit. He did all the Birds' extra-base hitting, with his second four-bagger in two days and a double.

The Bucs gave Paul Dean a terrific shellacking in his first big league appearance. Dizzy's younger brother, who pitched only six innings during spring training, lasted only two yesterday, Pittsburgh rushing 4 runs across on 5 hits, including home runs by Pie Traynor and Gus Suhr.

Young Dean, however, did not lose his first start. The Cards tied the score in the seventh only to have 19-year-old Harry Lavagetto crash a homer off Burleigh Grimes in the eighth to decide the battle. That was the only hit Grimes allowed in three innings, but it cost the big leagues' lone remaining spit-ball pitcher the game. [*This was the first major league home run for Lavagetto, who is best remembered for his final big league hit in the fourth game of the 1947 World Series, when, with two outs in the ninth inning, he struck a pinch-hit double against the right field fence of Ebbets Field to give the Dodgers a victory over the Yankees and deprive pitcher Floyd Bevens of a no-hit game.*]

Martin J. Haley, St. Louis *Globe-Democrat*

Nine home runs on opening day and 16 on the second day is a fine commentary on the new "stabilized" ball.

At the first two opening days' rate of home run hitting, the grand game, already thoroughly emasculated of speed and strategy by the magnates' craze for creating sluggers, will be a fine joke before the season is far advanced.

Any bush league outfielder could stick in his hip pocket most of the Polo Grounds hits that are counted as home runs, especially those into the right field stand. They should be two-baggers at most, though a single would be quite liberal. [*At the foul line, the right field fence at the Polo Grounds was only 257 feet from home plate, the shortest such distance of any park in major league history.*]

At the rate of 13 or so a day, there may be 2,000 homers hit by the end of the season, making the game more and more a matter of slug and run home. It seems as if all one has to do to hit a homer is to let the bat meet the ball.

Damon Runyon, New York *American*

° *Friday, April 20* °

[*On April 19, in St. Louis, the Cardinals lost to Pittsburgh, 14–4. Winning pitcher, Ralph Birkofer; losing pitcher, Bill Hallahan. Cardinals' standing: 1 win, 2 losses, in sixth place.*]

For four innings yesterday Bill Hallahan pitched like the Hallahan of 1931 [*when he won 19 games, tops in the National League, and then scored 2 victories against no losses in the World Series*], but in the fifth he was just a thrower, and so were his successors, Flint Rhem, and Jim Mooney.

Martin J. Haley, St. Louis *Globe-Democrat*

Odds bodkins! Zounds! Gadzooks! And what else have you in quaint expressions of surprise, annoyance, and alarm? While it's not exactly sporting to condemn a ball club for losing two straight games, the haphazard manner in which the boys waltzed, stumbled, and sprawled yesterday irked the chilled customers. If there was anything artistic, inspiring, or even amusing in their antics, it entirely escaped the notice of the fans, most of whom vanished long before the imbroglio was over.

The Red Birds' defense was as wide open as a Venice crap-game, and their batting attack made you wonder if a left-handed fellow advertised as Ralph Birkofer wasn't the great Giant southpaw, Carl Hubbell, in disguise, taking a fling on the mound for the Pirates.

Ray J. Gillespie, St. Louis *Star-Times*

○ *Saturday, April 21* ○

[*On April 20, in St. Louis, the Cardinals' game with Chicago was postponed because of cold weather.*]

○ *Sunday, April 22* ○

[*On April 21, in St. Louis, the Cardinals lost to Chicago, 2–1. Winning pitcher, Charlie Root; losing pitcher, Tex Carleton. Cardinals' standing: 1 win, 3 losses, tied for fifth place.*]

If ever a pitcher deserved to win, it was Tex Carleton yesterday. The tall right-hander struck out 11 Cubs, issued not a single pass and permitted only 5 hits. The Cards collected 9 safeties off veteran Charlie Root, including 3 doubles and a triple, and yet the Cubs won.

Carleton had "everything." His curve broke sharply, and there was a real hop to his fast ball. His strikeout record is the best of the new season.

The third Chicago hit, a homer into the left field seats by none other than Root, and the last pair of hits did the damage. In the ninth, Woody

English opened with a single. Bill Herman sacrificed, and Klein singled to right for the winning run.

However, there was compensation, for Carleton proved himself a great pitcher, ready for the campaign. And, on Carleton rests much of the Cardinals' flag hopes. [*The twenty-seven-year-old James "Tex" Carleton was beginning his third year as a Cardinal; in 1933 he had won 17 games and lost 11. He grew up on a cattle ranch in Comanche County, Texas, and, along with Frisch, he was one of the two principal Redbirds who had been to college. Carleton graduated from Texas Christian University. On July 2, 1933, in the Polo Grounds, Carleton was a leading participant in one of the best pitched games in baseball history. He pitched 16 scoreless innings against Carl Hubbell and the Giants, after which he was removed for a pinch hitter. In the eighteenth inning, the Giants won, 1–0.*]

James M. Gould, *St. Louis Post-Dispatch*

A lady scribe who smokes cigarets, drinks milk, and carries a score book the size of a family Bible, has a place in the Sportsman's Park press coop. Her gems are printed by an East St. Louis paper.

Chicago *Tribune*

John Heydler, president of the National League, has sent out his annual literary work, "Instructions to Umpires," a copy of which found its way to this desk.

Mr. Heydler's book confines itself to umpires, except for one paragraph. On page 9, Mr. Heydler writes, "If photographers are on the field, do not allow them to hover in groups around a base or the plate. If interference by a photographer prevents a catcher or infielder from making a catch, call the batter out. In all other cases, a ball hitting a photographer is in play. [*At this time, newspaper photographers regularly did their work while standing or crouching on the field.*]

Chester L. Smith, Pittsburgh *Press*

° *Monday, April 23* °

[*On April 22, in St. Louis, the Cardinals lost to Chicago, 15–2. Winning pitcher, Lon Warneke; losing pitcher, Dizzy Dean. Cardinals' standing: 1 win, 4 losses, tied for sixth place.*]

As a baseball-minded public attended post-mortems for the Cardinals, the players were packing their toothbrushes and collar-buttons preparatory to being shipped away. Since they got that opening day victory, our Redbirds have lost the winning touch. Accordingly Secretary Clarence F. Lloyd has been ordered to deport the Cardinals to see if a change of scenery, climate, and even adverse treatment by the fans might encourage them to alter their tactics. So it is off to Pittsburgh, then on to Chicago.

Only yesterday, in the unobstructed view of 14,000 spectators, the Cards combined a cream-puff batting attack with pitching that was no pitching at all, to make a great man of Lonnie Warneke, who pitched his second one-hit game in as many starts.

The Dean boys apparently were trying to win some sort of booby prize, and Diz, by virtue of seniority, made off with the grapes, allowing 8 hits and 6 runs in the first three innings, compared to Brother Paul's meager record of 6 hits and 2 runs in two innings.

Ray. J. Gillespie, St. Louis *Star-Times*

The attendance at Sportsman's Park was around 14,000, but it wasn't a money crowd because about half were in the 50-cent seats. The way most of them howled after the Cubs started after Dean indicated they would like to have had the four-bit pieces refunded.

Chicago *Tribune*

The dope is Jimmy Foxx signed for $16,000, only three grand more than he received last year. In which case the dope is Jimmy Foxx.

Dan Parker, New York *Daily Mirror*

NATIONAL LEAGUE STANDINGS

	W	L	PCT	GB		W	L	PCT	GB
Chicago	5	0	1.000	—	Boston	2	3	.400	3
New York	5	1	.833	½	St. Louis	1	4	.200	4
Brooklyn	4	1	.800	1	Cincinnati	1	4	.200	4
Pittsburgh	3	2	.600	2	Philadelphia	0	6	.000	5½

° *Tuesday, April 24* °

[*On April 23, the Cardinals were not scheduled to play.*]

At three o'clock on the Forbes Field stage, the curtain will rise on the first of a series of plays to be given by the Pittsburgh Pirates in collaboration with visiting troupers from St. Louis. [*It was opening day in Pittsburgh.*]

A work of an American composer, Francis Scott Key, "The Star Spangled Banner," and a folk song of the Republic entitled "Take Me Out to the Ball Game" [*which was written in 1908*] will be interpolated in the sketch, while numerous supernumeraries, in the character of pop boys, hot-dog merchants, and peanut vendors, will round out a cast of excellence.

As part of the prologue, Mayor William N. McNair will toss out what is known in baseball slang as "the first apple," a performance usually hailed with enthusiastic delight or gleeful derision, according to the political philosophies of the shouters.

While the umpires will pretend to be patriotic as they gaze on the ceremony, the American flag will be hoisted atop the flagpole in center field, while Danny Nirella's band will play the national song. Part of the crowd will join in the singing, starting out boldly, "Oh, Say Can You See . . . De De Dum Dum De Dee," and then stopping to see if the guy next to him knows all the words.

As the last strains float into nothingness over the Schenley acres, hard by the Pirates' ball park, there will arise cries of "Who wants ice cold pop?" or its American cousin, the hot-dog.

Harvey J. Boyle, Pittsburgh *Post-Gazette*

While Lon Warneke was pitching his second one-hit game of the season against the Cardinals on Sunday, the brothers Dean were taking a terrific lambasting. Dizzy started but soon had to give way and was followed by Paul, and shortly thereafter the brothers met under the showers.

It must have been an afternoon of anguish for the young men, but it may react to their benefit. It should have demonstrated that life isn't one round of pleasure and that it isn't always possible for a Dean to win by tossing his glove into the box.

Chances are the other Cardinal pitchers secretly were pleased at the spectacle and will occasionally refer to it as a means of piping Dizzy down when his bragging becomes annoying.

Joe Vila, New York *Sun*

[*The above item came from one of the last columns written by the longtime sports editor of the* Sun *and correspondent for* The Sporting News. *On April 27, the fifty-one-year-old Vila would suffer a heart attack and die.*]

° *Wednesday, April 25* °

[*On April 24, in Pittsburgh, the Cardinals lost to Pittsburgh, 5–4. Winning pitcher, Leon Chagnon; losing pitcher, Jesse Haines. Cardinals' standing: 1 win, 5 losses, tied for sixth place.*]

They tore one out of the story books today to bring to a fitting climax the opening of Pittsburgh's twenty-sixth baseball season at Forbes Field.

With it they tore the heart out of old Jess Haines, making his first start of the season, when the Pirates, by virtue of Freddie Lindstrom's home run over the left field fence, with two on in the ninth, won 5 to 4. [*Since joining the Cardinals in 1920, Haines, a forty-one-year-old knuckleball pitcher, had won 190 regular season games and 3 World Series contests. He was a 20-game winner three times, reaching his high point in 1927 with 24 victories. He was now used primarily as a relief pitcher.*]

Martin J. Haley, St. Louis *Globe-Democrat*

° *Thursday, April 26* °

[*On April 25, in Pittsburgh, the Cardinals' scheduled game was postponed because of cold weather.*]

Because he neglected to eject an autograph seeker from the Cardinals' clubhouse after Tuesday's game in Pittsburgh, while he was sputtering and fuming, Manager Frankie Frisch faced the first 1934 report of dissension in the ranks. The fan passed along his story, and the Cards' pilot was asked to explain whether or not there had been fights, bitter words, or a free-for-all battle behind the scenes.

"No!" Frisch barked. "But there will be if I catch any snoopers around my clubhouse."

"Did you second-guess any players after their defeat?" Frisch was asked.

"Why should I?" he replied. "Wouldn't I be a swell manager to say that a curve ball should have been pitched after a batter had hit a fast one? No, siree, I won't second-guess my players."

Ray J. Gillespie, St. Louis *Star-Times*

∘ *Friday, April 27* ∘

[*On April 26, in Pittsburgh, the Cardinals won, 10–1. Winning pitcher, Bill Hallahan; losing pitcher, Ralph Birkofer. Cardinals' standing: 2 wins, 5 losses, in sixth place.*]

The Pirates yesterday took a flogging. Colonel Buster Mills, the recruit outfielder, annexed four blows including a triple and a double, while Catcher Virgil Davis was credited with a homer, a two-sacker, and a single.

Frankie Frisch gave his team a healthy shakeup and when he was through every man who faced Birky [*Lefty Ralph Birkofer*] was able to bat right-handed. Martin was assigned the lead-off position, and Joe Medwick took care of the cleanup job, with Rip Collins following him. Mills was stationed in center [*replacing left-handed batting Orsatti*] and he took his turn in seventh place. Collins and Frisch, as well as Johnny Rothrock, who guarded right field, are turn-around hitters [*switch hitters*]. They swung from their right shoulders against Birkofer, but went into reverse when facing [*his right-handed relievers*] Chagnon and Smith. [*This was Mills's finest day as a Cardinal. Not long afterward he would return to the minor leagues, and his future major league career would be spent with other teams.*]

Edward F. Balinger, Pittsburgh *Post-Gazette*

Latest developments indicate that Cardinal officials have relented slightly on their ban of broadcasting games.

Radio stations now may announce the score at the end of the third, sixth, and ninth innings.

St. Louis *Star-Times*

○ *Saturday, April 28* ○

[*On April 27, in Chicago, the Cardinals, in 11 innings, lost, 3–2. Winning pitcher, Lon Warneke; losing pitcher, Bill Hallahan. Cardinals' standing: 2 wins, 5 losses, in sixth place.*]

There's nothing unlucky about No. 13 for Gabby Hartnett. The veteran went 12 times without a hit, and when he came up for No. 13, after his talent had been slandered by an intentional pass to the preceding batter, he drove out a single to score the winning run and decide an argument between two pitching experts, Lonnie Warneke and Tex Carleton. [*Carleton was taken out for a pinch hitter in the eleventh inning, and his reliever, Bill Hallahan, gave up the winning run.*]

Irving Vaughan, Chicago Tribune

Women fans in Chicago take no chances of not getting a seat. Despite cold weather several hundred lined up outside the park before the noon hour. [*Games began at three o'clock.*] Altogether about 15,000 took advantage of the free gate. [*Friday was ladies' day at Wrigley Field.*]

Chicago Tribune

[*The following is a letter to the sports editor.*]

Dear Sir,

I'm an avid Pirate fan. I get down in the dumps when they lose and shout with joy when they win.

Despite this enthusiasm, I have entered the sacred confines of Forbes Field but once during the past three years. I'm an average citizen, and so how, in the name of goodness, can I see a major league game with the exorbitant price of 55 cents staring me in the face? And that amount gets me the worst seat in the park. On top of everything, car fare from Swissvale costs me 20 cents.

Why doesn't the Pirate management reduce the assessment to within reach of EVERYONE's pocketbook? A 25-cent general admission charge would bring thousands of fans from Pittsburgh and the suburbs, who, like myself, must shy away from the half-dollar price.

If major league clubs continue playing behind locked doors (55 cents and up), baseball is doomed to lose its position as America's most popular sport.

Pittsburgh *Press*

◦ *Sunday, April 29* ◦

[*On April 28, in Chicago, the Cardinals lost, 7–1. Winning pitcher, Guy Bush; losing pitcher, Dizzy Dean. Cardinals' standing: 2 wins, 7 losses, tied for seventh place.*]

The Cubs refuse to concede that Jerome "Dizzy" Dean is an expert in the art of pitching. They polished him off again yesterday in an easy struggle featured by Guy Bush's highly efficient mound work and Chuck Klein's fifth homer of the season. It was the second blast given Dizzy by the Cubs this year and the fourth in a row since last July, when he buried them under 17 strikeouts.

Dizzy Dean's tenure was confined to three innings, the same as when he faced the Cubs last Sunday. Five runs were registered before he could be removed. Then Paul Dean appeared, and he too suffered again. He was limited to a two-inning stretch, during which Klein hit the homer, which was almost a record breaker for distance.

Irving Vaughan, Chicago *Tribune*

There has never been a more astounding comeback in baseball than John Leonard Martin's. The toast of St. Louis in 1931, Pepper saw the bottom drop out of everything in 1932. A .300 batting average went down to .238, and by October the Cardinals were looking for a convenient ash heap. But Martin had the stuff, and today there is hardly a better third baseman in the National League. Martin hit .316 last season, but if he had missed that mark by 30 points he still would be invaluable.

Bow-legged, broad-shouldered, as loose as Dillinger [*the most famous gangster still on the loose, who would be killed in Chicago on July 22*], and with an unquenchable yen to be in the thick of things, Martin possesses a rifle arm, and although he was once wild he is now one of the most unerring throwers in the business. Moreover he is regaining his blustery braggadacio. Trying to lasso him on the bases is almost hopeless. They ought to turn the job over to Frank Buck, who has had considerable success with pythons and lions. [*Frank "Bring 'Em Back Alive" Buck was noted for procuring wild animals for zoos and circuses.*]

Chester L. Smith, Pittsburgh *Press*

Stick ball is a new name to me. I heard it for the first time Thursday evening.

Stick ball is a third cousin to baseball, played with a soft ball and a broomstick on the sidewalks of New York. It is one of the most popular pastimes of boys gathered in various settlement houses. With sand lots getting scarcer and scarcer the youth still find a way to emulate Babe Ruth and get their start in baseball.

[*In 1951, the game of stickball would gain its most famous competitor, Willie Mays, who, during his first season with the New York Giants, often played the game on the streets of Harlem until he was advised by club officials to give up this leisure-time activity.*]

George Daley, New York *Herald-Tribune*

◦ *Monday, April 30* ◦

[*On April 29, in Chicago, the Cardinals won, 9–4. Winning pitcher, Bill Walker; losing pitcher, Pat Malone. Cardinals' standing: 3 wins, 7 losses, tied for sixth place.*]

The St. Louis Cardinals finally did something about the Cubs. They treated Pat Malone and young Bill Lee to base hit shower before 30,000 folks who came out to admire the home team.

Bill Walker performed with such marked skill that only one run was scored against him in seven innings. In the last two innings he apparently saw no need of bearing down, and this probably accounts for the Cubs' final three runs. [*A thirty-year-old left-hander, Walker was a Giant for six years before being traded to St. Louis for the 1933 season, when he won 9 and lost 10. The only native son among the Cardinals, Walker learned his baseball on the sandlots of East St. Louis, and, the owner of thirty tailor-made suits, he was once called "the Beau Brummel of the entire National League."*]

Irving Vaughan, Chicago *Tribune*

NATIONAL LEAGUE STANDINGS

	W	L	PCT	GB		W	L	PCT	GB
Chicago	9	2	.818	—	Brooklyn	5	5	.500	3½
New York	7	3	.700	1½	Cincinnati	3	7	.300	5½
Boston	6	4	.600	2½	St. Louis	3	7	.300	5½
Pittsburgh	5	4	.556	3	Philadelphia	2	8	.200	6½

° *Tuesday, May 1* °

[*On April 30, in St. Louis, the Cardinals defeated Cincinnati, 10–6. Winning pitcher, Burleigh Grimes; losing pitcher, Allyn Stout. Cardinals' standing: 4 wins, 7 losses, in sixth place.*]

In a purely second-division contest, featured by inferior playing by both teams, the great battle for sixth place resulted in a ragged Cardinal victory.

The pitching was strictly minor league, and the game was so tiresome and long drawn out many fans left long before it was over. The starting pitchers, Paul Derringer and the alleged great Dizzy Dean, were knocked off the hill, the talkative Dizzy leaving in the seventh after the Reds had overcome a five-run lead and tied the score.

The only pleasing feature from the Red standpoint was the sincere walloping administered to Dizzy, who announced before the season opened that he and his brother Paul would turn in no less than 45 victories.

Well, Dizzy won his first game, and since then he has been slammed off the mound every time he mounted it. Paul has not won anything yet and has been hit hard on the few occasions when he ventured into action.

If the Dean brothers are going to win the pennant for the Cardinals, the Frisch outfit may as well resign itself to defeat.

Jack Ryder, Cincinnati *Enquirer*

° *Wednesday, May 2* °

[*On May 1, in St. Louis, the Cardinals defeated Cincinnati in 11 innings, 3–2. Winning pitcher, Burleigh Grimes; losing pitcher, Silas Johnson. Cardinals' standing: 5 wins, 7 losses, tied for fifth place.*]

May Day found the Reds of Cincinnati very troublesome, but Jim Collins kept them under control, and the Cardinals won after 11 innings of spirited battling.

The Reds, with Silas Johnson pitching a whale of a game, had the Cards blanked 1 to 0 for eight innings, but Collins, in the last half of the ninth, deadlocked the struggle with a home run to the pavilion roof.

The Reds again looked like winners when they forged ahead, 2 to 1, in the eleventh. Then Collins again came to the rescue with a home run, after which DeLancey's double and Burgess Whitehead's single ended the bitter fight, 2 hours and 57 minutes after it had started. [*Jim "Ripper" Collins, who gained his nickname from the way in which he "ripped" the ball when batting, was thirty years old and had come to the Cardinals in 1931 after eight years of playing in the minor leagues. He succeeded Jim Bottomley as the Redbirds' regular first baseman in 1932, and he was now regarded as the team's principal home run threat. In this game, incidentally, the winning pitcher in relief, for the second day in a row, was the major leagues' only surviving spitball pitcher, Burleigh Grimes. Since he would not win again, this victory was the last to be gained by a pitcher who could legally throw a spitball.*]

Martin J. Haley, St. Louis Globe-Democrat

Umpire Dolly Stark says Carl Hubbell is the hardest pitcher to work with. Hubbell's screw ball, aimed at the corners of the plate, calls for plenty of concentration.

New York World-Telegram

◦ *Thursday, May 3* ◦

[*On May 2, in St. Louis, the Cardinals defeated Cincinnati, 4–1. Winning pitcher, Tex Carleton; losing pitcher, Benny Frey. Cardinals' standing: 6 wins, 7 losses, in fifth place.*]

Tex Carleton pitched another good game, and this time the Cardinals won for him. The Reds of Cincinnati got 8 hits and managed to drive Carleton to shelter in the ninth inning, but Tex pitched a tight game, nevertheless, and when he needed help he got it from Dizzy Dean, who rushed to the rescue and quickly locked out the intruders.

Martin J. Haley, St. Louis Globe-Democrat

"Is Brooklyn still in the league?" asked Bill Terry last winter.

It would have been poetic justice had the Dodgers answered Terry's taunt with three straight victories [*in a just-completed series*]. Instead the Giants slapped three straight defeats on the Dodgers, which means, "No, Brooklyn is not in the league."

However, it's a long lane that has no ashcan and Casey Stengel doesn't forget easily. Maybe Bill will live to rue his remarks before the season is over. It's bad business stirring up the fighting blood of a team that in the past has specialized in knocking off the Giants in the home stretch when they were pennant contenders and victories were as precious as radium.

Dan Parker, New York *Daily Mirror*

∘ *Friday, May 4* ∘

[*On May 3, in St. Louis, the Cardinals defeated Philadelphia, 8–7. Winning pitcher, Paul Dean; losing pitcher, Phil Collins. Cardinals' standing: 7 wins, 7 losses, in fifth place.*]

Jimmy Wilson's Phils piled up 14 hits, but the Cardinals won with a more condensed attack and superior defense.

One hit stood out above the others, Joe Medwick's home run into the left field bleachers with the bases loaded in the fourth inning. That broke a 2 to 2 tie, but the Birds needed a double by Jim Collins to drive in a pair of sixth-inning runs to make the day secure.

As in their three previous victories, the Cards needed relief hurling. They opened with Flint Rhem, who had enough after three rounds. His successor, Paul Dean, also was cuffed around and had to be relieved by Jess Haines. [*Although he gave up 7 hits and 5 runs in the five innings that he pitched, Paul Dean received credit for his first major league victory.*]

Martin J. Haley, St. Louis *Globe-Democrat*

∘ *Saturday, May 5* ∘

[*On May 4, in St. Louis, the Cardinals defeated Philadelphia, 3–1. Winning pitcher, Bill Walker; losing pitcher, Curt Davis. Cardinals' standing: 8 wins, 7 losses, in fourth place.*]

Bill Walker, the East St. Louis boy who took great delight in beating the Cardinals while with the Giants, proved to a ladies' day crowd that he was not particularly partial about his victims as he left-handed the hard-hitting Phillies into defeat. The women fans, seeing their first game of the year [*as free patrons*], numbered 2,000. [*Ladies' day, inaugurated in Brooklyn in the 1890's, was introduced to the feminine fans of St. Louis in 1917, and, despite the women's movement, it is still maintained in Busch Stadium.*]

Walker's performance was almost matched in brilliance by the recruit right-hander, Curt Davis, whose lack of control in the first inning cost him the game. It was won on two bases on balls, an error, and Spud Davis' two-run single. [*Virgil "Spud" Davis was regarded as baseball's hardest hitting catcher. In 1933, playing his sixth season with the Phillies, he batted .349, a National League average that was second only to that of his teammate Chuck Klein. During the winter of 1933–34, Klein was traded to the Chicago Cubs, and Davis was sent to St. Louis in exchange for Jimmie Wilson, who then became Philadelphia's manager.*]

Giving Davis a helping hand in producing runs was Joe Medwick, the free-swinging left sentryman [*outfielder*], who clouted a home run into the left center field bleachers in the fourth, his fifth homer of the season and his second in two days.

Raymond V. Smith, St. Louis Globe-Democrat

◦ *Sunday, May 6* ◦

[*On May 5, in St. Louis, the Cardinals defeated Philadelphia, 7–1. Winning pitcher, Dizzy Dean; losing pitcher, Cy Moore. Cardinals' standing, 9 wins, 7 losses, in fourth place.*]

Averaging better than two bases on their 10 hits, the Cardinals slugged Philadelphia into submission for their seventh straight victory, the first for Dizzy Dean since opening day and Diz's first complete game since the inaugural. He limited the Quakers to 7 hits, fanned 7, and had a shutout until the ninth inning.

The Cards again showed a fine defense. They turned 2 more double plays, giving them 6 in 2 games and 12 in the last 5.

Martin J. Haley, St. Louis Globe-Democrat

∘ *Monday, May 7* ∘

[On May 6, in St. Louis, the Cardinals lost to Boston, 3–2. Winning pitcher, Fred Frankhouse; losing pitcher, Bill Hallahan. Cardinals' standing: 9 wins, 8 losses, in fifth place.]

In a bitter battle dotted with verbal disputes, Boston's Braves ended the Cardinals' seven-game winning streak.

Bill Hallahan pitched perfect baseball until one out in the sixth, when an error and Bill Urbanski's double produced one run. The Braves then landed on the veteran left-hander for another run in the seventh, but in the end the Braves needed a homer by Joe Mowry off Burleigh Grimes in the eighth to win the game. *[One of the National League's foremost left-handed pitchers in the early thirties, the thirty-one-year-old Bill Hallahan had pitched regularly for the Cardinals since 1929. Sometimes called "Wild Bill," he had led the league three times in bases on balls, but he had also led twice in strikeouts.]*

Martin J. Haley, St. Louis *Globe-Democrat*

NATIONAL LEAGUE STANDINGS

	W	L	PCT	GB		W	L	PCT	GB
New York	12	5	.706	—	St. Louis	9	8	.529	3
Chicago	12	6	.667	½	Brooklyn	7	9	.438	4½
Pittsburgh	10	6	.625	1½	Philadelphia	4	12	.250	7½
Boston	9	7	.563	2½	Cincinnati	3	13	.188	8½

∘ *Tuesday, May 8* ∘

[On May 7, in St. Louis, the Cardinals defeated Boston, 10–5. Winning pitcher, Tex Carleton; losing pitcher, Bob Brown. Cardinals' standing: 10 wins, 8 losses, in fourth place.]

Summer weather found the Cardinals in a truculent hitting mood, and they slugged their way to an easy victory over the Braves. The Birds had a 10 to 0 lead after seven innings, and then Tex Carleton eased up. With one out in the seventh, Carleton had visions of a no-hit game, but Baxter Jordan shattered his chance for fame by slapping a ground single past Jim Collins. Then Carleton coasted along, and the Braves wound up with 7 hits.

Collins' fifth home run of the season, Jack Rothrock's first, and Carleton's triple were the longest Cardinal blows, but the most decisive was Joe Medwick's bases-loaded double in the third.

Martin J. Haley, St. Louis Globe-Democrat

Southpaw Bill Walker will be lost for at least six weeks because of a broken ulna bone in his left forearm. Bill suffered the break on Sunday when he was struck by a ball Joe Medwick hit during batting practice.

This is a tough break, for Walker had just boosted the Cards' chances with two straight victories. In an effort to get a left-hander to fill his place, Manager Frisch will give Jim Mooney a chance to show his starting ability this afternoon.

St. Louis Globe-Democrat

◦ *Wednesday, May 9* ◦

[*On May 8, in St. Louis, the Cardinals defeated Boston, 5–4. Winning pitcher, Jesse Haines; losing pitcher, Benny Cantwell. Cardinals' standing: 11 wins, 8 losses, in fourth place.*]

Four runs behind after three innings, the Cardinals shaded Boston, 5 to 4, to climb within two games of the league-leading Giants.

Jess Haines' brilliant relief pitching made possible the uphill victory. Haines went to work in the third inning after Boston had knocked out Southpaw Jim Mooney. Jess pitched so effectively he undoubtedly will be given a starting assignment in the near future. When he entered the struggle, the Braves, besides being four runs to the merry, had two men on base, but Jess quickly stifled that rally and blanked Boston for the last six innings, as he registered his first victory of the season.

Martin J. Haley, St. Louis Globe-Democrat

Bill Terry thinks that in August and September Frankie Frisch and his Cardinals will represent a threat to the pennant hopes of the Giants. Personally, I've never thought the Cardinals were quite the team Terry and other observers think.

Admittedly they possess playing qualities that catch the eye. Flash and dash, speed and an ostentatious aggressiveness. But it takes more than that to win a pennant.

The Cardinals run too much to the Leo Durocher type of player. Too much of what they do doesn't mean a thing, theatrical and pleasing to watch, but actually pointless.

Garry Schumacher, New York *Evening Journal*

Tom Yawkey is the first club owner in major league history to place his players on a profit-sharing basis. [*Yawkey owned the Boston Red Sox.*] Yawkey told his men that if they finished third or better he would declare them in on the net balance at the close of the season. [*The Red Sox had not finished in the first division since 1918 and in nine of the preceding twelve seasons they had ended in last place.*]

Dan Daniel, New York *World-Telegram*

◦ *Thursday, May 10* ◦

[*On May 9, in St. Louis, the Cardinals defeated New York, 4–0. Winning pitcher, Dizzy Dean; losing pitcher, Johnny Salveson. Cardinals' standing: 12 wins, 8 losses, in fourth place.*]

When Jerome "Dizzy" Dean is right he makes any team look futile, and "Dizzy" was right enough yesterday to limit the Giants to 5 hits and fan 7.

It was a tough spot for [*twenty-year-old rookie*] Johnny Salveson to make his first start of the season. The "Dean" of the Deans rated a more experienced opponent unless the reasoning was, why waste a good pitcher when Dean is likely to win anyway? It was certainly a long shot gamble, Salveson not having done any work in more than two weeks except in the bull pen. [*On the following day Salveson was sent down to the minor leagues.*]

Will Wedge, New York *Sun*

The Yankee network broadcast a testimonial dinner given Tom Yawkey, owner of the Boston Red Sox, last week. As the dinner cost eight bucks there was lively competition among announcers to get the assignment, since eight-buck dinners are not every-day occurrences even with the most affluent of the mike family.

The Sporting News

○ *Friday, May 11* ○

[On May 10, in St. Louis, the Cardinals defeated the Giants, 5–4. Winning pitcher, Jim Mooney; losing pitcher, Hal Schumacher. Cardinals' standing: 13 wins and 8 losses, tied for third place.]

St. Louis—Dimly through the dust cloud, which has swept southeastward from Nebraska and the Dakotas to envelop this town in a murky haze, the Giants today found themselves sharing third place with the Cardinals. The world champions bounced in here in first place two days ago, but since then the Cards have done all the bouncing, with the Giants in the unfamiliar role of bouncees.

The Cardinals think they're going some place this summer, and they certainly act like it. The Redbirds are now the most impressive club in the league.

Frankie Frisch has a strong club, and it's fast with Frisch himself among the least speedy of the regulars. Martin, Medwick, Orsatti, and Rothrock all can outfoot Frisch, which is a tip-off, not on Frisch, but on the general speed of the team.

If the pitching holds up, and it should grow even stronger when Bill Walker's broken arm heals, the Cardinals will be tough.

Right now the Giants are contributing to their downfall by mistakes. They won the pennant last year by winning games they could just as easily have lost. This year they may blow it by losing games they could just as easily have won.

Yesterday the Giants offered an excellent illustration of how NOT to protect a lead. At the end of three innings Bill Hallahan had been driven to cover and Hal Schumacher was pitching easily, with a 3–0 lead. The Giants eventually lost, and here's how the Cardinals got their first four runs:

No. 1. Durocher hit a pop fly in front of the plate. Catcher Gus Mancuso and third baseman Johnny Vergez both started for it and pulled back, the ball falling for a single. Comment: The Giants have a working arrangement with Nashville but apparently have no working arrangements among themselves. *[At this time the Giants maintained a farm team in Nashville, in the Southern Association.]*

No. 2. This same Durocher hit a pop fly to right, which Homer Peel lost in the wind. Comment: Some slugger, that Babe Durocher!

No. 3. Martin singles and second baseman Blondy Ryan walks to the pitcher's box to console Schumacher, leaving second base uncovered. Martin steals second and scores when Rothrock singles. Comment: Conferences should be held in the clubhouse, not on the diamond. Don't write, telegraph. [*In the mid-thirties Western Union's advertising slogan was "Don't write, telegraph!"*]

No. 4. Medwick walked and reached third on Virgil Davis' single. With one out the infield is playing in close. Orsatti slashes sharply at Ryan, who throws home too late to get Medwick, although he could have made a double play by stepping on second and throwing to Terry, ending the inning. Comment: Did you ever see a dream walking? [*One of the most popular songs of 1934 was "Did You Ever See a Dream Walking?"*]

Tom Meany, New York World-Telegram

○ *Saturday, May 12* ○

[*On May 11, in St. Louis, the Cardinals defeated New York in 10 innings, 3–2. Winning pitcher, Paul Dean; losing pitcher, Carl Hubbell. Cardinals' standing: 14 wins, 8 losses, in third place.*]

The famous "Dean Act" is beginning to pay dividends. Dizzy pitched his best game of the season on Wednesday, and now Paul comes up to claim his share of honors. Matching ball for ball with the great Carl Hubbell, Paul Dean came through like a thoroughbred to thrill a ladies' day crowd of 6,500. He had to travel ten innings before victory was his, the vital thrust being a long single by Jack Rothrock that scored Orsatti.

Time and again Paul Dean worked himself out of dangerous spots and had the 2,500 women and 4,000 paying fans gasping.

Raymond V. Smith, St. Louis Globe-Democrat

Aiding and abetting the Cardinals yesterday was a quota of soprano-shrill female customers, who yipped and yammered at everything, making a fearful din which helped the Cardinals to get a break in the tenth inning.

The score was tied with one down and Durocher on second. Paul Dean hit a fly over short right, and Ryan and Frank "Lefty" O'Doul both tried for it. Each yelled he had it, but neither could hear the other because of the feminine fans making such a racket. Each slowed up, fearing a collision, and the ball fell free. [*Durocher subsequently scored the winning run.*]

Will Wedge, New York Sun

Ben Chapman, Yankee outfielder who was under fire for making derogatory remarks about Jews at Yankee Stadium last summer, has again stirred up the resentment of Yankee fans of Hebrew extraction.

On Thursday, after Chapman had missed a ball in left field, he exchanged words with fans behind the Yankee dugout and, singling out one in particular, called him a "Jew b------."

A number of witnesses of the incident have telephoned the *Mirror* and several called in person to complain. They all agree on the details.

Chapman let a drive get away from him while trying to make a one-hand catch, and a fan shouted, "Why don't you use both hands and stop grandstanding?" [*At this time, unlike the present, outfielders regularly used both hands to catch fly balls.*]

Thereupon Chapman uttered his insulting epithet. [*Chapman, who was born in Tennessee and grew up in Alabama, would achieve notoriety in 1947 when, as manager of the Phillies, he shouted vicious racial slurs at the major leagues' first black player, Jackie Robinson.*]

New York *Daily Mirror*

◦ *Sunday, May 13* ◦

[*On May 12, in St. Louis, the Cardinals lost to New York, 6–4. Winning pitcher, Al Smith; losing pitcher, Tex Carleton. Cardinals' standing: 14 wins, 9 losses, tied for third place.*]

With an effort born of despair the Giants rose majestically over a lot of serious obstacles, not least of which was some atrocious play on their own part, and hurled back the Cardinals.

Five Giant tallies were bludgeoned across in the final two innings as the world's champions routed Tex Carleton and finished the job against Willie Hallahan, the highlights being two doubles by Travis Jackson, the second of which came in the ninth with the bases full.

John Drebinger, *The New York Times*

∘ *Monday, May 14* ∘

[*On May 13, in St. Louis, the Cardinals defeated Brooklyn, 12–7. Winning pitcher, Dizzy Dean; losing pitcher, Dutch Leonard. Cardinals' standing: 15 wins, 9 losses, in third place.*]

The almost daily practice of fattening rival batting averages was resumed by Brooklyn Dodger pitchers as the Cardinals slammed the offerings of Emil "Dutch" Leonard, Walter Beck, Phil Page, and Charlie Perkins for 18 hits and Dizzy Dean's fourth victory of the season.

Arthur E. Patterson, New York *Herald-Tribune*

NATIONAL LEAGUE STANDINGS

	W	L	PCT	GB		W	L	PCT	GB
Pittsburgh	15	7	.682	½	Boston	12	11	.522	4
Chicago	17	8	.680	—	Brooklyn	8	15	.348	8
St. Louis	15	9	.625	1½	Philadelphia	7	15	.318	8½
New York	14	10	.583	2½	Cincinnati	5	18	.217	11

∘ *Tuesday, May 15* ∘

[*On May 14, in St. Louis, the Cardinals' scheduled game with Brooklyn was postponed because of rain.*]

Burleigh Grimes, the last major league spitball pitcher, was given his unconditional release today by President Sam Breadon of the Cardinals.

Grimes was credited with two victories this year, won in relief on successive days, and he suffered one defeat. He appeared in four games and pitched eight innings. Only 3 runs and 5 hits were made off him.

Grimes' release was due to the club's necessity of getting within the player limit by midnight tonight, according to Breadon.

[*In 1921, the spitball became illegal in the major leagues, but an exception was made for seventeen pitchers, including Grimes, who were permitted to continue to use the pitch. In 1934, there were still two spitball pitchers in organized baseball, Frank Shellenback and Clarence Mitchell, who performed in the Pacific Coast League. In the depression year of 1931, the number of players a team was permitted to carry was lowered from twenty-five to twenty-three. The twenty-five-player limit would be restored in 1939 and has remained unchallenged.*]

St. Louis Post-Dispatch

○ *Wednesday, May 16* ○

[*On May 15, in St. Louis, the Cardinals lost to Brooklyn, 6–5. Winning pitcher, Ray Lucas; losing pitcher, Jim Mooney. Cardinals' standing: 15 wins, 10 losses, in third place.*]

Casey Stengel became a master mind, and his Dodgers defeated the Cardinals. Casey danced a sedate fandango on the dugout steps as the final put-out was made, and then hurried away for the home-bound train. [*Brooklyn's current road trip ended with this game.*]

The winning run was carried across in the eighth by Lonnie Frey in a successful double steal ordered by his boss, with Danny Taylor on the first base end of the play. Here, with Hack Wilson, who three times had failed to hit with men on base, at bat, Casey made his master stroke. Taylor broke for second with the pitch and Frey started home. By the time Frisch had run forward to take Spud Davis' short throw Taylor was on the bag and Frey had crossed the plate.

Roscoe McGowen, *The New York Times*

Yesterday Joe Medwick and Tex Carleton showed a new punch but not with their bats. They used fists.

During batting practice Carleton objected to Medwick taking a turn while the pitchers were hitting, and Medwick shouted, "I'm tired of taking your abuse!"

"Well, let's go," Carleton shouted back.

Round one was on. They both swung wild, Medwick leading with a hard right that grazed Carleton's left eye. The pitcher came back with a right hook that caught the outfielder flush on the chin. They sparred. Medwick connected with a hard right, and Carleton missed an uppercut. By this time other players intervened and pulled them apart.

Later the two men shook hands and agreed to bury the hatchet, but not in each other's head. Both insisted the row arose on the spur of the moment and was not the aftermath of two defeats suffered by Carleton due to fielding mistakes by the man with whom he scuffled.

Ray J. Gillespie, St. Louis *Star-Times*

◦ *Friday, May 18* ◦

[*On May 16, the Cardinals were not scheduled to play, and they traveled to Boston. On May 17, in Boston, the Cardinals won, 5–3. Winning pitcher, Paul Dean; losing pitcher, Huck Betts. Cardinals' standing: 16 wins, 10 losses, in third place.*]

"Huck" Betts, after pitching a sweet game for six innings, lost his control, and the Cardinals got away with the game.

"Huck" tried to get the opposition to go after bad balls, but they were not good enough to tempt them, and so the Boston pitcher got himself into holes and had to throw up cripples, and the Cardinals connected for two home runs and a triple.

Davis and Frisch hit the homers, Frisch's coming in the eighth with "Pepper" Martin, who had walked on four straight balls, on second with the tying run. Betts tried to get Frankie to go after bad balls, but the "Fordham Flash" disdained his offerings and got to three and one. Betts had to put the ball over, and Frisch, laying for it, eased it into the right field bleachers, and the jig was up.

James C. O'Leary, Boston *Globe*

It is obvious that Frank Francis Frisch, the erstwhile Fordham Flash, has instilled a new spirit of determination and camaraderie into the Cardinals. The spirit infused their locker room as they dressed. The jibing and ribbing was evidence of this new spirit.

Harrison J. "Doc" Weaver, rotund, bespectacled trainer, hastened about the room, taking care of "his boys" by splashing lotions over their lithe bodies as protection against the east winds of the Hub. "Butch" Yatkeman, the diminutive clubhouse boy whom the Cardinals always bring with them, hustled about doing odd jobs. [*"Butch" Yatkeman started with the Cardinals as the visiting club batboy in 1924, and he remained uninterruptedly in the club's employment until his retirement on December 31, 1982.*] Everywhere were signs of energy and enthusiasm.

"It's shoah nice to win a game like that," drawled James Otto "Tex" Carleton in his best Comanche, Texas, accent.

Spud Davis broke in with a Birmingham inflection. "Ah may have hit longer hom-ahs, but ah don't know when ah hit any tha' felt anah bettah."

"It doesn't matter if they just drop into the bleachers," offered sage Jesse Haines, "or go clear to Cambridge, they all count for a homer."

"Ouch," suddenly came from Frisch as Weaver vigorously rubbed a sore-looking left ankle. "That's from one of Davis' throws," explained the Cardinals' manager.

"What's the mattah," drawled Davis, "can't ya take it?"

"Oh," groaned Frisch, "somebody throw something at him."

"I wonder how the other clubs made out," interposed Miguel Gonzalez [*who served, along with Clyde "Buzzy" Wares, as one of the team's two coaches.*]

"The hell with the other clubs," exploded Frisch. "When you win, they've got to chase you. We've got enough problems with our own club instead of worrying about the others." There seemed the philosophy of the late John McGraw in his words. [*McGraw had died on February 25, 1934.*]

Frisch seems like "one of the boys" who can do everything he asks of his players. Certainly they must admire his courage. In addition to the ankle injury, he had a nasty-looking black and blue spot on his chest (hit by a pitch), a bandage on his right elbow, another on his left leg and the usual crop of "raspberries."

Gerry Moore, Boston Evening Transcript

∘ *Saturday, May 19* ∘

[*On May 18, in Boston, the Cardinals lost, 6–2. Winning pitcher, Fred Frankhouse; losing pitcher, Jim Winford. Cardinals' standing: 16 wins, 11 losses, in third place.*]

Boston—Gambling on his recruit pitcher, Jim Winford, starting his first game in the majors, Manager Frankie Frisch lost, and the Braves walked off with a victory.

Raymond V. Smith, St. Louis Globe-Democrat

The fans haven't responded greatly to the improvement in National League hitting. Owners are moaning all around the circuit. It takes more than a home run to bring out the fans—such as a little pocket money.

St. Louis Post-Dispatch

∘ *Sunday, May 20* ∘

[*On May 19, in Boston, the Cardinals won, 2–1. Winning pitcher, Tex Carleton; losing pitcher, Ed Brandt. Cardinals' standing: 17 wins, 11 losses, in third place.*]

James Otto Carleton, the young man from Comanche, Tex., who has had trouble going the nine-inning route recently, turned in a pitching masterpiece yesterday. His curve never crackled through the strike zone more effectively, and except for two pop fly doubles the slender Texan would have had a shutout.

In the fourth inning Hal Lee popped a dinky fly over Jimmy Collins' head and reached second. Walter Berger then sent a high pop fly to short left. Joe Medwick could have caught it, but Captain Leo Durocher, who has one of the loudest voices in baseball, announced so that it could be heard down Chelsea way, that he had it, he had it. [*Durocher was the team's field captain.*]

But he didn't have it. At the last moment he looked around for help, but none was there and the ball plunked into the turf for a two-base hit and Lee scampered home.

J. Roy Stockton, *St. Louis Post-Dispatch*

∘ *Monday, May 21* ∘

[*On May 20, in New York, the Cardinals won, 9–5. Winning pitcher, Dizzy Dean; losing pitcher, Carl Hubbell. Cardinals' standing: 18 wins, 11 losses, in second place.*]

That merry madcap, that Zany, that belligerent buffoon, Dizzy Dean, methinks, is as looney as Bre'r Fox. Leastwise, he is too smart for our Giants. He slit the sleeves of his undershirt, waved his flapping arms above his head and kept pouring that little white onion in there yesterday and coasted to a victory. [*Pitchers now are forbidden to work with a torn, flapping undershirt.*]

Dean completely baffled our sluggers, giving them one hit until the sixth. By then the Cardinals had very thoroughly shellacked Carl Hubbell. Ripper Collins bashed a home run in the fourth with Ducky Medwick aboard. Frank Frisch slammed a triple against the wall in left-center in the fifth with the bases full. Shortly after, Ducky batted again and hit the longest home run of the season to score his boss ahead of him. The ball whisked like a rifle shot high into the left field tier of seats above the St. Louis bullpen. [*The visitors' bull pen in the Polo Grounds was in deep left-center field, well over four hundred feet from the home plate, and Medwick's drive went into the upper of two tiers of stands.*]

After that Dean relaxed. He grinned good humoredly into the glowering face of Manager Bill Terry, impudently capered at the plate, and passed the time of day with the umpires. He strutted, he boasted, and he dominated the diamond before 40,000 fans, the largest crowd yet this season.

It was the first time Hubbell has been knocked out this year.

Jimmy Powers, New York Daily News

Spitball pitching, the picturesque if inelegant development in the science of slinging, soon will be in the limbo of the forgotten, along with the free lunch, the Republican party and the bicycle built for two.

Dan Daniel, New York World-Telegram

NATIONAL LEAGUE STANDINGS

	W	L	PCT	GB		W	L	PCT	GB
Chicago	20	11	.645	—	Boston	14	13	.519	4
St. Louis	18	11	.621	1	Brooklyn	12	16	.429	6½
Pittsburgh	16	10	.615	1½	Philadelphia	9	17	.346	8½
New York	17	13	.567	2½	Cincinnati	6	21	.222	12

∘ *Tuesday, May 22* ∘

[*On May 21, in New York, the Cardinals lost, 5–2. Winning pitcher, Joe Bowman; losing pitcher, Bill Hallahan. Cardinals' standing: 18 wins, 12 losses, in third place.*]

A fellow named Joe licked the Cards yesterday. This fellow Joe (his name is Bowman) got into the game by accident.

You see, pals, it was this-a-way. Freddy Fitzsimmons, the regular pitcher, was warming up in front of the grandstand, minding his own business, when suddenly a bat flies out of the hands of Jim Mooney and cracks our Fitz plunk in the kidneys. He fell like a stuck ox.

Bowman was then asked to step in and do his stuff. And did he curl that cantaloupe? Just take a quick squint at the boxscore. Two clean runs he gives those tough babies who had just murdered Hubbell. [*During the entire year Bowman had only five victories and pitched just three complete games.*]

Jimmy Powers, New York Daily News

Frank Frisch inspected the Cardinals' hotel restaurant checks today and wanted to know why several players hadn't taken last evening's meal at the hotel. It's a club rule.

St. Louis Post-Dispatch

∘ *Wednesday, May 23* ∘

[*On May 22, in New York, the Cardinals won, 7–4. Winning pitcher, Paul Dean; losing pitcher, Al Smith. Cardinals' standing: 19 wins, 12 losses, in third place.*]

Joe Medwick delivered for the Cardinals. With the count 3 and 2 and the bases jammed to capacity in the ninth, the lithe Hungarian smacked one of Adolf Luque's fast balls for a triple to center, three Redbirds spiking the rubber, providing the margin of victory. [*Born Joseph Mikal in Carteret, New Jersey, Medwick was the son of Hungarian immigrants.*]

For Paul Dean it was the fourth victory and the third time in succession he finished his starting assignment.

Manager Terry's strategy in the final chapter proved the turning point. With Dean on third and Rothrock on second, Terry and his lieutenants held a consultation, and they decided to pass the dangerous Frisch and try their luck with Medwick. If Terry recalled that the same Medwick hit for the circuit in St. Louis several weeks ago after Frisch had been purposely passed to crowd the bases he might have changed his mind. But he may have figured Medwick easy for right-handed pitching, for he waved to the bull pen for veteran Luque, who replaced left-handed Al Smith on the parapet. Medwick then came through with that blasting triple. [*Almost forty-four years old, Adolf Luque, a Cuban, was the oldest player in the major leagues.*]

Raymond V. Smith, St. Louis Globe-Democrat

◦ *Thursday, May 24* ◦

[*On May 23, in Brooklyn, the Cardinals lost, 5–3. Winning pitcher, Ray Benge; losing pitcher, Jim Mooney. Cardinals' satnding: 19 wins, 13 losses, in third place.*]

That pathetic old geezer did it again, Cuthbert. Yes, sir, he stood there with his bay window draped above the plate, unwound his long-handled broomstick and wafted that onion on a non-stop flight to the right field screen, and that's how the Dodgers won a game from the Cardinals.

That aforementioned old geezer, none other than Hack Wilson, sewed the game up for Cousin Casey Stengel in the fifth with his fifth homer of the season. [*In 1930, with the Chicago Cubs, Wilson batted .356, hit 56 home runs (still a National League record), and drove in 190 runs (still a major league record). After 1930, Wilson suffered an astonishing reversal of form. He never again hit .300, and when Brooklyn released him a little later in the 1934 season, he would leave the major leagues for good.*]

Earlier ol' Hack had scared Jim Mooney into two free passes. When he strode to the plate in the fifth, the game was deadlocked, 2–2. Mooney gambled that the Hacker, with none down and Linus Frey on second, would whiff. Instead he whaled it, and there was the game.

George Kenney, New York *Daily News*

Does anyone appreciate the resentment small town people hold for citizens of big cities? This explains more than anything the success of the Dean brothers. When you hand Paul or Jerome a baseball and tell them they are to pitch a nine-inning contest they more or less mechanically turn in an excellent job. If you tell them to pitch against the New York Giants their eyes glow fanatically, they snatch the horsehide and stride to the mound, nostrils breathing fire. Until the world champs appeared in St. Louis the younger Dean was just another performer. Most of the western clubs had knocked him out of the box. Now, he is made. He has beaten us twice, and so has his bigger brother. Both are tank towners from Texas who look upon themselves as consecrated Saint Georges turning back the Metropolitan dragons. If the Giants do not win the pennant and the Cardinals do, credit the remarkable Deans.

Jimmy Powers, New York *Daily News*

Frankie Frisch does a John McGraw when Paul Dean works, wig-wagging every pitch for the youngster. [*McGraw habitually called all pitches in a game.*]

Dick Farrington, *The Sporting News*

"Not a championship club." So Casey Stengel sums up the Cardinals. The reasons: "Frisch isn't what he once was, the shortstop can't hit, they have a good hitting catcher, and one swell outfielder."

The last two items sound like boosts, but they aren't. They are Casey's way of saying, "Davis is a good hitter, but they will miss Jimmy Wilson's defensive strength and his smartness in handling pitchers." Also, "Medwick's a star, but the rest of the outfield falls below par."

Harold Parrott, Brooklyn *Eagle*

◦ *Friday, May 25* ◦

[*On May 24, in Brooklyn, the Cardinals won, 7–3. Winning pitcher, Tex Carleton; losing pitcher, Dutch Leonard. Cardinals' standing: 20 wins, 13 losses, in second place.*]

The Dodgers had an unpleasant time yesterday, and so did the fellow who kept calling Leo Durocher the "All-American Out." [*Early in his major league career, when he played with the Yankees, Durocher acquired the nickname "All-American Out." Actually, his lifetime batting average of .247 is higher than that of some highly touted modern players. In 1981, for example, the owner of the Yankees, George Steinbrenner, paid an outfielder named Oscar Gamble a few hundred thousand dollars to hit a baseball, and Gamble repaid his boss by batting .238.*] He might better have termed the St. Louis shortstop "Leo the Lion," because Durocher delivered the blow that scuttled the Brooklyn ship.

After listening to the leather-lunged fan for five innings, Durocher stepped to the plate in the sixth with two on, two out, and the score tied. Once again the cry "All-American Out" floated over Ebbets Field, but this time the jibe must have struck home. Durocher lashed out with all the fury in his slender body and drove it into left field for a two-bagger. Both men raced home.

The boisterous fan wisely decided to let Durocher alone after that and concentrated on Frisch, calling him "Lucky!" That also worked out badly because the Flash made three hits and had a great afternoon.

They can say what they want about Frisch slowing up, but not many second basemen could turn in the play Frisch made on Ralph "Buzz" Boyle's shot in the third. Frisch raced back of second, scooped up the ball with one hand and still had time to toss out the fastest man on the Dodgers.

Frisch also outwitted Lonny Frey on a steal of second. The Brooklyn youngster was waiting with the ball, but Frisch slid around him to safety.

Murray Tynan, New York *Herald-Tribune*

Frisch is the strictest manager in either league. He makes the Redbirds check in by 11, insists they eat at regular hours, and he does a bit of snooping. Yet the Cardinals all swear by him.

Harold Parrott, Brooklyn *Eagle*

∘ *Saturday, May 26* ∘

[*On May 25, in Brooklyn, the Cardinals' scheduled game was postponed because of rain. The team moved on to Philadelphia for its next series, beginning today.*]

Philadelphia—Jerome Herman "Dizzy" Dean and his brother Paul are on the verge of a two-man strike for higher wages.

Manager Frank Frisch refuses to take the threatened strike seriously, even declining to admit that he has discussed arbitration with the two pitchers, but according to the best information, only the suggestion that the office of Sam Breadon is the proper place for fighting out the question of a compromise prevented the Dean boys from issuing an ultimatum· that if more money isn't forthcoming, there won't be any more Dean pitching.

Dizzy is scheduled to face the Phils tomorrow, and apparently he will go through with his assignment, content to postpone negotiations until the team returns home. And if local No. 1 of the Dean Brotherhood doesn't take an unexpected strike vote Paul will oppose the Phils Monday. But the atmosphere is charged with potentialities as only atmosphere around two Dean boys can be charged, and the most optimistic agree that anything can happen.

It will be remembered that Dizzy and Paul engaged in extended negotiations with Cardinal officers in March. Paul was offered $3,000, and the offer didn't please him. He held out for a long time, but eventually signed, with Dizzy acting as adviser.

Now, it seems, Dizzy feels that Paul made a mistake. That a man who can win four straight without a defeat should not have signed for such a paltry figure and that Dizzy himself should be paid more than his contract calls for.

When the team reached Boston, grumblings and mutterings were heard in the clubhouse and hotel lobby. Manager Frisch had a talk with Dizzy, but he declines to discuss the conference.

"Sure, everybody would like to have more money," Frank said last night. "But I don't know anything about a revolt or any promise that I'd recommend an increase. I have enough to do managing a ball club without taking a hand in the business of salaries. Sure, I have talked with Dizzy and Paul. I talk with all my players. Such conferences are confidential."

Had Frisch heard of a threat by the Deans to quit unless their contracts were revised?

"No, I never heard of any such threats. If anybody doesn't want to play on this club, they can go home. We sign our contracts in February or March, and it is not the custom to revise contracts in May or June."

"Let's forget it," Dizzy answered when asked about the strike. "Everything is going to be all right."

Paul also was reluctant to discuss the strike, but intimated that he had reason to suppose that a new contract would be offered.

Other players on the team do not take the strike threat seriously. Almost to a man they echo Frisch's thought that February is the time to engage in conversations over salaries.

J. Roy Stockton, *St. Louis Post-Dispatch*

∘ *Sunday, May 27* ∘

[*On May 26, in Philadelphia, the Cardinals' scheduled game was postponed because of rain.*]

The All-Star game between picked National and American League teams, inaugurated last year in Chicago for the benefit of old and indigent ball players, will be held on July 10 in the Polo Grounds, it was decided yesterday at a conference between President John A. Heydler and Will Harridge.

As was the procedure last year, the nation's fans will be asked to vote for their favorite players, although the final decision as to the line-up will rest with the two managers who will soon be chosen. Each team is limited to 20 players.

John Drebinger, *The New York Times*

∘ *Monday, May 28* ∘

[*On May 27, in Philadelphia, the Cardinals, in 10 innings, won, 5–2. Winning pitcher, Dizzy Dean; losing pitcher, Phil Collins. Cardinals' standing: 21 wins, 13 losses, in second place.*]

If Jerome Dean is "dizzy," let's hope all the Phillies suddenly go haywire.
   Not only did the long, lean, eccentric right-hander hold the Phillies in the palm of his hand on the pitching mound, he also hammered out a home run, a mammoth clout into the left field bleachers against a 40-mile gale in the tenth inning. This clinched the contest and sent the visitors bouncing up the ladder to second place. [*For a pitcher, Dean was a better than average hitter. He compiled a career batting average of .225, including 8 home runs.*]

Stan Baumgartner, Philadelphia *Inquirer*

NATIONAL LEAGUE STANDINGS

	W	L	PCT	GB		W	L	PCT	GB
Pittsburgh	20	11	.645	—	Boston	16	16	.500	4½
St. Louis	21	13	.618	½	Brooklyn	15	18	.455	6
Chicago	22	15	.595	1	Philadelphia	11	20	.355	9
New York	20	15	.571	2	Cincinnati	7	24	.226	13

∘ *Tuesday, May 29* ∘

[*On May 28, in Philadelphia, the Cardinals won, 10–0. Winning pitcher, Bill Hallahan; losing pitcher, Curt Davis. Cardinals' standing: 22 wins, 13 losses, in first place for the first time.*]

There isn't much to say about a 10–0 defeat, unless you are a soap box orator needing practice or a married man whose wife is on vacation, allowing him freedom of speech for the first time in months.

The writer, not being the first nor lucky enough to be the second, will content himself with brevity.

The score tells the story of the game. Your imagination may supply the rest.

If you crave details, we might say that "Wild Bill" Hallahan turned the steam on his left arm and exploded fast balls and curves in devastating fashion.

Stan Baumgartner, Philadelphia *Inquirer*

∘ *Wednesday, May 30* ∘

[*On May 29 the Cardinals were not scheduled to play.*]

The two-man strike of the Dean brothers came to a sudden end. "That's just Dizzy popping off," explained Owner Sam Breadon.

Much of Dizzy's time with the Cardinals has been devoted to popping off. But when game time rolled around and a man was needed to throw the old ball past enemy batters, Dizzy, before anyone else, volunteered.

The Deans love to complain, but they love to pitch better. And it's the heart they have for the game, their real zest for playing, that makes fans and owners forget their popping off. Too bad there are not a few more players with the Dean heart and spirit.

John E. Wray, *St. Louis Post-Dispatch*

On the inner side of the door of the Cardinals' dressing room at the Phillies' ball park was an arresting placard bearing the names, games won and lost, and games behind the leader of the various clubs in the league.

At the bottom in huge red letters were the words "WIN TODAY'S GAME."

"That's something new, a good idea," we remarked to Virgil Davis.

"Yes," he agreed. "That's Frankie Frisch's battle cry—so the trainer printed it on the card so we would see it just before going on the field."

It seemed, from the chatter in the clubhouse, that the Redbirds were enjoying themselves.

Dizzy Dean, reaching in locker 13 (he always insists on No. 13 locker) uttered a shrill mock cry of anguish. "Hey, who took that dirty sock out of my locker? I can't pitch unless I find it. I can't pitch unless I find it. Haven't worked a game this season without having it in my pocket."

For three minutes the clubhouse was in turmoil as Dean turned lockers upside down in an effort to locate the missing sock.

"You never had more than two socks in your life," growled Frisch. "You'll probably find it on your foot."

Dean looked at his right leg and then looked sheepishly at the charmed dirty sock hiding his No. 12 foot.

A baseball clubhouse is a perfect cross-section of American life. The Cardinal clubhouse is no exception.

The young fellow industriously tying his shoe string, for instance, is Joe Medwick, a young Hungarian who first learned to balance peas on his fork, not his knife, when he went into baseball.

If you asked him who Kant was, he would probably say that the word "can't" is not in his vocabulary. But now he can hit that baseball!

Other players in the league say that he is a bit "chesty." "Why shouldn't he be," retorted a teammate. "If I could hit as far and as often as he does you would have to send your name into the office boy before I would speak to you."

Next to Medwick is a frail looking lad who is the only Phi Beta Kappa man playing baseball. He probably could answer every question you asked on philosophy, psychology, and astronomy and then tie you in knots with a few of his own. If you seated him at a banquet table he probably would not make one mistake if they put seven different forks in front of him. He is Burgess Whitehead from the University of North Carolina. [*Playing his first full season with the Cardinals, and serving as their principal utility infielder, twenty-three-year-old Burgess Whitehead was indeed the only major leaguer with a Phi Beta Kappa key, earned, as indicated, at the University of North Carolina, from which he graduated in 1931.*]

A peep into the clubhouse would not be complete without a glance at Pepper Martin, probably the best liked member of the Cardinal ensemble. He is a true product of the West, a broncho buster, a hunter, a plainsman, who has not been tarnished by the East.

In Medwick, Whitehead, and Martin we have three types of men as far apart in temperament, education, and social standing as one can hope to find.

So on any major league club might we find as wide a divergence. Yet they mingle on even terms, fraternize joyfully, and fight for a common object. Baseball without doubt is the world's greatest melting pot of humanity.

With the Cardinals every difference is submerged and made secondary to that bottom line on the bulletin: "WIN TODAY'S GAME."

"The Old Sport," Philadelphia *Inquirer*

° *Thursday, May 31* °

[*On May 30, Memorial Day, in Cincinnati, the Cardinals won a dou-*
bleheader, 9–6 and 9–2. Winning pitchers, Paul Dean and Tex Carleton;
losing pitchers, Si Johnson and Tony Freitas. Cardinals' standing: 24 wins,
13 losses, in first place.]

The weather man predicted showers, and he guessed right. It rained in
such torrents that Crosley Field was virtually flooded. It was a base-hit
deluge, and when the field was finally cleared Skipper Frankie Frisch and
his Cardinals had two more victories to crow over and a firmer grip on first
place.

In the first game the Reds drove Paul Dean from the box in the eighth,
but brother Dizzy came to the rescue and saved the day. Paul got credit for
his fifth victory of the season. The second game was a breather for lean
Tex Carleton, who won under wraps with 7-hit pitching. In this second
game Joe Medwick, the strong-armed Hungarian, rang up a perfect score
with 5 hits in 5 trips.

Raymond V. Smith, St. Louis *Globe-Democrat*

There is one man in the Cardinal camp whose war club has played a most
important part in the Redbirds' drive to the top of the National League.
Joseph Michael Medwick is the slugger, and during the 12 games on the
road he has clouted the old American apple for 26 hits in 53 times at bat,
including a home run, 4 triples, and 4 doubles.

Hostile pitchers have tried every trick in the bag. They have pitched
inside, and Joe has whacked the ball against the left field fence. They have
pitched outside, and he has banged extra base hits down the right field
line. They have pitched high and low, fast and slow, and they haven't
found a weakness.

"I just smell the lettuce," Joe explains. "I have two good friends in this
world. Buckerinos and base hits. If I get base hits I will get buckerinos. I
smell World Series lettuce, and I'll get my two or three a day."

Pitchers are calling Joe Medwick the most dangerous hitter in the
league. Last year he tended to fold up in the pinches, largely because he
was so eager he would swing at bad balls. Now he makes the pitcher get
the ball within reach of the bat. It doesn't have to be in the strike zone. But
he must be able to reach it. He won't swing any more if the pitchers roll
the ball to the catcher or bounce it in front of the plate, but when it is

within reach he is likely to slam it against the fence.

Frisch deserves much credit for Medwick's improvement. Joe follows Frank in the batting order, and Frank never misses an opportunity to caution him.

"Make them give you a good one to hit," he tells Medwick. He has repeated that warning so often Joe has taken heed. And the Cardinals will wager that when the base hits are counted in October, Joisey Joe will lead the parade. [*Medwick has sometimes been called baseball's all-time best bad-ball hitter.*]

J. Roy Stockton, St. Louis Post-Dispatch

A tourist from California insists that the best young ball player in the game plays with the San Francisco Seals and will soon be astonishing the major leagues. The hero of the story is Joe De [*sic*] Maggio, 19 years old, 185 pounds, 6 feet, and a right-handed outfielder all the way, hitting, throwing, and thinking. "The team that gets Joe DeMaggio," said the tourist with pride, "will have a prize package for the next ten years."

Paging Colonel Ruppert! [*Jacob Ruppert, owner of the Yankees.*] Paging Mr. Stoneham! [*Charles A. Stoneham, president of the Giants.*] Paging Judge McKeever! [*Stephen W. McKeever, president of the Dodgers.*] [*Joe DiMaggio, now playing in his second season for the Seals, would be purchased by the Yankees in the winter, for delivery in 1936.*]

John Kieran, The New York Times

∘ *Friday, June 1* ∘

[*On May 31, in Cincinnati, the Cardinals, in 10 innings, won, 3–2. Winning pitcher: Flint Rhem; losing pitcher, Paul Derringer. Cardinals' standing: 25 wins, 13 losses, in first place.*]

As is almost invariably the case with a tail-end club, nothing clicks at the right time. When the team is hitting, the other side is hitting harder, and when a well-pitched game is delivered the trailers fall into a slump to offset it.

So it was yesterday when the league-leading Cardinals shaded the tottering Reds.

It took the Frisch outfit an extra round to put on the finishing touches, and they had to use three pitchers, but they stuck it out and put over the deciding tally in the tenth, when an unlucky Paul Derringer shoot grazed a batter's shirt, entitling him to first base, and Link Blakely misjudged a line drive from Frisch's bat which went for a double and pushed over the winning marker.

Jack Ryder, Cincinnati *Enquirer*

Anyone who questions the esprit de corps of Frankie Frisch's team should have seen yesterday's game. They should have seen Paul Dean go to the hill to hurl the tenth frame, although he worked 7⅓ hard innings the day before. And as Paul powered the ball through the strike zone, throwing with all his strength, his brother Dizzy was warming up. And Dizzy wasn't alone.

Tex Carleton worked nine innings on Memorial Day, but he was ready, too, to serve in an emergency. And Jim Mooney was doing bull pen duty should a left-hander be needed.

That is the spirit of the Cardinals, a spirit that will be hard to beat. It doesn't matter whose turn it is, or how hard a man worked yesterday or the day before. Every Redbird is willing and eager to work whenever he can help; that is why the Frisch team has made this trip through the enemy's country a triumphant one.

J. Roy Stockston, *St. Louis Post-Dispatch*

Pittsburgh [*where the Cardinals had arrived for a series beginning today*]— Rumblings of internal dissension broke into open revolt today when the Dean brothers defiantly announced that they would pitch no more until their salary differences are settled.

Dizzy, scheduled to face the Pirates today, refused to pitch, informing Manager Frisch of a "conveniently" sore arm.

The outburst was an aftermath of Vice-President Branch Rickey's visit to Cincinnati, where he held a conference with Frisch yesterday. Dizzy, eager to procure higher wages for his younger brother, called on Frisch in his hotel room, hoping to settle his controversy.

Frisch laid down the law and told Dizzy that he (Frisch) would not ask President Sam Breadon to give Paul a salary boost. Dizzy said he then gave Frisch a thorough verbal tongue lashing, after which the manager said, "If you don't want to pitch, go home."

"If Paul had my nerve," Dizzy remarked as he strutted up and down in his room, "we'd both be back in St. Louis. I don't need a second invitation to leave when I'm not appreciated."

Paul then entered the discussion and announced that he too has a sore right arm and will be unable to pitch for some time to come.

"Paul must get $1,000 cash in the hand, and there will be no compromising," Dizzy said. "When Paul and I went on strike in New York, Frisch promised he'd go to the office in St. Louis and plead our case. Now Frank has turned his back on us.

"Paul and I aren't running out on the other players—we'd do everything possible to help win the pennant and an extra $5,000 apiece, but we feel that we're getting the run-around by the club, and if the management doesn't care about the extra money, why should we?"

Dizzy emphasized his point by stating that his salary, $7,500, plus that of Paul, $3,000, does not equal the stipend of many other pitchers who will be lucky to win half as many games as one of the Dean boys will turn in this summer. "Hallahan gets $12,500.55," he complained.

The Dean boys reiterated their statements of a week ago, when they stated that they had refused to pitch until Frisch had promised to help Paul get a salary adjustment.

"I'm satisfied with my own pay—which is what I got last year," Diz said, "but Paul must get $2,000 more, or the Cards won't win the pennant. Neither Paul nor I will pitch any more under present circumstances."

Frisch stated that he did not care to discuss the situation.

Ray J. Gillespie, St. Louis *Star-Times*

∘ *Saturday, June 2* ∘

[*On June 1, in Pittsburgh, the Cardinals lost, 4–3. Winning pitcher, Waite Hoyt; losing pitcher, Bill Hallahan. Cardinals standing: 25 wins, 14 losses, in first place.*]

Pittsburgh—Manager Frankie Frisch is claiming a victory in the row with the Dean brothers.

After Dizzy Dean had threatened to take his brother back to St. Louis, Frisch conferred with President Sam Breadon over the long-distance telephone. Breadon assured Frisch that he would be supported by club officials in handling the situation. When Dizzy was informed of Breadon's attitude, he abandoned plans to quit the club.

The settlement was reached at a late hour last night, when Frisch, in conference with his arbitration board, consisting of Secretary Clarence Lloyd, Coaches Miguel Gonzalez and Buzzy Wares, and Pitcher Jesse Haines, called Paul Dean and then Dizzy, and heard their complaints.

Frisch had ordered Dizzy to pitch yesterday's game, but when Diz began to argue about Paul's salary and announced that he had a sore arm, the manager ordered him to discard his uniform and leave the clubhouse. Accordingly Dizzy departed and Hallahan took his place on the mound, and lost, 4–3, when the Buccaneers scored three runs in the ninth inning.

Ray J. Gillespie, St. Louis *Star-Times*

Pittsburgh—Back to the mines, boys, the strike is over.

"My arm's getting better fast," Dizzy announced last night. "Tell Frank that I'll throw this arm off to win for Old Frank and the boys.

"Gee, those Cardinals are swell fellows, and there never was a fellow like Frisch. Isn't he a pip? You know there must be something wrong with anybody who wouldn't pitch his arm off for Old Frank. Show me a guy who says a word against Old Frank, and I'll bash his face in."

J. Roy Stockton, *St. Louis Post-Dispatch*

The Cincinnati Reds are the biggest disappointment in the majors, hopelessly out of the running.

This proves once more that a millionaire's bank-roll cannot create a winning ball club. Powel Crosley, Jr., a young sportsman of considerable wealth, bought control of the Reds shortly before the current season opened. When he made his first appearance as the new owner at a banquet in his behalf, he announced that he would "give Cincinnati a winner." Much applause followed his statement.

Certified checks, however, do not win games. Each member of the Reds announced he was satisfied with his contract, and I heard several Rhinelanders praise their magnate when they were here early in the season.

"We're traveling like world champions," said Jim Bottomley. "The best hotels, lower berths in traveling for everyone, and we are accommodated whenever we ask for advance money." [*Usually only half of the team slept in lower berths, which were assigned to those who were playing regularly or who had seniority. The manager customarily rode in a compartment.*]

Despite this luxurious treatment, the Reds are in last place.

Sid Keener, St. Louis *Star-Times*

◦ *Sunday, June 3* ◦

[*On June 2, in Pittsburgh, the Cardinals split a doubleheader, winning 13–4 and losing 6–3. Winning pitchers, Dizzy Dean and Larry French; losing pitchers, Red Lucas and Jim Winford. Cardinals' standing: 26 wins, 15 losses, in first place.*]

Jerome Herman Dean, President of Local No. 1, Dean Brotherhood of Right-handed Pitchers, held the Pirates in check while the Cardinals lambasted four pitchers for 18 hits in the first game of a double-header, but Jim Mooney and Jim Winford were wild in the second contest, and when Paul Dean, Vice-President of Local No. 1, was called on in the eighth, Walter Roettger tripled with the bases filled, giving the Pirates the game.

Dizzy Dean and a devastating attack, with Jimmy Collins setting the pace, tell the story of the opener. Collins hit two home runs and a triple to dive in seven runs, each four-bagger coming with two comrades on base, and through the late innings Dean's lead was so commanding he just coasted along.

J. Roy Stockton, *St. Louis Post-Dispatch*

When Dizzy Dean went on "strike" with the object of increasing his brother's salary, it set a precedent. Leave it to Dizzy to set the pace.

Players have "struck" for higher wages before signing contracts and were called "holdouts." But no player ever had the nerve to present a demand for more pay while under contract.

Dizzy may or may not have had a grievance. But his antics approximated the wriggling of a fish that has been thoroughly hooked. True, the biggest fish gets away. But it takes a whale to get away from the barb that Organized Baseball sinks into the player, once he signs on the dotted line.

And even if he wriggles off the hook, where does he go? Only with the consent of the owner against whom he is "striking" can he play baseball at all.

Dizzy contended that his brother, at $3,000 a year, was underpaid and that his salary should be increased at once. However, Paul's salary was the usual increase over his minor league pay of $2,400. He received a 25 percent raise, even though the club owner was by no means certain that the promise of his minor league career would be sustained in the majors.

Paul is off to a good start, but five victories don't guarantee success. There's many a slip between May and September.

Dizzy seems to have been hiding behind the plea for his brother. Dizzy receives $7,500 a year. In view of the many retrenchments made in recent years, this writer doesn't know whether that is today a good salary for a good pitcher or not.

Baseball players have been likened to chattels because their services are bought and sold without profit to the players themselves. They have no voice in the price or in their destination. As their "owner" directs, so must they comply. The player is bound to his original owner from year to year and has no right to sell his services to the highest bidder.

Strange as it seems, baseball exists on this seeming unfairness. If players could annually peddle their services for the highest price, club owners could not hold their teams together.

The reserve clause, which binds the player to one owner from season to season, and the ten-day clause, by which an owner can release a player on ten days' notice, are violations of contract mutuality. In fact, it is said that the baseball contract would not stand if tested in court, but players recognize that baseball could not go on without the reserve clause. So they consent to become chattels and, as a rule, to abide by contracts. [*In fact, of course, baseball has been without a reserve clause for more than ten years, and it has managed to survive rather nicely.*]

John E. Wray, St. Louis Post-Dispatch

◦ *Monday, June 4* ◦

[*On June 3, in Pittsburgh, the Cardinals lost, 4–2. Winning pitcher, Heinie Meine; losing pitcher, Tex Carleton. Cardinals' standing: 26 wins, 16 losses, in first place.*]

Those tough Pittsburgh Pirates, who have made life miserable for the Redbirds, continued to wield black magic over the men of Frisch and took the series final. However, the Cards boarded a train for St. Louis in first place by a few points over the Giants and Cubs.

Heinie Meine pitched air-tight ball and had a shutout until Pepper Martin belted a tremendous home run over the score-board in the seventh. [*In Forbes Field at this time the scoreboard rose about 20 feet just inside the left-field foul line, 360 feet from home plate.*]

Raymond V. Smith, St. Louis Globe-Democrat

The strike of the Deans was a bloodless affair, undertaken with no motive save that of financial gain and settled without the help of scabs, strike-breakers, or Pinkerton operatives.

Dizzy's last walkout was such a nice, clean, sentimental thing, no one but a magnate would have the heart to criticize it. He did it for the wife and kiddies, or, to be specific, for his brother Paul. Diz would be surprised and mildly shocked if his walkout should exert an influence on other players and other clubs. Skilled labor, in his mind, is identified exclusively with the Dean family. "Strike a blow for the Deans!" is Dizzy's motto—not "Strike a blow for oppressed ivory everywhere!"

Organized baseball hasn't had much experience with organized labor. When a ball player holds out for a bigger pay check, he holds out alone. It never occurs to Babe Ruth, for instance, to join forces with Higgins, Foxx, the Deans, Lopez, and other solo agitators. The Babe would laugh at the theory of mass demand because, after all, that is not what the Babe is interested in.

Baseball unions have been suggested in the past. Mr. Heydler, Ban Johnson [*president of the American League from its formation in 1901 until his retirement at the end of the 1927 season*], and the club owners always received the suggestion with a smile.

"I think the players are pretty well satisfied with the present system," Mr. Heydler said.

Yet there is reason to suspect that the players would be stronger under a unified front than either they or the magnates imagine, for the present rules of the industry put the individual player at the mercy of the owners.

John Lardner, *New York Post*

Before the start of yesterday's game, Frankie Frisch, sitting on the Cardinal bench, was discussing the team's trip through the East.

"We kept on the pressure, and knocked 'em all off," Frisch, who can break into a sweat when he's sitting back relaxing, said.

"It's fellows like Pepper Martin who make us a good club," he went on. Look at Pepper now [*taking part in pregame fielding practice*]. He's going after pop flies as though it was the ninth inning of the last game of the World Series."

Martin was racing back toward the left field bleachers. He reminded you of a herd of elephants stampeding through the jungle. You'd have thought that catching that ball was all that mattered in his life. He nabbed it with a last-second leap that all but carried him near the tarpaulin, rolled up along the wall, and into the concrete. [*Major league clubs were not required to have warning tracks in their parks until the early 1950's, and padded fences did not begin to appear until the 1970's. It was in this season of 1934 that Yankee outfielder Earle Combs ran full speed into the concrete wall in Sportsman's Park and fractured his skull.*]

"See that," Frisch continued with a grin. "Well, Pep's that way from the time he gets up in the morning until he dives into bed at night. Some day, I expect to see him knock down somebody's grandstand. Put him on first base and you've got to call the cops to keep him off second. And the rest of the boys are the same way."

The reporter was about to reply that they must have gotten all that life from watching the wild man at second whose name, in case you didn't know, is Frankie Frisch.

Chester L. Smith, Pittsburgh *Press*

NATIONAL LEAGUE STANDINGS

	W	L	PCT	GB		W	L	PCT	GB
St. Louis	26	16	.619	—	Boston	22	17	.564	2½
New York	27	17	.614	—	Brooklyn	17	24	.415	8½
Chicago	27	17	.614	—	Philadelphia	12	26	.316	12
Pittsburgh	23	17	.575	2	Cincinnati	9	29	.237	15

○ *Tuesday, June 5* ○

[*On June 4, the Cardinals were not scheduled to play.*]

Included in the Cardinals' squad, returning from a pennant-driving road journey, were the Dean brothers. Ordinarily there would be nothing unusual about two members of a ball club parading back to town with the entire ensemble, but the Dean brothers are utterly different from the usual run of ball players. Especially Dizzy.

On the last lap of the club's tour, the Deans were talking about a two-man strike. But when the Cardinals returned yesterday, Dizzy and Paul were walking arm-in-arm with other members of the first placers. For some unknown reason the strike was called off. My opinion of the affair is that the Deans were putting out more of their ballyhoo. [*In the thirties the word "ballyhoo" was widely used as a slang synonym for noisy, exaggerated talk.*] The senior member of the Dean firm thrives on publicity, and when things become too quiet for his showmanship he can be counted on to pop up with something.

On the field, Dizzy is a tireless worker, loyal to the cause, and a pitcher extraordinary. I have never seen a player, except possibly Ty Cobb, put more vim and energy into his labors than Dizzy. Besides being an artist on the hill, Diz will run his fool head off in an attempt to sneak an extra base, and, unlike the average hurler, he's a hitter of considerable power.

Why can't Dizzy cut out his comedy and confine his bid for fame to his performance on the field?

Sid Keener, St. Louis *Star-Times*

It must be assumed that the strike of the pitching Deans was a success, for both are back in the foundry, forging hot, fast ones and steaming hooks for the trade.

You know, of course, about pitching Deans, earnest commoners who toil for the baronial Breadon in the capitalistic National League. They struck for more money, of all things. To be more correct, the older brother, who is called Dizzy as a sort of flattery, struck because the younger brother, who is called Nutsey by way of minimizing confusion, was underpaid.

In their strike the Deans respected established principles of labor. They issued an ultimatum. They came and said they would strike unless their demands were met.

"And we ain't kidding," said Mr. Dizzy. "I'm underpaid, but my brother is worse underpaid, and something has to be done. My brother must have $2,000 more or we don't pitch."

The strike didn't last long, and, as I say, the pitching Deans must have got what they wanted, for they are back in uniform. The outcome seems to indicate that the Deans are neither dizzy nor nutty. They know what they want and, more important, they seem to get it.

You can bet all the ships in the Hudson that they wouldn't have got it in this instance if they hadn't been militant. Baseball owners aren't disposed to sweeten the ante out of the bigness of their hearts.

There are no standards for baseball values. Mostly, the size of the pay check is determined by geography and expediency. A third base coach in New York is likely to be paid more than a star in St. Louis or Cincinnati.

Mr. Dizzy would be getting twice as much pitching for the Giants, and he would be worth it. And he is worth it in St. Louis, but because salaries have never been high there he doesn't get it. Mr. Nutsey was started at a beginner's pay as it is figured in St. Louis. By now it is apparent that he is a real pitcher worth much more than $3,000.

I am glad the Deans struck, and I think this sort of striking should be encouraged. I see no reason why a young ball player should have to wait a full year for adequate recognition at the cashier's window once he has established his class.

That the Deans were not permitted to walk out is proof enough that the management recognized their value and realized it all the time. Without the Deans St. Louis would be lucky to finish in the first division.

At the gate the difference between a potential pennant winner and an ordinary ball club is about $100,000. Thus it is easy to understand Breadon's amused tolerance over a strike involving a mere $2,000.

Baseball being a team proposition rather than an individual performance, its outstanding men never get all their talents warrant. At one time Babe Ruth was getting more than the President. That may have been cock-eyed in comparison with what men engaged in more important pursuits were getting. And yet the Babe, in my mind, was underpaid. [*In 1930 and 1931, Ruth's salary reached its peak, $80,000. At this time the President's salary was $75,000. After the 1930 season, someone told Ruth that he had been paid more than the President, Herbert Hoover, to which Ruth is supposed to have replied, "Well, I had a better year than he had."*]

From the point of view of attendance, Babe Ruth was the backbone of the league. He broke every attendance record in every city. Had he been a fighter, an actor, even a tennis professional, he would have shared in those receipts instead of working on a flat guarantee, and his returns, considerable as they were, would have been much more weighty.

Joe Williams, New York *World-Telegram*

∘ *Wednesday, June 6* ∘

[*On June 5, in St. Louis, the Cardinals defeated the Cubs, 6–3. Winning pitcher, Paul Dean; losing pitcher, Lon Warneke. Cardinals' standing: 27 wins, 16 losses, in first place.*]

It looks more and more like a Dean year. As Jerome and Paul go, so go the Redbirds.

Paul yesterday turned in his most impressive performance of the season. He stopped dangerous sluggers, and he stopped them after a first inning home run gave the enemy a lead that would have discouraged a more imaginative pitcher.

With one out in that first inning, Woody English singled. Paul burned strikes over the corners of the plate, and Chuck Klein struck out. But Paul became a bit too sure of himself, and he threw a half-speed ball to Floyd "Babe" Herman that was too good. Herman swung from Spring and Dodier and hit the change of pace into the center field pavilion. [*Spring and Dodier Streets intersect at a point near the site of home plate in Sportsman's Park.*]

That perturbed Paul Dean no little, and when Hazen "Kiki" Cuyler followed with a single, Paul became rattled, committed a balk, and the crowd thought that Dizzy's younger brother was about to be given a sound beating.

But the Deans concede nothing. The Cubs may be great hitters to you and you and you, but to Dizzy and Paul they are just palookas, and to Paul that home run by Babe Herman was just a fluke. [*Although the hero of the comic strip* Joe Palooka *was a champion, the term* palooka *was used in the twenties and thirties to denote a mediocre boxer and, by extension, a commonplace person.*] And even the balk didn't bother Paul. He struck out Dolph Camilli to end the inning, and before the game had progressed much farther, Paul was at the controls and Lonnie Warneke was the pitcher who took the whipping.

J. Roy Stockton, *St. Louis Post-Dispatch*

◦ *Thursday, June 7* ◦

[*On June 6, in St. Louis, the Cardinals, in 13 innings, lost to Chicago, 12–6. Winning pitcher, Pat Malone; losing pitcher, Tex Carleton. Cardinals' standing: 27 wins, 17 losses, in second place.*]

The Cubs battled through 13 terrific innings before flattening the Cardinals with a 6-run rally. The locals curled up and dropped out of first place after apparently exhausting themselves in an assault on Umpire Charles Rigler. The final score might have been 7 to 6 for the Cards in 12 innings if the veteran umpire hadn't made what seemed the wrong guess on a play at the plate.

The baby riot broke when Joe Medwick, with two out in the twelfth, tried to score the deciding run on Jim Collins' double off the right field wall. Gabby Hartnett had the plate blocked, but it appeared as if Medwick had one foot on the corner. Rigler called him out, and the big war was on.

Manager Frankie Frisch raced from the dugout, slammed into Rigler, and grabbed him by the lapels. Rigler staggered back and swung his mask, which crashed against Frisch's jaw. Then Rigler grabbed the belligerent manager and was shaking him lustily when Coach Mike Gonzalez tried to pry himself between them. Medwick, indignant over the decision, pulled at Rigler from behind. The four men squirmed in a mass for a few seconds before they were pulled apart. The St. Louis players then took the field with a patched up lineup and were annihilated by the Cubs' final rally.

Irving Vaughan, Chicago *Tribune*

Observers yesterday generally agreed that while Frankie Frisch "rushed" the umpire and grabbed his sleeve, the first fighting gesture was made by Rigler when he hit Frisch with his mask.

"You know I'm not a fighter," Frisch said when asked if he had punched the umpire. "I was rushing up to kick at the decision. He swings his mask at me, and I'm put out of the game, but he's permitted to stay on the field.

"What am I supposed to do when I get a bad decision? Am I supposed to laugh it off? Medwick beat the throw and touched the plate before Hartnett got the ball down. Hartnett knew Medwick was safe and figured the game was over. He was on his way to the dressing room when he turned and saw that Rigler had called Medwick out."

Umpire Rigler said that Frisch was responsible for the outbreak.

"Did Frisch try to hit you?" he was asked.

"No, but he put his hands on me," Rigler replied, "and the first rule in the book is that you mustn't put your hands on an umpire."

"Do you feel you were justified in doing what you did?" he was asked.

"Whenever anybody lays a hand on Charley Rigler," he replied, "Charley Rigler will defend himself. You saw Charley Rigler protecting himself. You saw that wild mob out there and those players rushing me."

At that minute, Dr. Robert F. Hyland, the Cardinal club physician [*from 1925 until 1950*], entered the dressing room with adhesive plaster and a finger splint.

"Pepper Martin threw his bat while at the plate in an earlier inning and hit me on my finger," Rigler explained. "The blow either broke it or dislocated it, and it stayed out of joint until I took that swing at Frisch with my mask."

[*Among National League umpires, Rigler was second in seniority to Bill Klem, having served since 1907. He weighed about 240 pounds, and Frisch weighed about 160.*]

J. Roy Stockton, *St. Louis Post-Dispatch*

For their part in yesterday's fistic exhibition, Frankie Frisch and Charley Rigler each received a fine of $100. This penalty was announced by National League President John Heydler in a message to Cardinal President Sam Breadon.

Frisch seemed satisfied with the decision, saying he was glad he was not suspended.

Rigler refused to comment on his fine.

Ray J. Gillespie, St. Louis *Star-Times*

Some members of the Cincinnati team will fly to Chicago tomorrow night from Cincinnati. Larry MacPhail, general manager of the Reds, explained that flying from city to city gives the players opportunity for more rest. Of the 25 men to report in Chicago, 6 have decided to go by train. [*This was the first time a major league team traveled together by air. Two regularly scheduled American Airlines planes carried the players. The Cardinals' first team flight, from Boston to Chicago, occurred in 1938.*]

The New York Times

∘ *Friday, June 8* ∘

[*On June 7, in St. Louis, the Cardinals lost to Chicago, 1–0. Winning pitcher, Jim Weaver; losing pitcher, Jim Mooney. Cardinals' standing: 27 wins, 18 losses, in third place.*]

Windmill Jim Weaver, freshman member of the Cubs' staff, was 239 pounds of pitching efficiency as he restricted the Cardinals to seven widely scattered singles, and the Cubs did just enough on offense to win. The lone run came in the third inning when Billy Herman singled, advanced to second on an infield grounder, and scored on Babe Herman's single against the right field wall.

Irving Vaughan, Chicago *Tribune*

° *Saturday, June 9* °

[*On June 8, in St. Louis, the Cardinals defeated Pittsburgh, 6–2. Winning pitcher, Tex Carleton; losing pitcher, Larry French. Cardinals' standing: 28 wins, 18 losses, in second place.*]

The Cardinals won on Tex Carleton's effective pitching and an ability to bunch their blows. Joe Medwick produced three hits, and Rip Collins planted a four-sacker on top of the right field stand.

Edward F. Balinger, Pittsburgh *Post-Gazette*

Mrs. Dizzy Dean insists on traveling with the Cardinals' ace pitcher in the interests of economy. She says it's cheaper than having Dizzy call her long distance every night.

Arch Ward, Chicago *Tribune*

° *Monday, June 11* °

[*After the June 9 game had been postponed because of rain, on June 10, in St. Louis, the Cardinals defeated Pittsburgh, 3–2. Winning pitcher, Dizzy Dean; losing pitcher, Larry French. Cardinals' standing: 29 wins, 18 losses, in second place.*]

It had to happen if the Cardinals were to remain a serious threat in the pennant race, and now that Frisch's Redbirds have won a series from the troublesome Pirates, they are more enthusiastic than ever about their prospects. [*For the first time in more than two years St. Louis played a series with Pittsburgh without losing a game. In the current series, of course, rain washed out one game.*]

"They really aren't tough, if you know how to pitch," Jerome Herman Dean explained after beating the Buccaneers for the third time this season before a crowd of 12,500. "And we Deans know how to do it. Paul would have beaten them sure if the rain hadn't shortened the series, and from now on you can depend on the Deans winning two games of each series we play with the Pirates. Why, those palookas are lucky whenever they get a run off me and Paul."

Dizzy gave an impressive exhibition of pitching in the pinches. The

Pirates collected 9 hits, but they were all singles, and, as Dizzy suggested, the Pirates needed a little luck to score 2 runs.

James "Ripper" Collins shared the day's honors with the elder Dean. Jimmy hit a home run to the pavilion roof, his thirteenth of the season, in the fourth inning, and he doubled in the eighth to start the winning rally.

J. Roy Stockton, *St. Louis Post-Dispatch*

NATIONAL LEAGUE STANDINGS

	W	L	PCT	GB		W	L	PCT	GB
New York	32	18	.640	—	Boston	24	22	.522	6
St. Louis	29	18	.617	1½	Brooklyn	20	29	.408	11½
Chicago	30	20	.600	2	Philadelphi	16	29	.356	13½
Pittsburgh	26	19	.578	3½	Cincinnati	11	33	.250	18

∘ *Tuesday, June 12* ∘

[*On June 11, the Cardinals were not scheduled to play.*]

Have you heard about Lefty O'Doul's double? Not a double that Lefty clouted in the pinch, but a guy who has been going around New York masquerading as Lefty and doing a good job of it. [*Lefty O'Doul, the Giants' outfielder-pinch hitter, who had twice led the National League in batting, once with an average of .398, was widely known as "the man in the green suit."*]

The imposter is fairly smart. He has decked himself out in the familiar green of O'Doul and presents himself at cafes and cabarets as the Giants' famous pinch-hitter. The green togs get him over immediately, the credulous believing that nobody but O'Doul or a guy who had lost a bet would wear a green suit.

The phoney O'Doul is affable. He is modest as to his baseball records and shows an amazing willingness to meet anybody, particularly anybody who will buy him a drink.

So far, the man who would be O'Doul has visited three spots in Greenwich Village—probably trying out in the provinces before opening on Broadway. The El Chico, Holtz's restaurant, and Haan's have forwarded *billets-doux* to the real O'Doul, telling him that they enjoyed his visit and that they are sorry to bother him, but would he please send a check to cover the enclosed statement?

Amazingly, none of the bills runs into a sawbuck [*ten dollars*]. They range from $3.85 to $8.25. The guy does 50 bucks' worth of acting for a ham sandwich and a martini.

So, as a tip to cafe and cabaret owners, if a chap comes in and says he's Lefty O'Doul, reach for the bung-starter [*a lid covering the hole, the "bung-hole," in a cask of beer*]. If it's the real O'Doul there'll be no harm done, for Lefty long ago learned the art of ducking back in Butchertown in 'Frisco. [*Located south of Market Street and seldom visited by tourists, Butchertown is a rough district in San Francisco, where O'Doul was born and raised.*]

Tom Meany, New York *World-Telegram*

° *Wednesday, June 13* °

[*On June 12, in St. Louis, the Cardinals defeated Boston, 7–3. Winning pitcher, Paul Dean; losing pitcher, Huck Betts. Cardinals' standing: 30 wins, 18 losses, in second place.*]

James "Ripper" Collins, the young man who left the Pennsylvania coal fields and made good with a first baseman's glove, is having the best year of his career, and if he continues at the pace he has been setting he will be a serious candidate for the league's most valuable player award.

Collins had a perfect day at bat yesterday, and his single, triple, and fourteenth home run of the year played an important part in Paul Dean's seventh triumph of the season.

Lately Collins has been almost a daily hero for the Cardinals. The Ripper's fine showing is another feather in Frankie Frisch's cap, for it is the first time that Collins has approximated the performance expected from him when he graduated from Rochester [*in 1931*].

Collins broke into the big league under unfortunate circumstances. He came up as an understudy to Jim Bottomley, one of the most popular players ever to wear a Cardinal uniform. And to make the situation more difficult, the Redbird advertising department did a thorough job of ballyhooing Collins. He was described as the greatest slugger since Babe Ruth, the fastest and best fielding of all first basemen.

It was too much for Collins. He thought he had to hit two or three home runs a day. When he didn't, his morale bogged. He thought no base hit should ever pass. And when they did, it pained him. Then, too, there was Bottomley ready to push him to the bench. [*In 1931, Bottomley appeared in 93 games at first base, Collins in 68; in 1932, Bottomley played in 74 games*] at first base, Collins in 81. After the 1932 season, Bottomley was traded to Cincinnati, and Collins became the Cardinals' unchallenged first baseman.]

And there was the question of how to handle the Ripper's temperament. Mistakes were made. Boyish gestures were interpreted as those of a play-boy, a clown, or a "Fancy Dan" grandstander, as the trade describes a fellow who goes in for trick pepper games and stuff like that. [*A pepper game is a practice exercise involving several players with gloves and one with a bat. The batter hits a ball to a fielder, who throws it to the batter, who again hits it to a fielder, and this exchange continues as long as neither the batter nor a fielder misses the ball. The game does provide an opportunity for exhibitionism.*] If an opposing player joked with Collins and the Ripper joked back, he was reprimanded for not taking baseball seriously.

Frankie Frisch decided that under the playful Collins exterior was a heart that would beat in two, three, and four base hit time. If no monkey wrenches in the form of harsh and unkind words were thrown into the machinery.

The Frisch policy has yielded fine results. Collins is among the league's leading hitters, and under Frisch's coaching the Ripper has overcome his worst fault. In past years he was so eager to live up to the reputation the ballyhoo department built around him he'd strike at anything in the pinch. Opposing pitchers took to bouncing the ball to the plate with men on base and Collins would swing.

But not this year. He makes the pitchers pitch. He insists on balls in the strike zone. And there's not a happier warrior than James Ripper Collins.

[*Joe Medwick, it will be remembered, had shared Collins' batting affliction until he too was cured by Frisch.*]

J. Roy Stockton, *St. Louis Post-Dispatch*

◦ *Thursday, June 14* ◦

[*On June 13, in St. Louis, the Cardinals lost to Boston, 9–0. Winning pitcher, Fred Frankhouse; losing pitcher, Bill Hallahan. Cardinals' standing: 30 wins, 19 losses, in second place.*]

Last Thursday the Cards were shut out, the first time this season, by Jim Weaver. Yesterday ex-Cardinal [*in 1927–29*] Fred Frankhouse blanked his old teammates on 6 hits, while Boston clubbed Hallahan, Haines, and Winford for 13. Hallahan also was the losing hurler in last week's shutout.

The Braves' shortstop Bill Urbanski equaled an all-time mark by facing Cardinal pitchers six times without being officially listed at bat. Urbanski walked four times and sacrificed twice.

Leo Durocher almost matched a modern mark when he committed four errors, one short of the record. Durocher fumbled a ground ball in the second, booted another grounder and made a wide throw in the sixth, and fumbled again in the ninth.

Martin J. Haley, St. Louis *Globe-Democrat*

° *Friday, June 15* °

[*On June 14, in St. Louis, the Cardinals defeated Boston, 12–9. Winning pitcher, Tex Carleton; losing pitcher, Leo Mangum. Cardinals' standing: 31 wins, 19 losses, in second place.*]

All is forgiven! Leo Durocher, who resembled a bush league rookie as he erred four times on Wednesday, batted himself back into the good graces of the fans. A home run with the bases filled proved sufficient to wipe out a multitude of sins and gave Lippy Leo an opportunity to trade in his goat-horns for a hero's mantle.

In the fifth, Medwick beat out a hit and Ripper Collins crossed up the opposition by doubling to left instead of right. Reserve catcher Bill De-Lancey was retired, and Signor Ernesto Orsatti was purposely passed to get at Durocher. What in insult! The very idea! Imagine the anguish our hero suffered by this humiliating piece of pitching humbug.

To make a long story longer, Durocher blasted the ball past Center-fielder Wally Berger and, trailing his three mates, circled the bases for a home run.

The usual hoopla went up in the Cardinal dugout where bench-warmers shook themselves and slid off their seats long enough to congratulate the shortstopper. He had driven in a run with a first inning single, but he said his day's work wasn't completed.

"I've got to drive in one more run to make it six," he snapped.

Then it was recalled that before yesterday's game Leo boasted, "I'll win the hecklers back today by driving in six runs!" This brought a round of ho-hos and ha-has.

Came the seventh and Orsatti doubled. Durocher quickly made good his promise by rifling a long single to right, and the hustling Italiano scrambled across the plate with the sixth run driven in by Lippy Leo. [*And thus the finest batting day in Durocher's career came twenty-four hours after his all-time worst fielding performance.*]

Ray J. Gillespie, St. Louis Star-Times

◦ Saturday, June 16 ◦

[*On Friday, June 15, in St. Louis, the Cardinals lost to Boston, 10–4. Winning pitcher, Ed Brandt; losing pitcher, Jim Mooney. Cardinals' standing: 31 wins, 20 losses, in second place.*]

[*The June 15 game may be summarized in one sentence: The Cardinals were weak in batting, weaker in fielding, and weakest of all in pitching.*]

◦ Sunday, June 17 ◦

[*On Saturday, June 16, in St. Louis, the Cardinals lost to Philadelphia, 8–2. Winning pitcher, George Darrow; losing pitcher, Dizzy Dean. Cardinals' standing: 31 wins, 21 losses, in second place.*]

Jimmy Wilson's Phils fattened up on Cardinal pitching to win their first game of the season from the Cardinals. The Phils amassed 14 hits off Dizzy Dean and Jess Haines.

Dean, knocked out in the ninth inning, was pounded for 12 hits and all the runs. Two were homers on successive times at bat by Dolph Camilli, recently traded to Philadelphia by the Cubs for Don Hurst. [*This trade is generally regarded as one of the best, or worst, in the history of baseball. Hurst batted .228 in 1934 and then left the major leagues for good. Camilli played regularly for the next ten years; in 1941, he led the National League in home runs and runs batted in and was voted the league's most valuable player.*]

Martin J. Haley, St. Louis Globe-Democrat

∘ *Monday, June 18* ∘

[*On June 17, in the first home doubleheader of the season, the Cardinals defeated Philadelphia twice, 6–0 and 7–5. Winning pitchers, Dizzy Dean and Paul Dean; losing pitchers, Curt Davis and Syl Johnson. Cardinals' standing: 33 wins, 21 losses, in second place.*]

There are days when Dizzy Dean's arm is not what the trade calls "right." There are days when he talks through is sombrero with the nonchalant abandon of a couple of Barons Munchausen. [Baron Munchausen's Travels *was a popular eighteenth-century book with highly exaggerated accounts of the author's alleged adventures. In the mid-thirties Jack Pearl starred in a weekly radio show inspired by this book, entitled* Baron Munchausen.] But come Whitsuntide, Shrove Tuesday or the Fourth of July, and Jerome Herman's heart is filled with the vodka of victory, esprit de corps, and the will to serve and win. And because he is what he is, the Cardinals turned a threatening defeat into a triumph and made the first double-header of the season at Sportsman's Park a twin victory. [*At this time, so-called synthetic doubleheaders, those played on days other than legal holidays, were prohibited before June 15. This rule was passed as a compromise to appease owners who were opposed to all doubleheaders and those who, like Sam Breadon, wanted the freedom to hold doubleheaders at any time.*]

Paul Dean was a shutout pitcher in the first contest. He held the Phils to five hits, with not a single base runner reaching third base.

After Paul had done his work, Bill Hallahan went to the hill in the second game, and the Phils knocked him out in the fifth inning when they moved in front, 5 to 3. Jim Lindsey replaced Hallahan and hurled hitless ball in the sixth, and then was withdrawn for a pinch hitter.

Dizzy Dean had pitched more than eight innings on Saturday. Nobody expected to see Dizzy on Sunday. But when the Phils went to bat in the seventh there was Jerome Herman on the hill. And how he pitched! His arm was as strong as his heart. The hard work of the day before seemed to be just what he needed. And Dizzy mowed down the enemy.

That was enough of an inspiration to make any team fight, and if further incentive was needed, Jimmy Wilson furnished it by working the Redbirds into a fury with the greatest exhibition of within-the-rules stalling this observer ever saw.

Pepper Martin opened the Cardinal seventh with a double against the left field wall. Dark clouds had been gathering, and as though Martin's wallop were a signal to the elements, a wind of near-cyclonic proportions whipped across the field and a stormy haze darkened the waning day.

A storm was about to break. When Rothrock flied out, Jimmy Wilson decided that if he could delay things the elements would come to his aid, prevent the game's completion and protect his team's lead.

And so, after Ed Holley had pitched two balls and a strike to Frisch, Wilson conferred with Holley and then with Coach Hans Lobert. The Cardinals complained loudly, and Umpire Ernest Quigley pointed an official finger at Jimmy's nose and told him that such tactics would not be tolerated.

But the rules provide that a manager can change pitchers as often as he wishes so long as each pitcher faces one batter. And so when Wilson sent Holley to the showers and called on the ambling Scandinavian, Sylvester Johnson, the Cardinals could only fume and fret and hope that the storm would hold off.

Johnson took his five practice pitches, and then Wilson and the Phils were hoist by their own petard, or something like that. Frisch hit a pop fly that would have been easy for Second Baseman Irv Jeffries a few minutes earlier. But the wind had increased in velocity and blew Frisch's fly out of Jeffries' reach for a single, Martin racing to third.

Wilson was not yet whipped. He waited until Johnson was about to pitch. Again the ubiquitous Lobert bow-legged from the dugout, again there was a conference. The Cardinals fumed and fretted, but it was rule-book baseball, and in due time Snipe Hansen meandered in to relieve Johnson. Hansen threw five practice pitches and then gave a splendid imitation of slow-motion pictures as he hurled four consecutive balls to Medwick, shaking his head after each pitch as though bemoaning his lack of control, and fingering the resin bag after each delivery.

The pass to Medwick filled the bases. The clouds were darker, the wind stronger, the rain seemed on its way, and the customers were wondering where they would take shelter if the threatening storm became a cyclone. [*Most of the seats in Sportsman's Park were uncovered.*]

Wilson stuck to his stall. Again he chatted with the waddling Lobert, and he called on George Darrow to relieve Hansen. Darrow pitched to Collins, and the Ripper hit a hot smash to Dick Bartell's right. The Phillie shortstop grabbed the ball and fired to Jeffries for a force-out, but Collins beat the relay to first and Martin scored the tying run.

When Chick Fullis came out to bat for DeLancey, Darrow was sent away, after the usual Wilson-Lobert ceremonies, and Austin Moore went to the hill, the fifth pitcher of the inning. Fullis hit a low line drive to left center for a double, Frisch and Collins racing home to put the Cardinals two runs ahead.

It was dark enough to call half a dozen games, but the umpires wanted to give Mr. James Wilson the pleasure of as much night baseball as possible, so they kept things going for another inning. After Dean turned back the Phils, Umpire Quigley finally capitulated, and the stentorian tones of Jim Kelley informed the remaining customers that the game had been called on account of darkness.

J. Roy Stockton, *St. Louis Post-Dispatch*

NATIONAL LEAGUE STANDINGS

	W	L	PCT	GB		W	L	PCT	GB
New York	37	19	.661	—	Boston	28	25	.528	7½
St. Louis	33	21	.611	3	Brooklyn	25	31	.446	12
Chicago	33	24	.579	4½	Philadelphia	19	33	.365	16
Pittsburgh	27	24	.529	7½	Cincinnati	13	38	.255	21½

∘ *Wednesday, June 20* ∘

[*On June 18, the Cardinals were not scheduled to play. On June 19, in St. Louis, the Cardinals lost to Philadelphia in 12 innings, 10–8. Winning pitcher, Curt Davis; losing pitcher, Paul Dean. Cardinals' standing: 33 wins, 22 losses, in second place.*]

Paul Dean, in a relief role, lost his first game of the season after eight straight victories, when Philadelphia defeated the Cardinals in 12 innings. Paul, the fourth of five hurlers used by Manager Frisch, blanked the Phils from the seventh until he was knocked out in the third extra round.

Johnny Moore's single, Camilli's triple, and a double by Curt Davis brought to an end the younger Dean's winning streak.

His conqueror, Davis, the fifth Philadelphia hurler, entered the game in the seventh and shut out the Cards for six innings, allowing only two hits.

Martin J. Haley, St. Louise *Globe-Democrat*

The introduction of the lively ball to the National League has meant a decided new deal for batters. A check of 45 regular players shows that they have made a total net gain of 1,227 points in their batting averages over their 1933 efforts at a corresponding date. That's not recovery, it's pure inflation.

The 45 leading batters in the American League, however, are pounding the ball only 240 points better than in 1933.

Caswell Adams, New York *Herald-Tribune*

Tickets for the All-Star game at the Polo Grounds on July 10 will be priced according to the regular scale. There will be 3,796 box seats at $2.20; 5,806 grandstand seats at $1.65; 40,000 grandstand seats at $1.10; and 4,000 bleacher seats at 55 cents.

New York *Sun*

∘ *Thursday, June 21* ∘

[*On June 20, in St. Louis, the Cardinals lost to Brooklyn, 9–5. Winning pitcher, Van Mungo; losing pitcher, Bill Hallahan. Cardinals' standing: 33 wins, 23 losses, in second place.*]

Bill Hallahan, once the fastest southpaw in the National League, has gone into a tailspin. With his decline the Cardinals have dropped from the lead and are five games behind the Giants.

Bad Bill was nominated to pitch the first game of the Dodger series, but, as in his three previous starts, he never saw the finish line, being knocked out in the fifth after yielding 11 hits.

If Hallahan remains in his slump, the Cardinals will be lucky to finish as high as third. Around the league, players agree that he isn't as fast as he used to be, and that his curve, once his forte in the pinches, has lost its deception. He doesn't wheel back and let go with might and main any more. The fact that he walked seven Phillies in less than five frames last Sunday was a tip-off.

Hallahan's toboggan slide has whittled Frisch's staff down to the Dean brothers, and nowhere do the books show a team winning the pennant with two pitchers.

Bill McCullough, Brooklyn *Times-Union*

∘ *Friday, June 22* ∘

[*On June 21, in St. Louis, the Cardinals beat Brooklyn, 9–2. Winning pitcher, Dizzy Dean; losing pitcher, Tom Zachary. Cardinals' standing: 34 wins, 23 losses, in second place.*]

The Cardinals rallied back into pennant-contending form yesterday to drub Brooklyn and reduce New York's league lead to four games. Pitching, punch, and a perfect defense dovetailed.

Dizzy Dean supplied the pitching. Joe Medwick returned to slugging stride, and Jim Collins to home-run range. The Dodgers gathered only 7 hits off Diz, who has 10 victories. Medwick, with only 1 scratch hit in 11 times at bat when the game started, hit a home run and a double. Collins boosted his home-run total to 15 when he pounded a pitch to the pavilion roof, his first circuit clout since June 12.

Martin J. Haley, St. Louis *Globe-Democrat*

The cash customers are burning the wires with this question: "What's the matter with Bill Hallahan?"

In two of the four pennants won by the Cardinals, Hallahan was the little jim-dandy, supreme in a crisis. When an important game was at stake, Bill received the assignment, and he usually succeeded. [*In 1930, Hallahan won 15 games, lost 9, and led the league in strikeouts with 177; in the World Series he won 1 game in 2 decisions. In 1931, as noted earlier, Hallahan was the Cardinals' most valuable pitcher, during the season and in the World Series.*]

Hallahan of 1934, however, is not the Hallahan of 1930 or 1931. He has 2 victories and 7 defeats, and the Cardinals say that Bill's fade-out is crimping their pennant prospects.

What's wrong with Hallahan? I asked him to come out in the open and tell his story. Bill shook his head. He had no excuses.

"I don't know what's wrong with me," he remarked. "I've lost a few games because I didn't get the breaks, but on the whole I've been a mess. Maybe I'm trying too hard. When a pitcher is losing he throws himself off his natural stride because of a mental hazard. I've been pressing—I admit it—because I'm trying to win, and I suppose I'm getting my stuff too close to the center of the line.

"But don't let anyone tell you I'm dissatisfied. Frisch is a great guy, and all the boys are giving me the best they have. A fellow blows himself to a bad year every now and then. Maybe this is the bad one for little Bill." [*Although not particularly small, Hallahan, at five feet ten inches, was the shortest of the Cardinal pitchers, most of whom were at least six feet tall.*]

I quizzed Frisch on Hallahan's erratic work. Perhaps Frankie possessed a hokus-pokus touch that would put the left-hander back on his stride.

"I've tried everything," Frisch said. "I've rested him. I've worked him oftener than his regular schedule. I've advised him to use more fast balls, and then I've asked him to specialize on the curve. When a great pitcher gets in a rut he has to pitch himself out of it. A manager can't help him."

Hallahan came to the rescue in 1930 and 1931, and it is not too late for him to save the 1934 flag for the Cardinals. Whadda ya say, Bill?

Sid Keener, St. Louis *Star-Times*

(AP)—The major leagues sprang a surprise by announcing the selection of the relatively youthful championship club managers, Bill Terry of the New York Giants and Joe Cronin of the Washington Senators, as pilots for the All-Star teams.

"By appointing the World's Series managers," said John A. Heydler, president of the National League, "we feel that we have established a precedent which perhaps will be carried out in future All-Star games." [*A precedent was indeed established for managers of World Series teams to direct the All-Star teams of the following year. In the first All-Star game, in 1933, the managers had been Connie Mack and John McGraw.*]

The New York Times

∘ *Saturday, June 23* ∘

[*On June 22, in St. Louis, the Cardinals defeated Brooklyn, 7–2. Winning pitcher, Paul Dean; losing pitcher, Ray Benge. Cardinals' standing: 35 wins, 23 losses, in second place.*]

Paul Dean, younger half of the Cardinals' "dizzy duo," kept step with brother Jerome by plastering a second straight defeat on the Dodgers. Paul had oodles of stuff. He spread 8 hits over the distance, and struck out 10 as he gained his ninth triumph, the nineteenth victory netted by the Dean brothers.

Although Rip Collins' sixteenth homer of the year with Frankie Frisch on base in the fifth produced the winning runs, the Cards' manager earned batting honors with 2 doubles and 3 singles in 5 trips to the platter.

Edward Zeltner, New York *Daily News*

Good as Dizzy was against our boys, Paul was even better, according to the men who batted against him.

"That fellow is a real pitcher," said catcher Al Lopez. "He just winds up and explodes dynamite in front of you, and don't let anybody tell you he isn't smart out there on the rubber. I don't think he made a mistake all afternoon. All of our players think he's a wow!"

Bill McCullough, Brooklyn *Times-Union*

Baseball has taken it mighty hard on the chin since that Old Debill Depression came along.

There's red ink on many baseball ledgers where red ink never went before. More money's in circulation than in the past two years. Why aren't baseball clubs getting their share of it?

Can you think of one attempt to make a ball game more attractive? (Leave out that boomerang idea of putting in the lively ball.) You can't.

No one will pay attention, but I'll make some suggestions.

1. Shoot the peanut, hot dog, cigaret, and pop vendors.

2. Replace them with attractive girls who don't have to shout something between a hyena's laugh and tribal chant to attract attention. (Preferably they should have husky brothers to bust the first guy who gets fresh.)

3. Replace the megaphone announcer with a public address system. No matter how good a voice megaphone wielder has, even Vallee, it can't always carry into the stands. [*The trademark of the highly popular crooner of the twenties and thirties, Rudy Vallee, was a megaphone.*]

4. Put games on the air. Make radio broadcasts interesting enough that fans won't want to take the thrills second handed.

5. Sell beer in the park. YOU'D be surprised how popular beer has become. The objection is, "Somebody'll get hit by a bottle." Well, a pop bottle hurts as much as a beer bottle, and throwing is about all the pop is good for anyway.

Chester L. Smith, Pittsburgh *Press*

° *Sunday, June 24* °

[*On June 23, in St. Louis, the Cardinals defeated Brooklyn, 5–4. Winning pitcher, Bill Hallahan; losing pitcher, Les Munns. Cardinals' standing: 36 wins, 23 losses, in second place.*]

Frankie Frisch's Cardinals, showing the courage of champions and fighting hardest when things looked darkest, finally found their batting eyes, overcame a four-run Brooklyn lead and defeated the Dodgers.

One of these days the Cardinals will mount victory hill without the aid of the Dean boys, but the story of this triumph under a broiling sun cannot be told except in terms of the ubiquitous Jerome Herman, the fourth Cardinal pitcher. Dizzy was not the winning pitcher, but his strong arm and determination, his pitching skill, and his fielding agility made it possible for the Cardinals to win.

J. Roy Stockton, *St. Louis Post-Dispatch*

Dizzy Dean, who blanked Brooklyn the last three innings yesterday to protect a one-run lead, may be credited with the victory. Martin J. Haley, official scorer, originally named Bill Hallahan the winning pitcher, but announced that he would set forth the facts in a report to President Heydler and ask him to make a decision.

St. Louis Post-Dispatch

[*Hallahan entered the June 23 game at the start of the sixth inning with Brooklyn leading, 3–0. In the sixth he gave up one run and two hits. He was then removed for a pinch hitter, and in the last of the sixth the Cardinals scored five runs. Ordinarily, a pitcher is credited with the runs scored by his team during the innings that he pitches, and since the five runs were scored in the one inning that Hallahan pitched, they would ordinarily have been credited to him, giving him the victory. But this may not have been an ordinary situation. In an instance where the nominal winning pitcher has not been particularly effective and he is succeeded by someone who pitches outstandingly well, the official scorer is permitted to declare the second man the winning pitcher. In this particular game Dizzy Dean allowed two hits and no runs in his three innings on the mound.*]

In yesterday's contest, for the first time in the memory of any observer present, the umpires worked without their coats. [*St. Louis was undergoing a heat wave that was rare this early in the summer; during the game the temperature reached 100 degrees Fahrenheit.*]

Roscoe McGowen, The New York Times

With the Giants steadily pulling away from the field, the only thing close in the National League is the St. Louis weather.

James C. Isaminger, Philadelphia Inquirer

∘ *Monday, June 25* ∘

[*On June 24, in St. Louis, the Cardinals lost to New York, 9–7. Winning pitcher, Dolf Luque; losing pitcher, Jim Lindsey. Cardinals' standing: 36 wins, 24 losses, in second place.*]

There can be no question that the Giants and Cardinals are embroiled in a hot series, for the weather man has taken care of that. Even if the two clubs were not fighting for the league leadership, this would be one of the hottest series of the season. The general effect is that of playing a double-header in a boiler room with full pressure up. If the far-flung Cardinal empire maintains a branch in Arabia, now is the time for Branch Rickey to call in the Bedouin farmhands. They'd be a cinch in this temperature. [*At three o'clock, when the game started, the temperature was 99 degrees Fahrenheit; an hour later it hit 100 for the second day in a row.*]

Even the natives admit that it is rather warm. The Cards felt the effects of the heat as much as the Giants, possibly more so, as New York's victory might indicate. Nine pitchers were used, five by St. Louis and four by the Giants. The excessive heat throws the burden entirely on the pitchers, for every flinger has to fight against the temperature as well as opposing hitters.

Bill Terry declared that he never played ball in hotter weather, and Bill is a veteran of the Southern and Texas leagues. Terry has been coming to St. Louis for a dozen seasons, and he never found it this hot before.

Tom Meany, New York World-Telegram

NATIONAL LEAGUE STANDINGS

	W	L	PCT	GB		W	L	PCT	GB
New York	40	22	.645	—	Boston	32	29	.525	7½
St. Louis	36	24	.600	3	Brooklyn	26	37	.413	14½
Chicago	38	26	.594	3	Philadelphia	22	38	.367	17
Pittsburgh	31	27	.534	7	Cincinnati	19	41	.317	20

∘ *Tuesday, June 26* ∘

[*On June 25, in St. Louis, the Cardinals lost to New York, 10–7. Winning pitcher, Carl Hubbell; losing pitcher, Bill Hallahan. Cardinals' standing: 36 wins, 25 losses, in third place.*]

Frankie Frisch is complaining.

And that is one of the very best things the erstwhile "Fordham Flash" does—complain. When he sets out to register a "beef," he cuts it an inch thick and asks a man to digest it.

His pitching staff is his present peeve. What was supposed to be the strongest heaving corps in the league has ceased to function.

"What's the matter with my pitching?" he countered a question before yesterday's game. "I'll tell you. And in a few words. My gang should be pitching hay instead of baseballs. At least they'd be earning their pay."

Frankie exaggerated, but he had reason to be aggravated. He had just learned that Jerome, the dizzier of the Dean brothers, had lost a decision to the heat and wouldn't be able to take the mound against Carl Hubbell.

"That leaves me with one pitcher," Frankie mourned, "and he won't be ready until tomorrow."

Frankie did not elaborate, but we inferred that he was talking about Dizzy's younger brother, Paul.

The two Deans have been pitching all the winning games lately. Tex Carleton and Bill Hallahan have been belted lustily, and the relief pitching has done nothing but relieve the other side of worry.

Later, after he'd cooled out a bit, and assigned Hallahan to Dean's place, Frisch adopted a more philosophical attitude, or maybe it was merely fatalistic.

"Maybe this thing is all for the best," he said. "We're not going any place, unless Carleton and Hallahan win some games, and they might as well start now."

Unhappily for Frisch, Hallahan didn't "start" yesterday. The left-hander was out of there and so was Jim Lindsey before the second inning had ended, an inning in which the Giants scored seven runs.

Garry Schumacher, New York *Evening Journal*

There was muttering and much complaining among the customers at Sportsman's Park yesterday when Bill Hallahan went to the hill instead of Dizzy Dean, who had been advertised as the day's hurler.

After five innings Announcer Kelley megaphoned that Dizzy was ill and under a doctor's care and that the club apologized for advertising that he would pitch.

Boos and jeers met the announcement.

Old-timers could not remember having heard such an apology before.

St. Louis Post-Dispatch

○ *Wednesday, June 27* ○

[*On June 26, in St. Louis, the Cardinals defeated New York, 13–7. Winning pitcher, Paul Dean; losing pitcher, Al Smith. Cardinals' standing: 37 wins, 25 losses, in third place.*]

Every season with the Cardinals is divided into two sections, and the Giants are in the second, or Dean phase today. Now that the National League schedule is around to four-game series, you see a Dean half the time. The other half of the series is devoted to pitching by softies. [*In April, May, and early June, a series generally included three games; from mid-June until mid-September, teams usually played a four-game series.*]

Frankie Frisch has been operating on the plan that if one of the softies can get by, the series is "in" for the Cardinals. He counts on the Brothers Dean to give him an even break at all times, which by the way is more than the Brothers Dean are getting from the Cardinal owners.

Frisch used his softies in group formation for the first two games of the current series, throwing them in en masse. The net result of the combined efforts of nine softies was two Giant victories. Then Frisch called Paul the Younger, and he tied knots in the Giants yesterday. Jerome the Elder goes to the wars today.

Paul scored his tenth victory against one defeat. Dizzy also has won 10, but has lost 3. Since the Cardinal record is 37 victories and 25 defeats, it can be seen that the Deans are handy to have around despite their eccentricities. Neither of 'em is the least bit silly on that hill when the gong sounds.

The rest of the Cardinal pitching has won 17 and lost 21, which is strictly second division. The Deans are not only keeping the Cardinals in the race—they're keeping 'em in the league!

Tom Meany, New York *World-Telegram*

Arthur "Dazzy" Vance, 41 years old, who has been flinging from that center knob on the diamond since 1912, is the answer to Frankie Frisch's urgent call for immediate pitching strength. With his hurling staff tottering and on the verge of a complete collapse, Frisch flashed an S.O.S. to headquarters at Sportsman's Park.

"We need pitching—we gotta get pitching!" shouted the Flash.

Whereupon Messrs. Breadon and Rickey bought the old Dazzler from Cincinnati. Wow—that deal's a honey!

Pitching 18 innings for the Reds this season, the old Dazzler has been bumped for 21 runs and 28 hits. Boiled down to the average of a nine-inning game, Vance has given more than nine runs per game. And he's the pitcher who's been added in a desperate move to save the pennant for St. Louis! [*Vance had done his best pitching for Brooklyn in the twenties. In 1924, he won 28 games and lost 6, and he led the league in strikeouts for seven consecutive years, 1922–28.*]

Sid Keener, St. Louis *Star-Times*

∘ *Thursday, June 28* ∘

[*On June 27, in St. Louis, the Cardinals defeated New York, 8–7. Winning pitcher, Dizzy Dean; losing pitcher, Dolf Luque. Cardinals' standing: 38 wins, 25 losses, in third place.*]

With the current heat wave steaming at its peak and the thermometer sizzling at 115 on the playing field, the Giants closed their Western campaign by crashing to defeat.

A homer by Bill DeLancey in the last of the ninth won the game and gave Dizzy Dean his twelfth victory of the season, although he required help from Jim Mooney to collect the third out in the upper half of the ninth after the Giants had tied the score, 7–7.

John Drebinger, *The New York Times*

In St. Louis the Deans rule, and their sway even affects the official scoring. Yesterday Dizzy Dean was hammered out by three successive singles in the ninth, tying the score with Lefty Mooney coming in and pitching to one batter and retiring the side. But when the Cardinals in the last of the ninth won on DeLancey's homer, did Mooney get credit for the victory? He did not. The St. Louis scorer said it was Dizzy Dean. [*This ruling would seem to have been indefensible. Rule 10.19 states, "Whenever the score is tied the game becomes a new contest insofar as the winning and losing pitcher is concerned." When Dean left to be relieved by Mooney, the score was tied, and so clearly the winning pitcher should have been Mooney.*]

Will Wedge, New York *Sun*

Most of the Cardinal players think Mooney should receive credit for yesterday's victory.

Some of them resent the acclaim and applause heaped upon the Dean brothers, insisting that their own part in the success of the Redbirds has been ignored. The Deans are all the St. Louis fans talk about. When anybody else starts on the mound, the fans chant in unison, "We want Dean." This attitude is supposed to explain much of Hallahan's recent ineffectiveness. Thus yesterday's victory awarded "Dizzy" won't please many Cardinal players. As one of them said, "You can bet that if the positions of Mooney and Dean had been reversed Dizzy still would have received the credit."

Garry Schumacher, New York *Evening Journal*

Getting credit for yesterday's decision was the day's second good stroke of fortune for the elder Dean. Earlier he received word from President John A. Heydler of the National League that he had been awarded last Saturday's victory over Brooklyn, a game originally credited to Bill Hallahan. [*In this instance, as noted earlier, the ruling was not improper.*]

Ray J. Gillespie, St. Louis *Star-Times*

St. Louis—No longer do advertisements in the local Gazettes begin with that age-old "Giants vs. Cards at Sportsman's Park today," not when our Jerome is to pitch. In bold type they read "Dizzy Dean—in person—vs. the Giants today." Farmers come out of the distant Ozarks and Mid-West traveling salesmen arrange their itineraries to catch him. Sam Breadon told me that had Dean pitched last Sunday it would have meant 15,000 extra admissions.

I met our Jerome last night at a little bulb-spangled amusement park. In an outdoor pavilion our hero was dancing with his wife. He wore a white polo shirt, open at the throat, and a night wind tousled his handsome head until his hair sprayed out in all directions like a busted whisk broom. The orchestra was playing a waltz, and Jerome was singing softly to his wife, cheek to cheek, his lips close to her ears. She is a very pretty woman, Mrs. Jerome Dean, and when you see her you realize what a great wave of love swept through the heart of the farmer-boy-rookie when he first met her.

Jimmy Powers, New York *Daily News*

Alas, there is a drawback with the Deans. When they are winning, the other members of the hurling staff sulk in their tents. Curbstone gossip would have us believe that Frankie Frisch is not getting 1,000 percent out of some of them. Perhaps this is true, and, if so, it can be traced to the success of the Dean boys.

Not all the Cardinal hurlers like the Deans for what they are worth in a material sense. They resent the publicity diverted from them to the Deans. And there was that "crack" Dizzy made in Pittsburgh about himself being more valuable to the ball club than Hallahan, who was getting about 40 percent more pay. This didn't help the Hallahan morale any, and there have been reports that Bill would like to be traded.

Dick Farrington, *The Sporting News*

○ *Saturday, June 30* ○

[*On June 28, the Cardinals were not scheduled to play. On June 29, in Cincinnati, the Cardinals lost, 7–1. Winning pitcher, Paul Derringer; losing pitcher, Tex Carleton. Cardinals' standing: 38 wins, 26 losses, in third place.*]

Red stood out all over the place during the super-heated matinee yesterday on the sun-baked turf of Crosley Field. The countenances of the athletes glistened under the violent rays of Old Sol, an umpire had to be removed in a parboiled condition, and our boys climaxed an afternoon of brilliant hue by soaking the Cardinals, their first victory over the Frisch faction this season.

Also were the faces of said Cardinals red when Tex Carleton was punched for six runs in the fourth round.

The Cardinals were completely subdued by their former teammate, Paul

Derringer, who allowed seven scattered blows. Derringer held up better than some of the other performers. He went all the way while Umpire Beans Reardon was overcome after the fourth inning. Beans said that the hot sun beating down on the back of his heavy blue coat disabled him.

Even Frankie Frisch felt the effects of the furnace-like environment and resigned his position at second base.

Jack Ryder, Cincinnati *Enquirer*

° *Sunday, July 1* °

[*On June 30, in Cincinnati, the Cardinals lost, 11–4. Winning pitcher, Si Johnson; losing pitcher, Paul Dean. Cardinals' standing: 38 wins, 27 losses, in third place.*]

Those surprising Reds, having discovered that the Cardinal pitching staff is not invincible, made another vicious attack on the Frisch faction yesterday, pushing over no less than nine tallies in the big eighth round. The victims of this rally were Tex Carleton, Paul Dean, and Jim Mooney, with Dean bearing the brunt of the slaughter and losing his second game of the season.

The beauty of it was that all nine tallies were scored after two were out by a combination of eight hard blows and a couple of passes.

Jack Ryder, Cincinnati *Enquirer*

° *Monday, July 2* °

[*On July 1, in Cincinnati, the Cardinals, in 18 innings, won, 8–6. Winning pitcher, Dizzy Dean; losing pitcher, Paul Derringer. Following this game, the two teams played five innings of the scheduled second half of a doubleheader, which was called, because of darkness, with the score tied, 2–2.*]

The Reds and Cardinals engaged in a titanic struggle yesterday, the Cards finally winning after 18 bitterly contested rounds.

The operation lasted four hours and a half, with Tony Freitas and the great Dizzy Dean working on even terms for 17 frames, after which both retired in favor of pinch-hitters.

The combat was followed by a pigmy game which went five rounds to a score of 2 to 2, just to keep faith with the 12,000 fans who had been promised a double-header.

The first game was a nip-and-tuck conflict, and because neither Tony nor Dizzy was so effective as usual there was a good deal of free hitting. The big hero was Joe Medwick, who broke a long batting slump by driving out a home run in the seventeenth, which kept the Cards in the game until they had a chance to win in the following round.

Then in the last half of the eighteenth Joe saved the day with a sensational one-handed catch of Bottomley's drive with two outs and two men on base. When the ball left the bat it looked good for three bases, but Medwick cut back toward the scoreboard like a startled hare, leaped high, and came down with the ball tightly encased in his glove.

Jack Ryder, Cincinnati *Enquirer*

Next Tuesday a picked team of American Leaguers will play a picked team of National Leaguers at the Polo Grounds. The players for the teams were designated by baseball fans of the country by means of a ballot. The final returns are in, and here are the teams selected, along with the votes.

NATIONAL LEAGUE			*AMERICAN LEAGUE*		
1b	Terry, Giants	121,110	1b	Gehrig, Yankees	117,789
2b	Frisch, Cards	120,141	2b	Gehringer, Tigers	120,781
3b	Traynor, Pirates	115,018	3b	Dykes, White Sox	102,673
ss	Jackson, Giants	82,430	ss	Cronin, Senators	116,326
of	Klein, Cubs	119,933	of	Ruth, Yankees	114,399
of	Medwick, Cards	80,744	of	Averill, Indians	97,657
of	Berger, Braves	79,743	of	Manush, Senators	82,410
c	Lopez, Dodgers	77,785	c	Dickey, Yankees	102,686
p	Hubbell, Giants	86,048	p	Gomez, Yankees	84,712
p	J. Dean, Cards	62,201	p	Whitehill, Senators	53,662
p	Warneke, Cubs	56,923	p	Grove, Red Sox	38,327

It now develops that maybe these players will play, and maybe they won't. The fans were merely shadow boxing with the ballot, and this election was no different from most elections which supposedly express the will of the people.

If the bosses agree with the fans, these players will play; if they don't, they won't. In this instance the bosses are Mr. Terry of the Giants and Mr.

Cronin of the Senators. They will pick the players they want regardless of the vote.

This smacks so much of the Tammany touch and is so characteristic of the American system of democracy that it should occasion no surprise. But that doesn't make it any less cock-eyed. Why ask the fans to vote if their judgment is to be ignored?

As I see it, the baseball people miss the point entirely, which is not astonishing, because baseball people are adept at missing points. For generations baseball people have lived on the island of Let-Well-Enough-Alone, completely surrounded by a large body of Stagnation.

All the ballyhoo leading up to the All-Star game has stressed interleague rivalry. Could anything be sillier? When and where did one game decide the relative merits of two leagues? From the standpoint of superiority the result of the All-Star game will be less important than Max Baer's opinion on the German situation. [*On June 14, Max Baer had knocked out Primo Carnera to become the heavyweight champion of the world.*]

If the All-Star game has any point at all, it is as a special occasion for the nation's grandstand managers to speak their voice and be heard.

Perhaps the fans' teams are not as strong as they might be, but what difference does it make? The important thing is that these are the teams the fans want to see. So where does anybody get off in overriding their desires?

If the fans' teams do not represent the best in the leagues, whose concern is that but the fans'? After all, they fill the parks, make the game possible, and perpetuate the sport. I agree with some of the more profound critics that some selections were based on sentiment—and I add, hurray!

Since when has there been a law against boys in the bleachers getting sentimental? I know that Ruth is no longer a first-rate player, but I am pleased to note that he got more votes than any other outfielder. I know that Lefty Grove's soup bone has lost its fire, but again I string along with the fans. I don't care to forget that he was once the king of pitchers. [*Grove had won twenty or more games in each of the preceding seven seasons, but in 1934 he would gain only eight victories against as many losses.*]

Please remember, Mr. Managers, this isn't your game. It's the fans' game.

Joe Williams, New York *World-Telegram*

NATIONAL LEAGUE STANDINGS

	W	L	PCT	GB		W	L	PCT	GB
New York	43	25	.632	—	Pittsburgh	35	29	.547	6
Chicago	41	27	.603	2	Brooklyn	27	41	.397	16
St. Louis	39	27	.591	3	Philadelphia	24	44	.353	19
Boston	37	30	.552	5½	Cincinnati	21	44	.318	20½

° Tuesday, July 3 °

[*On July 2, in Chicago, the Cardinals lost, 7–4. Winning pitcher, Lon Warneke; losing pitcher, Paul Dean. Cardinals' standing: 39 wins, 28 losses, in third place.*]

Was it an infield fly, or wasn't it? They are still arguing about it. Umpire Bill Klem's decision in the seventh inning yesterday still was a moot point.

Four singles off Paul Dean in the seventh sent one run in to make the Cubs' lead 4 to 1 with the bases filled and one out. Then Chuck Klein lifted a high pop fly near the plate along the first base line. Catcher Bill DeLancey threw off his mask, ran out, and poised himself. The wind carried the ball foul, and then back fair. DeLancey had poised himself two points to the rear of where the capricious wind finally decided to send the ball. The sphere popped to the ground, Klein reached first, and Warneke, on third base, scooted home. DeLancey retrieved the ball but made a wild throw and Warneke was safe.

Immediately Frisch started making faces out loud at Klem. Why wasn't Klein out under the infield fly rule? The faces he made were too disrespectful. He was invited to leave the premises. Whereupon Coach Mike Gonzalez and Dizzy Dean, scenting a chance to do some talking, came charging out of the dugout. "And you, too," Klem said, impolitely doing some finger-pointing in their direction at the same time. They "too-ed."

Later Klem explained that Rule 44, Section 8 (the infield fly rule) says that the batter is out if, with first and second occupied or the bases filled, he hit a fair fly ball other than a line drive that can be "handled" by an infielder. In that word "handled" lies Klem's explanation. The "infielder" in this case, DeLancey, wasn't in a position to handle the ball, he says. If he wasn't in a position to handle the ball, he couldn't trap it and by trapping it start a double play, which is what the rule seeks to prevent. Therefore it was not an infield fly.

James M. Gould, *St. Louis Post-Dispatch*

National League President John Heydler delayed his ruling upon the Cardinals' protest of yesterday's Chicago victory, but he did fine two Redbirds for their part in the row.

Manager Frank Frisch was fined $100 for "extremely bad conduct in defying a league umpire by repeatedly refusing to resume play" and Coach Mike Gonzalez $25 "for unreasonable delay of game and repeated threats to punch an umpire."

Frisch immediately telephoned Heydler and protested vigorously. He pointed out that it was Umpire Klem's conduct and his failure to properly interpret the infield fly rule that delayed the game.

"You're making a joke of the National League by permitting your umpires to assume a belligerent attitude," Frisch shouted to Heydler over the phone. "I can't understand why you don't make your umpires stay awake, attend to business, and call plays right."

The league president hung the receiver upon the hook.

Regarding Klem's statement that Klein's fly was a difficult chance and hence did not come under the infield fly rule, Frisch sharply commented, "If I had men in my infield whom I thought incapable of catching this so-called difficult chance, I'd fire them at once."

[*Bill Klem was the senior National League umpire, having joined its staff in 1905, and he would continue to be active until 1941. He has often been called the best umpire of all time.*]

St. Louis *Star-Times*

○ *Wednesday, July 4* ○

[*On July 3, in Chicago, the Cardinals won, 7–3. Winning pitcher, Bill Hallahan; losing pitcher, Guy Bush. Cardinals' standing: 40 wins, 28 losses, in third place.*]

Guy Bush had nothing with which to annoy the St. Louis Cardinals, and the Cubs could not devise any ways to bother Bill Hallahan. Under the circumstances the Cubs were forced to curl up and accept an even break in the series.

Irving Vaughan, Chicago *Tribune*

∘ *Thursday, July 5* ∘

[*On July 4, in St. Louis, the Cardinals split a doubleheader with Chicago, winning the first game, 6–2, and losing the second, 6–2. Winning pitchers, Tex Carleton and Jim Weaver; losing pitchers, Bill Lee and Jim Mooney. Cardinals' standing: 41 wins, 29 losses, in third place.*]

Makers of fancy bouillons, consommes, and odd broths of all kinds will no doubt be disappointed to learn that the pitching soup bones of Bill Hallahan and Tex Carleton are not yet ready for the boiling pot. These mound aces of other days have suddenly found new life in those pitching wings, and thus we find renewed hope in Cardinal baseball circles. If this pair can consistently duplicate their hurling performances of the past two days, they should add considerably to the 45 victories the Dean brothers have set out to score.

Prior to their recent form reversal, this pair had been knocked from the mound in nine straight starts. Hallahan had been blasted five times in a row before he subdued the Cubs on Tuesday. Carleton had yielded to enemy bats on four successive occasions before he forgot his losing complex, resembled the hard-to-touch 1933 Carleton, and let the Cublets down on six hits in the opening half of yesterday's double-header. [*In 1933, Carleton won 17 games and lost 11, and in total strikeouts he was surpassed only by Dizzy Dean and Carl Hubbell.*]

Then, to add to this sudden, unexpected pitching prosperity, Southpaw Jim Mooney graduated from the bullpen in the second game, and held the Cubs on even terms for five innings. However, he folded up shortly afterwards under a deluge of hits that resulted in a Cub victory. [*The twenty-seven-year-old Mooney was in his fourth major league season, his second with the Cardinals. In 1933, he won only two games while losing five. Along with Frisch, Carleton, and Whitehead, Mooney was one of the team's four college graduates, having attended East Tennessee Teachers' College, in Johnson City.*]

Manager Frankie Frisch, as tickled as a kid with a new sandpile, said of the winning efforts of Hallahan and Carleton, "That answers the question, 'What's been wrong with the Cardinals?' Hallahan and Carleton won 21 games between them at this time last season. This year Hallahan has won 3 and Carleton has won 8."

Ray J. Gillespie, St. Louis *Star-Times*

Why was Manager Frisch's every appearance yesterday greeted with cheers that have made the name "Bronx" so well-known? [*The Bronx cheer is a loud, derisive type of noise that is the direct opposite of applause. The term may have originated in the National Theater, in the Bronx.*] The Flash is playing good ball and, as pilot, is doing an excellent job. Maybe the booers didn't have any firecrackers to explode and just wanted to make some noise. Whatever the reason, the jeers were untimely and entirely undeserved.

James M. Gould, *St. Louis Post-Dispatch*

◦ *Friday, July 6* ◦

[*On July 5, the Cardinals were not scheduled to play.*]

The only conclusion one can draw about the All-Star game is that no one connected with baseball is in a terrific lather to run this affair. The magnates and league presidents apparently have decided that something in which baseball fans take such interest could not possibly be good for them and the sooner the idea is abandoned the better. The game has become baseball's stepchild. The players don't like it because they don't get paid for it. The managers don't like it because they are afraid of the risk to star players. The owners don't like it because they just ain't smart enough, and the league presidents don't like it because they didn't think of it themselves. [*The creator of the All-Star game was Arch Ward, sports editor of the* Chicago Tribune, *who conceived of it as an adjunct to the Chicago World's Fair of 1933.*] Arrayed against this stiff-necked outfit are the fans, the dear peepul, the public that supports baseball. They like it. But they don't count.

For three days we have tried to find someone with sufficient authority and consideration for the voting fans to instruct the appointed managers, Terry and Cronin, to use the starting lineups as indicated by the national poll of baseball lovers. We have encountered a magnificently organized passing of the buck, winding up in the statement by President Harridge of the American League that the matter lay between the fans and the managers, which is nothing but hooey. What does he expect the fans to do except stay away from the game? Or is that what he wants?

This game, played for the first time last year, is the first practical all-star game ever devised because it is completely feasible. It is possible to have a fans' team, one that they asked for, and it is possible to show this team in action. Whereupon baseball people proceed to gum it up. Terry's team is close enough to the vote of the fans to accept without much fuss. [*For one of his starting outfielders, Terry chose his own Mel Ott over the fans' choice, Wally Berger, of the Braves, and one of his pitchers was Fred Frankhouse, of the Braves, who received very few votes. He also indicated that his starting shortstop might be Arkie Vaughan, of the Pirates, rather than the top vote getter at that position, Travis Jackson, of the Giants. Otherwise Terry adhered to the fans' selections.*] Cronin's selections, however, are arbitrary and don't follow the poll. Why not? Because Cronin wants to win the game? Who cares who wins? It is all a dream, a baseball fan's beautiful dream about to come true. Keep out of our dreams, you managers! [*Although White Sox manager Jimmy Dykes received ten times as many votes, Cronin named Pinky Higgins of the Athletics to play third base, and he picked Al Simmons, of the White Sox, as an outfielder rather than the popular choice, Earl Averill, of the Indians. In forming a pitching staff, Cronin ignored three of the top four vote getters— Earl Whitehill, of the Senators; Lefty Grove, of the Red Sox; and Willis Hudlin, of the Indians—and selected, instead, Red Ruffing, of the Yankees; Mel Harder, of the Indians; and Tommy Bridges, of the Tigers.*]

Paul Gallico, New York *Daily News*

Baseball, which has been battling against depression and other ills, must soon or late consider what to do about this thing called softball.

Up to this season the magnates have yawned when softball was mentioned.

"Just something for women and children to fool around with," some suggested.

"It's a fad that will wear out like miniature golf," commented others.

As a threat to baseball it was a laugh.

But you can't laugh off a paid attendance of 8,612 with hundreds turned away because the capacity had been reached, last Sunday night. And probably 15,000 turned out at other softball parks throughout the district on that one night.

Anything that interests those who spend money on sports is certainly a rival of baseball, especially since admission to softball games is within reach of almost everyone.

John E. Wray, *St. Louis Post-Dispatch*

∘ *Saturday, July 7* ∘

[*On July 6, in St. Louis, the Cardinals lost to Cincinnati, 16–15. Winning pitcher, Don Brennan; losing pitcher, Jesse Haines. Cardinals' standing: 41 wins, 30 losses, in third place.*]

Frankie Frisch used seven hurlers yesterday in an effort to stop the wholesale manufacture of hits and runs, but six of them were mauled, with Tex Carleton, who worked the ninth, the only one who didn't feel the sting of Rhineland war clubs.

Jess Haines, Jim Lindsey, Dazzy Vance, Dizzy Dean, Bill Walker, and Jim Mooney were the other pitchers who paraded from the mound to the showers.

Ernest Lombardi, the Big-Horn catcher of the Reds, was the outstanding slugger of the base-hit picnic. [*"Big-Horn" is a reference to Lombardi's gargantuan nose, which gained him other nicknames such as "Schnozz" and "Beezer."*] Lombardi singled in 2 runs in the first inning, hit a homer in the third, drove in 2 more with a triple in the fourth, singled and scored in the sixth, and singled in the seventh to drive a runner home. With a perfect day at bat he pounded 6 runs across the plate and scored 4 himself. [*Twice, in 1938 and 1942, Lombardi would lead the National League in batting.*]

The outcome of the game was in doubt to the last second of play, when Leo Durocher was thrown out trying to score from second on an infield single by Tex Carleton.

J. Roy Stockton, *St. Louis Post-Dispatch*

Frankie Frisch is preparing to carry on in the footsteps of John McGraw and fight for the rights of managers and players to question the judgment of umpires and league executives.

"Something must be done with these temperamental umpires," said Frisch. "They refuse to listen to a fair discussion. They insist they are always right and the manager or player who is arguing is wrong. One word from us, and we're out of the game. This condition should be changed immediately, or the fans will lose interest.

"Umpires are under the jurisdiction of President Heydler, but even Mr. Heydler can be wrong. He is wrong when he supports umpires who remove players when a decision is open to debate. The club owners should convince President Heydler that his system is making a 'sissy' game out of baseball."

I heartily endorse Frisch's stand. Managers and players are entitled to a fair hearing before an umpire.

What happens now? A majestic wave of an arm and a player is removed from the scene simply because the man in blue felt that no one should question his judgment.

Umpires can err. They do repeatedly. What makes them so important that they cannot listen to a complaint without creating a scene?

Presidents Heydler and Harridge should advise their umpires to be more lenient when a heated discussion pops up. The umps can look and listen—and then take a walk. The heated exchange will cool, and then everything will be all right.

Sid Keener, St. Louis *Star-Times*

The heat wave has served one purpose. It has revealed the "boner" baseball moguls committed when they tampered with the ball.

The new, dynamite-laden pellet has made a travesty of baseball. It has taken the science and skill from the game. Luck is now the determining factor—and the individual player needs only batting power, or what passes for it—sheer strength.

Here are a few recent scores. They tell their own story. New York 15, Boston 0. New York 13, Brooklyn 7. Philadelphia 14, Boston, 11. Boston, 16, Philadelphia, 13. Cincinnati, 16, St. Louis, 15.

The ball explains it, though the protracted heat spell has aggravated the situation for pitchers. The tired and weakened pitchers have lost some of their edge. The batters, thoroughly in stride, are taking fullest advantage of their handicapped foemen.

No better illustration of what the ball has done to baseball could be found than in the sixth inning of the Giants' game yesterday against the Dodgers. Dodger first baseman Sambo Leslie's home run with the bases filled was as artificial and "phoney" as a home run can be. It was only a single to center, a bouncer through the diamond, but the "rabbit" in the ball insisted on a couple of extra bounds which carried it high over center fielder George Watkins' head. [*One wonders what this writer might say about some of the base hits that nowadays are made on fields with artificial turf.*]

Garry Schumacher, New York *Evening Journal*

∘ *Sunday, July 8* ∘

[*On July 7, in St. Louis, the Cardinals defeated Cincinnati, 10–4. Winning pitcher, Bill Hallahan; losing pitcher, Tony Freitas. Cardinals' standing: 42 wins, 30 losses, in third place.*]

Bill Hallahan's second straight complete nine-inning victory was a close battle until the sixth inning, when, with the score tied, Lady Luck smiled sweetly. Hallahan, permitted to bat for himself after Durocher doubled with two out, hit an easy grounder which hopped over third baseman Tony Piet's head for another double. That break sent the Birds ahead, and thereafter they simply mopped up.

Martin J. Haley, St. Louis *Globe-Democrat*

Casey Stengel will someday be recognized as one of the great managers. Underneath his clowning is a keen perception of what it takes to win and an ability to lead that are found in few men.

Chester L. Smith, Pittsburgh *Press*

∘ *Monday, July 9* ∘

[*On July 8, in St. Louis, the Cardinals split a doubleheader with Cincinnati, winning the first game, 6–1, and losing the second, 8–4. Winning pitchers, Dizzy Dean and Benny Frey; losing pitchers, Paul Derringer and Paul Dean. Cardinals' standing: 43 wins, 31 losses, in third place.*]

Closing their home stay, the Cardinals broke even with Cincinnati, Dizzy Dean winning the first game and Paul Dean losing the second. It was Dizzy's fourteenth victory against three defeats. Paul's loss was his third straight. He has 4 defeats and 10 triumphs.

In the second game the big blow came in the third inning when Harlin Pool hammered Cincinnati into a commanding lead with a bases-loaded home run. Just before the homer, Paul Dean had bawled out Umpire Charles Pfirman for calling a ball on what Paul thought should have been the third strike. After the homer, Durocher talked his way out of the game by a belated "beef" over the aforementioned pitch.

Then suddenly Paul Dean started for the Cincy dugout. He objected to something said to him, and invited his tormentor onto the field. Paul was trotting to the dugout when Jim Collins restrained him. Ray Kolp [*a thirty-nine-year-old pitcher*], one of the best-known "jockies" in baseball, was identified as the bold, bad villain.

Soon Dizzy Dean was over near the Cincy bench, asking somebody to "come out and fight," and being held back by Mike Gonzalez. The scene died out, Paul resumed his pitching, lost his control, and was stung for two more runs.

Martin J. Haley, St. Louis *Globe-Democrat*

Dizzy Dean has not won a game from the Cubs since establishing his strikeout record of 17 against them last July 30. He has been beaten five times since that remarkable performance.

Sid Keener, St. Louis *Star-Times*

NATIONAL LEAGUE STANDINGS

	W	L	PCT	GB		W	L	PCT	GB
New York	48	28	.632	—	Boston	39	37	.513	9
Chicago	46	30	.605	2	Brooklyn	31	45	.408	17
St. Louis	43	31	.581	4	Philadelphia	30	47	.390	18½
Pittsburgh	38	33	.535	7½	Cincinnati	24	48	.333	22

∘ *Tuesday, July 10* ∘

[*On July 9, the day before the All-Star game, no games were scheduled in either major league.*]

This writer sees as the main purpose of today's All-Star game the fact that the proceeds go to a meritorious cause. They go to an association devoted to the relief of sick and distressed veterans of baseball. Any effort that contributes to the amelioration of human suffering and distress the writer deems worthy of support.

The game itself means nothing to competitive sport. It is merely a novelty parade of star players. Neither club could beat any second division team in the two leagues in a best four-out-of-seven series.

But as a spectacle the game should be well worth seeing, and the writer sincerely hopes that the fund for which it is played will be enriched by many thousands of dollars.

Years ago the writer often suggested that big league ball players, while in their playing prime, make some provision for the upkeep of the aged and infirm of the game. Among the ideas advanced was taking a small percentage each year off the World's Series receipts.

The active players laughed off these suggestions. They did not need assistance. Why should they provide for improvident old timers who had failed to save their money?

Many of these then active players later found themselves in the very predicament of the old timers whose cause they had spurned. One of baseball's greatest all-time stars, now long dead, who criticized the suggestions, saw the day when he was glad to accept the proceeds of a benefit game.

There is something of his attitude among some baseball stars of today with reference to the All-Star game. They are luke warm toward the game, for which they receive no immediate reward.

They should reflect that their reward is the consciousness of a kindly deed, of effort toward a worthy cause. In years to come, some of them may be glad that they assisted in building this fund.

The baseball magnates are not particularly enthusiastic toward the game. The magnates never have done much to help superannuated players. Yet they should welcome the game as solving one of baseball's oldest problems. [*It was not until after World War II that major league players gained the rights to a pension, which did not cover anyone whose career had ended before 1947.*]

Damon Runyon, New York *American*

The most charming feature of today's All-Star game if Hubbell is right and his arm red hot will be the spectacle of American League sluggers snapping their spinal cords in an attempt to hit his screw-ball.

Paul Gallico, New York *Daily News*

Is batting a lost art? Sometimes old-timers growl and grumble to that effect. And, after watching futile efforts to bunt or work the hit-and-run, you think perhaps the graybeards are right.

And then along comes Frankie Frisch and reminds you that some players can wield the ash today as skillfully as Willie Keeler or Jess Burkett. [*Keeler and Burkett, who played late in the nineteenth and early in the twentieth centuries, were two of baseball's all-time best hitters, and both were noted for their skillful place hitting. Keeler is supposed to have explained the secret of his success by saying, "I hit 'em where they ain't."*]

If you saw Sunday's doubleheader, you saw Frisch place a hit to left field as scientifically as Keeler himself could have done. Batting left-handed, Frank saw a gap between the third baseman and shortstop, and he popped one right through it and just above the hands of either fielder.

Frisch, incidentally, is the surprise of the year, both as a player and as a manager.

Frisch was all over the lot on Sunday, making wonderful stops and going after forlorn hopes as if they were at his finger tips. Once he ploughed up the dirt with his nose when he missed knocking down a hit to right field.

As a leader Frisch has the world popeyed. It had been freely predicted that he would be a flop because he was not temperamentally suited to be a manager and his players were not in sympathy with him. Both charges have been completely disproved. Frisch is getting 100 percent support from his men and is playing better than he has for two or three seasons.

John E. Wray, St. Louis Post-Dispatch

∘ *Wednesday, July 11* ∘

[*On July 10, in the Polo Grounds, New York, the American League won the All-Star game, 9–7. Winning pitcher, Mel Harder; losing pitcher, Van Mungo. Home runs: Frank Frisch, Joe Medwick.*]

Mel Harder, who never attained such great heights that his selection worried the National Leaguers, was the Gibraltar of the American Leaguers' hurling staff as the stars representing the Will Harridge circuit defeated the National League's team.

Going to the relief of Charley Ruffing, of the Yankees, in the fifth inning with none out and two men on base, Harder quelled the National Leaguers' uprising and then went on to hurl a splendid exhibition of baseball to have his name put alongside that of Babe Ruth, the hero of the first All-Star game.

A crowd of 52,000, which had come with the expectation of seeing brilliant pitching from Carl Hubbell, Van Mungo, Lon Warneke, Lefty Gomez, et al, were amazed as it watched the Cleveland right-hander hold the National Leaguers to one hit in the last four innings, a double by Billy Herman in the ninth. Only one other runner got to first in those innings, Chuck Klein, who reached the bag on a wide throw from Lou Gehrig to Harder. [*Perhaps surprisingly to present-day fans, most of the immediate re-*

ports of the game devoted far more space to Harder than to any other player. But, as shown by the next item, not everyone concentrated on Harder.]

Charles Segar, New York *Daily Mirror*

Well, you may close the books on the All-Star game. A slim fellow with No. 14 on his back trotted off the field towards the locker room while a crowd of 48,363 covered his departure with cheers that lingered long after the figure in cream-white had taken the last pat on the back from ecstatic bleacherites who leaned far out of the stands by the locker room door in center field to touch the wonderful shoulder of the man who, with two men on base and none out in the first inning, had struck out Ruth, Gehrig, and Foxx in succession. It was, of course, Carl Hubbell, the great left-hander of the Giants. [*In the Polo Grounds, the Giants' clubhouse, used in the All-Star game by the National League, was under and beyond the center field bleachers. To reach it, a player would cross the field and go through a passageway from which he could be touched by nearby fans.*] When Hubbell waved good-bye to the adoring thousands, after pitching three innings, he left the Nationals in the lead by 4 to 0. He had given two hits and had fanned, in addition to the first three named, Messrs. Simmons, Cronin, and Gomez.

Those who watched him will treasure the brief period as some of the greatest innings of baseball pitched. Hubbell's complete mastery of the hitting stars of the American League was all the more sharply outlined against what happened to his successors, Warneke and Van Lingle Mungo. Two innings after Hubbell turned his back on the field that he had held in the hollow of his left paw, the score was 8 to 4 in favor of the American League. They may tell you that Hubbell was bearing down because he had only three innings to go and that he couldn't have continued at that pace. Bunk and nonsense. He'd have taken them for nine innings the way he took them for three, because when he struck out Ruth, Gehrig, Foxx, Simmons, and Cronin in succession, the American League was whipped. All he had to do was to feint at the boys. The American Leaguers were jumping at his windup the way Primo Carnera nearly jumped out of his skin the time Max Baer feinted at him and hollered "Boo!" Of all the stars on the field, Hubbell was the brightest.

Two minutes after the game opened, Hubbell was in as deep trouble as he will ever be in his pitching life-time. Charley Gehringer, first man up, singled to right and took second on Berger's sloppy handling of the ball. Heinie Manush walked. None out, men on first and second. And Ruth, Gehrig, and Foxx up. What odds that the Americans wouldn't score at least one run? Hundred to one? Don't be cheap. It is difficult to figure the exact odds, but it must have been close to a 500 to 1 shot. The first man he had to face had hit 699 home runs during his career. The second was the greatest slugger in the American League today. The third was once one of Connie Mack's wrecking crew and is still one of the most powerful hitters in the game. Brrrr! Night mares! Shivers! Jitters! How would you have liked Hubbell's spot? A hundred thousand eyes burning little individual spotlights on his reputation.

Babe Ruth looked at one, took one, and looked at a third, and that was that. There was a great yell from the crowd as Ruth walked away and Hubbell stood hitching his pants and pulling down his cap and weighing the next man up, Lou Gehrig. Hubbell struck out Gehrig swinging, but Gehringer and Manush pulled a double steal and were on second and third. The crowd was simply insane. If it was 500 to 1 that Hubbell would get by scoreless, it was 1,000 to 1 that he would strike all three men out. Oh, but here was magnificent duelling of eye and skill and courage and steady nerves, no longer team against team, but man against man, Hubbell against the hitters. Now the hitter was Jimmy Foxx, but by that time Hubbell's magic had become too potent. It filmed Foxx's eye and slowed his muscles. The old dipsie-doodle ball was swooping and dipping. There was red hot magic on it. It was turning into a rabbit, or a humming bird, or a bunch of flowers on its way to the plate. It would come up in front of Foxx's eyes and then vanish completely. Foxx struck out swinging. The crowd lifted the Polo Grounds six feet off the ground with a roar and then set it down again. [*In the second inning, Hubbell struck out the first two men he faced, Al Simmons and Joe Cronin.*]

Paul Gallico, New York *Daily News*

When Joe Medwick got that home run yesterday, he hit a ball high over his head. How anybody can get so much power on a ball at that height is a mystery.

Dan Daniel, New York *World-Telegram*

○ *Thursday, July 12* ○

[*On July 11, in Philadelphia, the Cardinals lost, 5–2. Winning pitcher, Phil Collins; losing pitcher, Tex Carleton. Cardinals' standing: 43 wins, 32 losses, in third place.*]

Having suffered a charley horse in the All-Star game, Frankie Frisch rode the bench as his Cardinals bowed to Jimmy Wilson's hustling Phils.

Fidgety Phil Collins, outpitching Tex Carleton and receiving better support, had a shutout until the ninth inning, when with two out and Virgil Davis on base, Bill DeLancey cracked a home run over the right field fence.

Martin J. Haley, St. Louis *Globe-Democrat*

Frankie Frisch isn't smiling much these days, not even at the antics of baseball's greatest clown, Dizzy Dean.

When a man can't laugh at Dean, the thunder clouds are hanging low and the lightning is about to strike.

Frisch looked as if he hadn't shaved for two days when we saw him peering out of the Cardinal dugout yesterday. Maybe the fact that he had "charley horses" in both legs had something to do with his fierceness of face.

The fact is, however, that the brilliant Redbird cast is in third place, and in the last 37 games has lost 19, certainly not a pennant stride.

Frankie, however, stoutly defends his club. "We're having bad breaks, but when they turn we'll be up at the Giants' heels," he remarked.

"Injuries haven't helped, either," he continued. "Bill Walker broke his arm when he was our most dependable hurler and cannot seem to recover his strength. Orsatti pulled a leg muscle, and Hallahan is just beginning to show something.

"The Deans are our only consistent pitchers, but Paul has lost his last three starts and he's starting to worry. It's too bad in a way that he hasn't Dizzy's happy-go-lucky disposition. Paul is more serious. Dizzy is just plain crazy, but a fellow has to be crazy to be a good ball player. If you aren't cuckoo when you start, you soon get that way.

"Look at Dean now," Frisch said, pointing to the Phillies' bull pen, where Dean was making eyes at "Southie," the famous lucky rabbit of the Wilsonmen.

"I suppose you might say, 'just a couple of dumb bunnies,' but don't fool yourself. Dizzy is as smart as a whip," said Frisch.

Dean then bounced into the dugout, shouting, "I've got it. I've got it."

"You got what?" asked Virgil Davis.

"I have the secret of how to eat grass, get fat and enjoy it," replied Dean.

"How is that?" queried Davis.

"Just become a bunny."

"The Old Sport," Philadelphia *Inquirer*

United Press International Photo

The Cardinals' field boss, who managed the team and was also a Hall of Fame second baseman: the "Fordham Flash," Frank Francis Frisch.

United Press International Photo

The most colorful pitcher in the history of baseball, Jay Hanna Dean, known to everyone as "Dizzy."

Dizzy Dean and Frankie Frisch during spring training in 1934. Could Dizzy be modestly predicting a great season for himself?

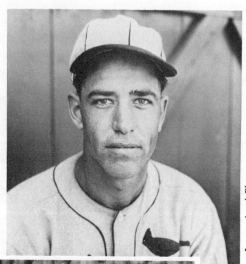

Dizzy Dean's younger brother, a rookie in 1934, who became one half of that famous pitching duet "Me and Paul."

United Press International Photo

United Press International Photo

The very first Dean family portrait, taken in February 1935. Dizzy and Paul stand with their older brother Elmer, who in 1934 had been a St. Louis ball-park peanut vendor. Their father is shown sitting with Dizzy's wife and Paul's bride.

United Press International Photo

He could hit with his fists as well as his bat: Hall of Fame outfielder Joe "Ducky Wucky" Medwick.

United Press International Photo

He generated excitement at bat, on the base paths, and in the field: the "Wild Horse of the Osage," Johnny Leonard "Pepper" Martin.

United Press International Photo

He was a pool shark, a flashy dresser, and a nonstop talker. He was also a fine shortstop: "Leo the Lip" Durocher.

United Press International Photo

Leo Durocher and his second wife, the former Grace Dozier, just after their wedding in September 1934.

United Press International Photo

The Cardinals' fun-loving home-run slugger: first baseman Jim "Ripper" Collins.

United Press International Photo

United Press International Photo

Two famous Cardinal pitchers: the southpaw strike-out artist "Wild Bill" Hallahan, and the Hall of Fame knuckleball hurler Jesse "Pop" Haines.

United Press International Photo

The Cardinals' owner, Sam Breadon *(left)*, and his general manager, Branch Rickey, who perhaps are conferring on what to do with their most tempestuous employee, Dizzy Dean.

United Press International Photo

The New York Giants' first baseman and manager, Bill Terry, who, on January 24, 1934, asked the notorious question, "Is Brooklyn still in the league?"

United Press International Photo

In his first year as manager of the Brooklyn Dodgers, Casey Stengel provided Bill Terry with the answer to his question.

United Press International Photo

United Press International Photo

◄ Bill Terry's two preeminent teammates: the left-handed hitter of home runs, Mel Ott, and the left-handed pitcher of screwballs, Carl Hubbell. ▲

Joe Medwick sliding into third base in the 1934 World Series, the play that
caused thousands of spectators to go berserk.

This party owes an apology to a party named Mel Harder, who throws curve balls for the Cleveland Indians. Somehow his work in the All-Star game didn't look as showy or exciting as Hubbell's performance, but it must have been. It looks much better on paper.

Harder faced the following sluggers: Mel Ott, Paul Waner, Arkie Vaughan, Al Lopez, Frank Frisch, Pie Traynor, Chuck Klein, Bill Terry, and Billy Herman. [*All of these players but Vaughan are in baseball's Hall of Fame. It is surprising that Vaughan, a shortstop with a lifetime batting average of .318, has not become a member of the Hall of Fame.*] To some of them he pitched twice. Only Herman hit him safely. The rest of the boys popped, grounded, fanned, and forced. Also Harder gave but one base on balls in five innings. There is a considerable pitching record.

Paul Gallico, New York Daily News

∘ *Friday, July 13* ∘

[*On July 12, in Philadelphia, the Cardinals split a doubleheader, winning the first game 8–5 and losing the second 8–3. Winning pitchers, Dizzy Dean and Curtis Davis; losing pitchers, Snipe Hansen and Bill Hallahan. Cardinals' standing: 44 wins, 33 losses, in third place.*]

Paul Dean sprained an ankle after two innings in the first contest yesterday, and when Jim Mooney couldn't hold the lead, Jerome Dean had to be called to the rescue.

Paul's injured ankle was X-rayed, and the photographs disclosed no fracture. But the young right-hander was limping badly, will have to use a cane for several days, and probably won't pitch again for ten days or two weeks.

Paul might have avoided injury if he had slid for third base instead of going in standing up. He opened the third inning with a grounder to Lou Chiozza and was safe on the second baseman's error. Then Pepper Martin singled to center, and Paul legged it for third, which was not smart base running, with nobody out. He might have beaten the throw and avoided injury if he had slid. He appeared to be undecided what to do, and at the last minute elected to stay up. His spike caught in the bag, and the sprain resulted. He had to be carried off the field.

The accident gave Dizzy the chance to hang up his fifteenth victory, and stupid base running by the Cardinals was a factor. If it had not been for the bad base running, they would have had a dozen runs and Mooney, who relieved Paul, would have coasted to a win.

The less said about the second game the better. Hallahan started, but was handicapped by a lame left ankle, injured when his foot caught in the slab at Sportsman's Park the last time he pitched. Bill was not right, and the Phils whacked him for seven hits and six runs in three innings.

Frisch was disgusted with his team's showing, and he had good reason to be. The base running alone made the Cardinals look like a team fighting for the cellar.

J. Roy Stockton, *St. Louis Post-Dispatch*

° *Saturday, July 14* °

[*On July 13, in Philadelphia, the Cardinals' scheduled game was postponed because of rain.*]

There isn't much doubt that the ball player of today is far more mercenary than he was 30 or even 20 years ago. In the last 15 years the major league star has been "in the big money," and to remain there is his first objective.

That does not mean that he plays less energetically or shirks or skulks, although in some cases he has done these things. However, you will have a hard time convincing some observers that present day players are working wholeheartedly.

A veteran was recently quoted as saying that "the reason so many players are required on a roster—23 is the limit—is that the players, especially pitchers, will not extend themselves or give their fullest efforts.

"Pitchers are especially delinquent. They believe that every hurler has only a certain number of throws in his arm, and that the more he conserves these the longer he'll last. You can't get pitchers to work out of turn except by ordering them, and if you do that you'll regret it.

"If pitchers gave as they should, they would pitch oftener and last longer. Those old boys like Cy Young, Walter Johnson, and Grover Cleveland Alexander lasted long years and gave everything they had. But our 'heavy sugar' boys of today dole out their stuff by the throw."

This is not a fair indictment of all players, certainly not Dizzy Dean. Dizzy gives everything he has every time he pitches, which is every day they will let him. He argues about his pay now and then, but he's in there doing his stuff right along.

John E. Wray, *St. Louis Post-Dispatch*

Carl Hubbell, sitting in a corner of the Giant dugout, was asked what he threw to Babe Ruth, Lou Gehrig, and Jimmy Foxx when he struck them out in the first inning of the All-Star game, and also Al Simmons, Joe Cronin, and Vernon Gomez in the second inning?

"Screw balls. That goes for Gehringer, Manush, and Dickey, too. I figured they saw fast balls and curves every day but that they didn't see a screw ball very often, and that as I would pitch only three innings they wouldn't have a chance to catch up with a strange delivery. So I gave them nothing but screw balls." [*The screwball is a pitch which, when thrown by a left-hander like Hubbell, breaks away from a left-handed batter, as his curve would break away from a right-handed batter. The man who is credited with perfecting this pitch is the Giants' great right-hander of the first fifteen years of this century, Christy Mathewson, who called it a fadeaway. Mathewson and Hubbell are the only masters of the pitch who are in baseball's Hall of Fame.*]

Was this the most he ever got from a pitching feat?

"No," he said. "I don't think of the game as anything but an exhibition that doesn't mean anything. I don't mind telling you I felt pretty good when I struck out the side in the first game of the World Series last fall—and when Cliff Bolton hit into a double play in the ninth inning of the fourth game. Getting those fellows out really meant something." [*In the very first inning of the first game of the 1933 World Series, Hubbell struck out the first three Washington batters, each of whom had won or would win an American League batting championship: Buddy Myer, Goose Goslin, and Heinie Manush. When Bolton hit his game-ending double-play grounder in the fourth game, the Giants were ahead, 2–1, and the bases were loaded with one out. Many years later, John P. Carmichael edited a series of articles in the* Chicago Daily News *entitled "My Greatest Day in Baseball," and for this series Hubbell chose, or Carmichael chose for him, the 1934 All-Star game. This shows the danger of relying upon reminiscences and explains why the present volume contains no retrospective recollections.*]

Frank Graham, New York *Sun*

∘ *Sunday, July 15* ∘

[*On July 14, in Brooklyn, the Cardinals lost, 10–2. Winning pitcher, John Babich; losing pitcher, Bill Walker. Cardinals' standing: 44 wins, 34 losses, in third place.*]

Missing on all cylinders, the Cardinals were taken by Brooklyn, the seventh loss in their last 11 games with the three worst clubs in the league—Cincinnati, Philadelphia, and Brooklyn.

The Cardinals made only 4 hits off Johnny Babich, a 22-year-old rookie in his first game since reporting from the Coast League. The Birds were handcuffed at the plate, and their own hurlers gave up 11 blows and 9 bases on balls. Also, the Cardinals continued their sloppy work afield, committing 3 errors for a total of 13 in their last 4 games.

Bill Walker, making his first start since early May, when he suffered a broken left forearm, was knocked out in the third inning.

Martin J. Haley, St. Louis *Globe-Democrat*

Have you ever seen Frank Frisch protest a decision at home plate? On our recent tour to St. Louis an umpire, one George Barr, had the temerity to overrule another umpire, one Bill Stewart, who had called a geezer out trying to sneak through a dust cloud with an important run. Frisch immediately skied his glove. It was an elegant motion. He seized the chocolate mitt between a thumb and forefinger and flipped it into the air. The leather had great spin, and it soared up until the relentless law of gravity broke its headlong flight. Then it stopped and, like a wounded bird, fluttered gently down to the grass.

That's a GREAT artist! That's symbolism and expression. That's the old sock and buskin, buddy. [*The shoe worn by ancient Greek comic actors was known as a sock; Greek tragic actors wore a half boot, called a buskin. Sock and buskin thus stand for comic and tragic drama.*] That's the stage for you.

Unfortunately this interpretive, flawless performance was lost on the unresponsive Umpire Barr. He hunched his shoulders, sullenly contemplated his aching feet and glowered. Did this discourage our newly discovered disciple of the late John Drew? [*John Drew, Jr., was a well-known actor who died in 1927. He was the uncle of the principal members of America's most celebrated family of actors, Lionel, Ethel, and John Barrymore.*] No, sirree! Off came the Frisch cap. Bingo! He hurled it to the earth. He looked at Barr. Still no response. Frisch took a running start. The A.A.U. regulations permit ten full strides [*for the broad jump, now known as the long jump*]. Frisch took 20 full strides. He leaped upon his recumbent headgear. He stomped it viciously with his spikes. Like a man "scotching" a loathsome snake he beat the ground, churning up a smoking volcanic eruption of clay. Get that? More symbolism! The cap is the umpire. Frisch is battering him. He is driving out the perverse devil that causes decisions to go willy, nilly against his beloved Cardinals. Ah, what a master.

I would like to describe this outburst further because Frisch began declaiming to the Roman Senate. He threw his arms about and used all manner of charming adjectives, adverbs, superlatives, and invectives. They came tumbling out of his throat on each other's heels, a gaudy assortment indeed. It was an extremely hot day, and our great artist unfortunately is bald. There is an immense white patch as big as a soup plate at the top of his skull. Umpire Barr was quite solicitous. He looked once at the sun and then at our hero's head. Frisch was instantly requested to withdraw from the premises. Umpire Barr, no doubt, feared he might catch a sunstroke.

Jimmy Powers, New York *Daily News*

° *Sunday, July 16* °

[*On July 15, in Brooklyn, the Cardinals won a doubleheader, 2–0 and 6–3. Winning pitchers, Dizzy Dean and Tex Carleton; losing pitchers, Ray Benge and Les Munns. Cardinals' standing: 46 wins, 34 losses, in third place.*]

Big Dean picked up the Dodgers in his big paw and dropped them bodily into seventh place. Big Dizzy shut out our boys with four hits, and in the eighth inning clouted a home run into the left field deck.

"A combination of Ty Cobb, Napoleon Lajoie, and Rogers Hornsby couldn't have hit that guy this afternoon," sighed Al Lopez. "That ball came up there so fast it jumped like a jackrabbit when it crossed the plate."

Tex Carleton beat the Dodgers in the nightcap, and when Len Koenecke hit a home run in the eighth, who do you suppose rushed to the bull pen to warm up? Dizzy Dean.

A few other pitchers were warming up at the time. Dizzy told them to sit down.

"Give me that glove," he said to one.

With Dizzy ready to go to the rescue, Carleton lasted it out.

Medwick completely ruined the Dodgers in the second game with 2 home runs and 5 runs batted in. The first homer he hit "off his ear." It was high and wide.

"The only way to fool that guy," said Boyle, "is to throw right over the heart of the plate. He hits wild pitches farther than he does good balls. His first home run went to left and his second hit the right field fence. What can you do with a fellow like that?"

Medwick seems to be the incarnation of that fabled fellow who reached over and hit the fourth ball of an international pass over the fence for the winning homer.

Harold Parrott, Brooklyn *Eagle*

NATIONAL LEAGUE STANDINGS

	W	L	PCT	GB		W	L	PCT	GB
New York	52	30	.634	—	Boston	41	42	.494	11½
Chicago	50	32	.610	2	Philadelphia	35	48	.422	17½
St. Louis	46	34	.575	5	Brooklyn	34	49	.410	18½
Pittsburgh	41	37	.526	9	Cincinnati	26	53	.329	24½

∘ *Tuesday, July 17* ∘

[*On July 16, the Cardinals were not scheduled to play.*]

One of baseball's oldest traditions, one of those "The king can do no wrong" edicts for lo! these many years, was knocked galley west yesterday when President John A. Heydler of the National League upheld a protest by Cardinal Manager Frankie Frisch and reversed a decision of his most venerable representative on the diamond, Umpire Bill Klem.

Klem decided that an infield fly batted by Chuck Klein last July 2 wasn't an infield fly at all. Heydler decided that Klem should have called the ball an infield fly immediately and ruled the batter out ipso facto.

Heydler added that the game must be replayed from the point where the dispute arose—the last half of the seventh inning—with the same players in the same positions as far as possible. It will be resumed prior to the scheduled game of July 31 between the Cubs and Cardinals.

George Kenney, New York *Daily News*

New York (United News)—Although 11 weeks remain in the season, it is apparent that the National League pennant race has developed into a two-team contest between the Giants and Cubs, with the Giants favored to retain the flag.

The St. Louis Cardinals, picked by many experts to cop the banner, played bang-up ball during most of the season's initial half. However, pitching and catching weaknesses have ruled out Frankie Frisch and his Redbirds as contenders.

Pittsburgh *Post-Gazette*

○ *Wednesday, July 18* ○

[*On July 17, in Brooklyn, the Cardinals lost, 7–6. Winning pitcher, Dutch Leonard; losing pitcher, Jesse Haines. Cardinals' standing: 46 wins, 35 losses, in third place.*]

Len Koenecke lifted the depression for the Dodgers and Casey Stengel at Ebbets Field when he propelled a home run high into the right field screen.

Koenecke's round-trip blow, cheered lustily by 4,000 fans, including 2,000 Boy Scouts in the left field stands, was hit in the seventh inning off the veteran Jess Haines, pitching in relief of Bill Hallahan, and broke a 6–6 deadlock. [*Len Koenecke was a promising young outfielder playing in his first year as a major league regular, and he would finish the season with an average of .320. In 1935, his performance fell off somewhat, and he was released early in September. A few days later, on September 17, as the only passenger in a private plane, he suddenly started to fight with the pilot and copilot, who in self-defense killed him.*]

Roscoe McGowen, The New York Times

The Cardinals may be sagging, but Joseph "Ducky-Wucky" Medwick, former New Jersey semi-pro, has the National League all heated up over his sensational hitting. Medwick, the son of a Hungarian millhand, was discovered by a St. Louis scout three years ago while the Giants, Yankees, and Dodgers slumbered.

Yesterday's pre-game conversation in the Brooklyn dugout centered around Medwick. Ducky had just belted two balls into the upper deck in left center [*in batting practice*], and this got a rise from the Brooklyn pitchers.

"I'd rather pitch to any other hitter in the league," declared Van Mungo. "He's bad news all the time. No game is ever won against the Cardinals until Medwick is out in the ninth. I'd rather face nine left-handed hitters all day than face Joe twice. He can do more harm with one swing than nine other guys." [*Mungo was a right-handed pitcher, and Medwick was a right-handed batter. In theory at least, right-handed batters are less troublesome than left-handed batters to right-handed pitchers.*]

"If you think he's tough for you, what should I say?" piped "Dutch" Leonard. "I'm a relief pitcher. He's a baseball murderer. You can't let up on him for a second. And the harder you bear down the harder he hits. I fooled him twice with knucklers at Sportsman's Park last month, and Sunday he hit the same pitch out into the street. I think the league should forbid his carrying a bat to the plate. Make Medwick use his fist to swing against us. Then he'd only smack out singles."

Bill McCullough, Brooklyn *Times-Union*

∘ *Thursday, July 19* ∘

[*On July 18, in Brooklyn, the Cardinals won, 5–3. Winning pitcher, Bill Walker; losing pitcher, John Babich. Cardinals' standing: 47 wins, 35 losses, in third place.*]

Ducky Wucky Medwick has left Ebbets Field for a while. Thank goodness the National League schedule permits him to play only 11 games in Flatbush each year. The Cardinals' star socker annihilated Brooklyn pitching during the five-game series that ended yesterday. His long-distance wallops were big factors in all of the games the Cards won, while in their 7 to 6 defeat Tuesday he kept them in the game with a homer and a single.

Medwick's four bingles yesterday enabled the Mound City troupe to win the rubber game. The well-built Ducky drove out a homer, a double, and two singles. During the series he made 10 hits, including 4 homers, a triple, and 2 doubles, and knocked in 11 runs. On the strength of his showing, Medwick is rated the outstanding visiting player to perform at Ebbets Field this season.

Bill McCullough, Brooklyn *Times-Union*

∘ *Friday, July 20* ∘

[*On July 19, in Boston, the Cardinals won, 4–2. Winning pitcher, Dizzy Dean; losing pitcher, Bob Smith. Cardinals' standing: 48 wins, 35 losses, in third place.*]

Dizzy Dean, who won his seventeenth game of the season yesterday, is a better pitcher this year than ever before, and to Frank Frisch and Coach Miguel Gonzalez must be given much credit for the splendid record Jerome Herman is building for himself.

When Dizzy broke into the big leagues he had enough to baffle most teams without worrying about the strength or weakness of this or that batter. Then the smart hitters began to study Jerome Herman. They learned what to expect, and last year he lost almost as many games as he won. [*In 1933, Dean won 20 games and lost 18.*]

But this season, under the patient urging and constant prodding of Frisch and Gonzalez, with the aid of the catcher of the day, Dizzy has been pitching to the weakness of each individual batter with the result that he wins the close games. [*A native of Cuba, Gonzalez had a long major league career as a catcher which ended in 1932. Regarded as one of the smartest men in baseball, he was chosen by Frisch at the beginning of the 1934 season to be one of his two coaches.*]

He has been in many a critical situation where one carelessly pitched ball could have beaten him and a few careless pitches, scattered through the season, could have made his record a mediocre one.

Bill McKechnie's Braves always seemed to be the toughest opposition for Jerome Herman, and when it was announced yesterday that he would pitch the series opener, the Braves made merry and the Boston press box experts quoted statistics to show that Frisch should have selected somebody else.

But Dizzy made few mistakes. He did make a careless pitch to Walter Berger in the fifth with two out, a man on base, and the score tied, 1–1, and Berger tripled to put the Braves ahead. But that mistake jarred Dizzy into a realization of the importance of pitching more carefully and that was the Braves' last hit. [*This game marked the first career victory for Dizzy Dean in Boston.*]

J. Roy Stockton, *St. Louis Post-Dispatch*

In his hotel room, Dizzy Dean, clown of the visiting St. Louis Cardinals, spoke of his latest trick. "This morning," he said, "I put a little sneezing powder back of the cigar desk. When the girl sneezed, she said, 'My goodness, everybody's got a cough or a sneeze today.'"

The telephone rang, and Dean answered at once before the other party could speak: "No, Dean ain't goin' to pitch today. There's not enough people in the park."

Pepper Martin was in the room, and after Dean had put down the phone, Pepper said, "Tell him about the time you broadcasted."

"I broadcasted a game between the Cardinals and Rochester once," Dizzy laughed. "Broadcasting is all right after you once get used to it. But there are some fellows on this club who'd fall over stone blind if they ever got near a mike. I guess Vance would be all right if he didn't stutter so much. Collins would be OK too, if he didn't have such a long nose that'd keep him away from the mike." [*In the forties, Dean broadcast for the Cardinals and Browns and gained fame for saying "he slud home" and "the runners has returned to their respectable bases." Later he broadcast nationally televised games of the week.*]

Does Manager Frisch approve of his clowning?

"Sure, Frank don't care, although he gets a little sore because he can't do it. As long as a guy's goin' all right. It's only fellows that's not going good that makes a joke out of the game."

The phone rang again. Paul Dean answered this time. Without waiting to see who was there, he shouted, "It's your nickel."

Robert Webb, Boston *Evening Transcript*

DIZZY GUNGA DEAN
(If Mr. Kipling Doesn't Mind)

You may talk of throwing arms that come up from Texas farms,
  With a hop upon the fast one that is smoking;
But when it comes to pitching that will keep the batter twitching
  I can slip you in a name that's past all joking;
For in old St. Louis town, where they called him once a clown,
  There's a tall and gangling figure on the scene,
And of all that Red Bird crew, there's one bloke that pulls 'em through,
  Just a fellow by the name of Gunga Dean.

> It is Dean—Dean—Dean—
> You human coil of lasso—Dizzy Dean!
> If it wasn't for old Dizzy
> They'd be worse than fizzy-wizzy,
> Come on and grab another—Gunga Dean.

He told 'em what he'd do, and they labeled him a screw,
  Just a blasted mug who took it out in boasting;
And one day they sent him back to the cattle and the shack,
  With a fair amount of panning and of toasting;
But the tall and gangling gawk, with a fast ball like a hawk,
  Keeps them standing on their heads along the green—
Brings back color to the game with a flash of crimson flame,
  So I'm slipping it along to Gunga Dean—

Yes—it's Dean—Dean—Dean—
He's a beggar with a bullet through your spleen.
Though at times some bat has flayed you,
By the Texas sun that made you,
You're a better man than bats are, Dizzy Dean!

Grantland Rice, New York *Sun*

○ *Saturday, July 21* ○

[*On July 20, in Boston, the Cardinals won, 5–1. Winning pitcher, Tex Carleton; losing pitcher, Flint Rhem. Cardinals' standing: 49 wins, 35 losses, in third place.*]

After pitching a perfect game for 6⅔ innings, Tex Carleton threw a home run ball to Wally Berger, but the Cardinals won their third straight game anyway.

Martin J. Haley, St. Louis *Globe-Democrat*

○ *Sunday, July 22* ○

[*On July 21, in Boston, the Cardinals won, 5–3. Winning pitcher, Jim Mooney; losing pitcher, Ed Brandt. Cardinals' standing: 50 wins, 35 losses, in third place.*]

Jim Mooney, the smiling schoolmaster from the hill country of Tennessee, went to the hill in the third inning yesterday when a line drive knocked Bill Hallahan's left index finger out of joint, and pitched the Redbirds to their fourth straight victory, Mooney's first triumph since May 10. [*Mooney had been a manual training teacher.*]

Mooney was in trouble many times. Dazzy Vance and later Dizzy Dean warmed throughout the contest, but Manager Frisch kept him on the hill, and the southpaw finally found himself, checked a seventh inning rally and breezed through the eighth and ninth.

Virgil Davis was the leading batter, with three singles, scoring two runs, and driving in two, but the Cardinal catcher says that the magic of Dazzy

Vance, the big medicine man from Homosassa, Fla., brought triumph to the Redbirds.

Davis is superstitious, and for several days each time he has gone to bat, Vance has said a Seminole Indian prayer over the Davis war club. On Friday Vance was in the bull-pen, and Davis went hitless. Yesterday Vance said the hocus-pocus Tamiami prayer, and Davis singled in the second and again in the fourth. Dazzy was then sent to the bull-pen, and when Davis went to bat in the fifth, with runners on first and third, his bat, without benefit of Seminole medicine, was impotent and he grounded out weakly.

And so when Davis saw that he was likely to bat in the seventh, with the score tied, he pleaded with utility infielder Pat Crawford, and Pat, much against his better judgment, carried the Davis war club out to the bull-pen for the Vance Seminole medicine. Vance willingly quit warming up for a minute, stroked the bat affectionately and muttered the words of the Seminole chiefs.

Crawford, feeling very foolish, carried the bat back to the dugout, and the happy Davis strode to the plate with the bases filled and whacked a single through the box. Two runs scored on the base hit of the Seminole medicine, and that, if you ask Davis, is the story of the victory.

J. Roy Stockton, *St. Louis Post-Dispatch*

Here's good news for Sam Breadon. Dizzy Dean says he is going to demand only $18,500 for next season.

Asked how he came to arrive at that figure, he pointed out that the highest paid Cardinal player since Diz joined the team has received $18,500 for a single season, and Dizzy reasons that he is worth at least that much. [*The Cardinal who received $18,500 was manager Frank Frisch.*]

St. Louis *Globe-Democrat*

∘ *Monday, July 23* ∘

[*On July 22, in Boston, the Cardinals won a doubleheader, 5–4 and 4–2. Winning pitchers, Bill Walker and Dazzy Vance; losing pitchers, Fred Frankhouse and Ben Cantwell. Cardinals' standing: 52 wins, 35 losses, in third place.*]

Six consecutive victories have rekindled the fires of the Cardinal pennant hopes, and Frankie Frisch and his men squared themselves with World

Series determination as they prepared to meet the Giants in the first game of a "little World Series" of four.

"We can win the pennant. We can win the pennant," was the keynote of all conversation on the train last night as the Redbirds journeyed from Boston where they completed a clean sweep of the five-game series by winning both ends of a double-header. And the Cardinals believe that they CAN win the pennant. And they feel that the pennant can be won or lost in the next four games.

"We all realize the importance of these games," Manager Frankie Frisch said last night. "The spirit of the club is great, and I am hopeful that we are going to climb from now on.

"Hallahan's injury was a tough blow. Bill was just beginning to regain his form. He was as fast as anybody would want him to be in that game Saturday. While his injury isn't serious, he'll have to miss a turn or two.

"I was delighted with the way Vance pitched yesterday, and I was also pleased with Walker's performance. I look for more good games from both of them in the days to come."

J. Roy Stockton, *St. Louis Post-Dispatch*

Arthur the Dazzler Vance pitched the entire second game yesterday, and when he fanned Wally Berger for the third out in the eighth, it was his fifth strike-out of the afternoon and the two thousandth of his big league career. He hurried up to Umpire Charley Moran and asked for the ball. He told Charley what it represented, and Uncle Charley asked Manager Bill McKechnie of the home team, which furnishes the balls, if it was OK. The magnanimous McKechnie, despite the way things were going, agreed that it was all right, and Dazzy got the ball for his souvenir case. [*This was the 216th, and last, complete game to be pitched by Dazzy Vance in sixteen major league seasons.*]

Burt Whitman, Boston *Herald*

"Oh, it's just loads of fun to cook and stew for the Dean boys," said the charming young housewife who is married to J. Herman "Dizzy" Dean. "I can speak for Paul since he lives and eats with us because he likes my cooking.

"They're such regular fellows. They love to eat, and that makes it enjoyable to prepare the dishes. Jay is especially fond of sauerkraut and frankfurters. [*As we shall learn from a later item, Dizzy Dean's actual first name was Jay, not Jerome.*] He likes cornbread, too, and roast lamb and fried chicken with cream gravy and good, thick steaks, and, oh, most any kind of meat and vegetables."

Jay's likes and dislikes, it was noted, wouldn't leave much room for special dishes.

"As soon as he finishes his meal he always takes a nap while I wash the dishes," continued Mrs. Dean, who seemed glad to say that "Diz" doesn't stand around and second-guess while she's clearing the table and tidying up.

"After I'm finished with my work I awaken him, and we play cards until 11 or 11:30," Mrs. Dean said, declaring they don't go out much because Jay doesn't like shows and he won't dance. "Sometimes friends drop in and we'll chat for a while, but we're never up after 11:30," she said.

Charles "Kid" Regan, St. Louis *Star-Times*

NATIONAL LEAGUE STANDINGS

	W	L	PCT	GB		W	L	PCT	GB
New York	57	32	.640	—	Boston	43	47	.478	14½
Chicago	54	35	.607	3	Brooklyn	39	50	.438	18
St. Louis	52	35	.598	4	Philadelphia	37	52	.416	20
Pittsburgh	41	43	.488	13½	Cincinnati	28	57	.329	27

○ *Tuesday, July 24* ○

[*On July 23, in New York, the Cardinals won, 6–5. Winning pitcher, Dizzy Dean; losing pitcher, Hal Schumacher. Cardinals' standing: 53 wins, 35 losses, in third place.*]

Jerome Herman Dean has won 18 games this year, 10 in succession and 4 against the world champion Giants. And when Dizzy checks back over his triumphs of 1934, he can be really proud and chuckle no little over the beating he gave the Giants yesterday.

Dizzy's arm wasn't right. But his heart was willing. His luck was also bad, but his will was strong. And when Bill DeLancey clutched a foul from Lefty O'Doul's dangerous bat for the final out, Dizzy ran after DeLancey, took the ball as one of his many souvenirs, and pounded Bill on the chest so hard that he all but knocked the wind out of the young catcher.

Dizzy will treasure that ball. He was happy after that victory. His winning streak was intact. The Cardinals were nearer to first place—only three games behind now—and it was a triumph despite a weary right arm that couldn't make the ball do its usual tricks.

If Dizzy had been his usual brilliant self, the game would have been a breeze.

"Give old Diz a lead of a run or two after five or six innings and the other fellows might as well fold up," he said in the hotel lobby yesterday morning. "It's just payday for Diz and the Redbirds, that's all." And he grinned as he visualized the enemy, mowed down by his cracking curve and blinding fast ball.

In this game he had a four-run lead after the Cardinals' fourth inning, and then the Giants and bad luck went to bat. Bill Terry started it with a pop fly to short left. Medwick fell trying for a shoestring catch, and the drive was good for two bases. Dizzy's curves wouldn't break, and Ott walked on four pitches. They wouldn't break for O'Doul, and Lefty singled to right, scoring Terry and sending Ott to third. Johnny Vergez, usually a mark for Jerome, cracked a double to left and Ott scored.

That should have ended the trouble, as Dean disposed of Ryan on a tap to the box. But Whitehead [*substituting at second base for Frisch, who had been inactive since the All-Star game because of his charley horse*], hurrying back for Gus Mancuso's pop fly, failed to hold it and the fluke double scored O'Doul.

Frankie Frisch left the dugout to learn first hand what was the matter with Dean, and he must have whispered magic words, for Dizzy struck out Pinch Hitter George Watkins on three burning pitches through the heart of the plate. Joe Moore, a dangerous left-handed sticker, was passed intentionally, and Dean again stuck to his fast ball and struck out Hughie Critz on four pitches.

J. Roy Stockton, St. Louis Post-Dispatch

Mr. Lively Baseball is all that the pitchers complain about. The National League has increased its batting average from .266 in 1933 to .282 in 1934.

Sid Keener, St. Louis Star-Times

∘ *Wednesday, July 25* ∘

[*On July 24, in New York, the Cardinals lost, 5–0. Winning pitcher, Roy Parmelee; losing pitcher, Tex Carleton. Cardinals' standing: 53 wins, 36 losses, in third place.*]

With no Deans, dizzy or otherwise, as distracting sidelights, the Giants swung sharply back into their normal gait yesterday.

Roy Parmelee pitched an amazingly fine game, Melvin Ott hit his twenty-fourth home run of the year, and not even the inspiring return of Manager Frankie Frisch to the Cardinal line-up could withstand this.

Parmelee allowed only four hits, all singles, and only three went to the outfield. Even more remarkable, aside from these three hits not a play was made by the Giant outfield. Parmelee fanned seven, and the other putouts were recorded by his comrades draped around him in the infield. Not a fly ball of any sort went to the outfield.

John Drebinger, *The New York Times*

"I hope they pitch Hubbell against me," Paul Dean said this morning. "I'll beat him sure, and then we'll take three out of four because if we beat Hubbell the Giants ought to fold up. Sure, my ankle is all right. I can run as fast as ever. I can throw my full weight on it when I pitch without feeling any pain, and after all this rest I ought to be able to throw a ball through a brick wall."

"You're right, Paul," Mike Gonzalez agreed. "You throw him through two brick walls. I know, because I catch you in warm-up, and my hand you almost knock him off."

J. Roy Stockton, *St. Louis Post-Dispatch*

New York (United News)—"Dizzy"Dean is co-operating with mother nature in a determined effort to provide the National League at last with another pitcher who can win 30 games in a season.

"Dizzy" has built up a reputation for goofiness. But his teammates say that he is "dizzy like a fox" after he leaves the clubhouse. He is one of the cleanest livers in the game and takes meticulous care of himself to prevent anything impairing his blinding speed and control.

Dizzy is as careful of his diet as a musical comedy star. He eats only two meals a day.

"I don't have to worry about weight," he said. "I'm about 180 now, and I never go above 188. I pitch best when I'm eating lightly. Light breakfast, no lunch, and then a good dinner with a nice steak. I don't drink coffee, use milk instead. Smoke cigarettes but only after meals. Don't touch liquor. Take plenty of exercise. Sleep in my pajamas, uppers and lowers, taking no chances of kicking off the clothes and catching cold."

Why does he pull off goofy stunts?

"I like to play around and let off steam. Baseball is a game, and I think players and fans should get as much fun as possible out of it."

Pittsburgh *Post-Gazette*

∘ *Thursday, July 26* ∘

[*On July 25, in New York, the Cardinals' scheduled game was postponed because of rain.*]

Just because he answers when you call him Dizzy is no sign that the elder Brother Dean doesn't know what the score is. This correspondent sought out the Cardinal ace, and the Diz was amenable, as usual. He will talk about anything at any time. Nobody will ever need a rubber hose to get information from the Diz.

What are Mr. Dean's ideas on pitching?

"Power and more power," advises Dizzy. "Smart pitching, this so-called pitching to weaknesses of hitters is the bunk. You finally get so that you're outsmarting yourself. I got myself in a jam trying to be smart against the Giants Monday. With a couple of men on base, guys flocked all around me giving advice. I listened and tried to do as I was told. And I only got in more trouble. Then I says to myself, 'Phooey on that smart stuff,' and I just reared back and let'er go. I struck out George Watkins and Hughie Critz, and we were out of that jam.

"If you can get the ball over with something on it, there's no call to be smart and try to get it to certain parts of the plate. That plate's only a few inches wide and the ball park is as big as all get-out. Watch batting practice and see how many balls are hit into the stands. Not many. And in batting practice the hitter knows what's coming and there's nothing on the ball. So how's he going to do it when you're wheeling 'em in with whiskers on 'em?

"And another thing—I think pitchers are a better judge of what to throw than catchers. The pitcher's throwing it, ain't he?"

Among other things the interview yielded was the information that the correct name is Jay Hannah [*actually, Hanna*] Dean, not Jerome Herman. He took the Jerome Herman out of friendship for a battery-mate in the San Antonio City League, Jerome Herman Harris, who looked something like him. And he was born at Lucas, Ark., not Holdenville, Okla, as the record books have it. He says that Chuck Klein gives him more trouble than any other hitter, and the Braves are his toughest club. The Giants are the easiest for him.

Tom Meany, New York *World-Telegram*

° *Friday, July 27* °

[*On July 26, in New York, the Cardinals split a doubleheader, winning 7–2 and losing 6–3. Winning pitchers, Paul Dean and Freddie Fitzsimmons; losing pitchers, Carl Hubbell and Bill Walker. Cardinals' standing: 54 wins, 37 losses, in third place.*]

Events in the affairs of the Giants were taking a serious turn in the humid atmosphere of the Polo Grounds yesterday, and a gala week-day crowd of 30,000 was feeling apprehensive.

In the opening clash of the double-header, Carl Hubbell, ace of aces, survived only four rounds of inept play by his comrades and went down before the combined efforts of the celebrated Dean brothers. Paul went the first seven rounds, then passed the baton to the more illustrious Dizzy, who covered the final two in nothing flat.

Paul, retiring with a five-run lead, received credit for the victory, giving this surprising young counterpart of the incomparable Dizzy his fourth triumph of the year over the Giants, to match the four recorded by Dizzy, while Hubbell suffered his third straight setback.

At this low ebb in the Giants' fortunes Stout Freddy Fitzsimmons brought his knuckle-ball into the arena and forthwith rightened things for the world's champions. [*Fitzsimmons threw almost nothing but knuckleball pitches.*] Stout Freddy hurled the Giants to a decision in the second game, and by nightfall all was serene again on the west bank of the Harlem.

John Drebinger, *The New York Times*

° *Saturday, July 28* °

[*On July 27, in Pittsburgh, the Cardinals lost, 4–0. Winning pitcher, Bill Swift; losing pitcher, Jesse Haines. Cardinals' standing: 54 wins, 38 losses, in third place.*]

Blanked by Bill Swift, the Cardinals dropped farther back in the pennant race and now trail the Giants by five games and the Cubs by two.

Swift held the Birds to 7 hits, fanned 7, and permitted only one man to reach second base and none to reach third.

Martin J. Haley, St. Louis *Globe-Democrat*

∘ *Sunday, July 29* ∘

[*On July 28, in Pittsburgh, the Cardinals lost, 5–4. Winning pitcher, Waite Hoyt; losing pitcher, Dizzy Dean. Cardinals' standing: 54 wins, 39 losses, in third place.*]

Dizzy Dean's winning streak of ten straight was broken, and the brilliant young right-hander was forced to accept his fourth defeat as he bowed to the control and skill of a veteran of baseball wars. Waite Hoyt, a boy wonder 18 years ago and youthful World Series hero as early as 1921 [*when he won two games for the Yankees against the Giants*], deserved his triumph over Jerome Herman the great.

Hoyt struck out 8, doled out 6 safeties, and were it not for 2 errors he would have romped to an easier victory.

Dean, on the other hand, was not right. By dint of hard work and a burning fast ball, he pitched out of numerous precarious situations to leave 12 Pirates stranded on base and hold down the score. But his control was bad. He issued 6 passes and could not break his curves. Lloyd Waner whacked Dizzy for 3 singles and drew 2 passes, and Paul Waner doubled and hit a home run.

If Manager Frisch had been interested in winning streaks or personal records, he probably would have derricked Jerome Herman with the score tied and save him until another day. But winning games is the thing, progress in the pennant race, and Dean stayed in there and lost a game fight.

J. Roy Stockton, *St. Louis Post-Dispatch*

"Here comes the pitch. Hale connects, swipes the ball hard. It's heading toward third base. Higgins goes after it. He scoops it up as Hale streaks toward first. It was a dandy stop. Higging straightens up and lets the ball go. It shoots straight into Jimmy Foxx's glove. Looks like it is going to be close. The umpire calls Hale out and that retires the side."

A broadcasters' account of Hale being thrown out by Frank Higgins on a schoolboy chance.

James C. Isaminger, Philadelphia *Inquirer*

° *Monday, July 30* °

[*On July 29, in Pittsburgh, the Cardinals won, 9–5. Winning pitcher, Tex Carleton; losing pitcher, Bill Swift. Cardinals' standing: 55 wins, 39 losses, in third place.*]

Pittsburgh—James "Ripper" Collins is a happy young man today, and the good people of Nant-y-glo, a little Pennsylvania mining community, are happy, too, and they are proud. Collins—"Lefty" to the folks back home— hit a home run for the old home town yesterday afternoon, and today his picture is in the Nant-y-glo paper—if they have a paper—and it's too bad there isn't more of this small town sentiment in major league baseball.

For weeks the good people of Nant-y-glo planned for their glorious excursion of yesterday. They saved up their dimes and quarters, which don't come easy in mining towns any more, if they ever did. They had little stickers printed saying "greetings to Collins." They painted one big one, with the Lions' Club insignia on one side, to stick on the grandstand wall in front of the delegation at the ball game to see "Lefty" perform.

Then there had to be money for tickets and gasoline and railroad transportation for those that couldn't find motor space, and by that time there wasn't any money left for a suitable gift for "Lefty."

The Lions' Club helped out by donating a life membership and even went further. The club engraved the membership certificate, framed it, and then decided that enough members of the Lions' Club band would be making the trip to make possible some music, so they took their trumpets and horns and drums along, and there's no mistake about it, it was the high falutenist time the folks had heard tell of in years.

The band played before the game, and they gave "Lefty" the membership certificate and a little membership button, and then they all sat back and waited for Lefty to do something worthwhile.

Doggone it, for a time it looked like Lefty was going to throw 'em all down, when he popped up in the second inning and grounded out in the third and popped up again in the fifth.

By that time, if you know musicians and how they feel with pent up emotions, all waiting to toot and blast away on their horns and tooters, you know how restless they were getting and how they kept wetting their lips and looking at each other.

Finally with the score tied, "Lefty" walked up to the plate in the eighth inning and hit the most beautiful home run that was ever hit, so help me any of the 275 Nant-y-glo-ers who attended that game, and you never heard such a joyous outburst from any band in your life. The contrapuntal effects would have delighted the most meticulous; tone and quality would have entranced you. It was a grand outpouring of harmonious joy released through brass and percussionals, and they played on through the rest of the inning.

Nobody from a big city ever enjoyed a ball game like those people from Nant-y-glo enjoyed this one, and the Cardinals took inspiration from their ecstasy and won their only victory of the three-game series.

J. Roy Stockton, *St. Louis Post-Dispatch*

NATIONAL LEAGUE STANDINGS

	W	L	PCT	GB		W	L	PCT	GB
New York	61	35	.635	—	Pittsburgh	44	47	.484	14½
Chicago	57	38	.600	3½	Philadelphia	41	55	.427	20
St. Louis	55	39	.585	5	Brooklyn	40	54	.426	20
Boston	48	49	.495	13½	Cincinnati	32	61	.344	27½

○ *Tuesday, July 31* ○

[On July 30, the Cardinals were not scheduled to play.]

Leading National League batter with a mark of .361, Pirate outfielder Paul Waner talked shop yesterday.

"The pitcher with more stuff than anyone in the league? That's easy," Waner said. "Paul Dean. If he gets proper control he will be a greater pitcher than his brother. Paul is learning faster than Dizzy learned, and within a couple of years he will be really great. He doesn't have to worry about curves or change of pace so long as he holds his speed. *[In 1934, Paul Waner would win the second of his three batting championships in his ninth consecutive year with an average of over .300.]*

Edward F. Balinger, Pittsburgh *Post-Gazette*

∘ *Wednesday, August 1* ∘

[*On July 31, in Chicago, the Cardinals lost, 7–2. Winning pitcher, Lon Warneke; losing pitcher, Bill Walker. Cardinals' standing: 55 wins, 40 losses, in third place. The two teams also replayed the last 2⅓ innings of the successfully protested game of July 2, with Chicago retaining its victory.*]

Chicago—If you had an hour of your life to live over again, would you be able to profit by your mistakes of the time before? But no one ever lives his life over, no one except, on rare occasions, ball players. And so at 2 o'clock today I looked down upon the amazing sight of 18 men turning back the written pages of time elapsed out of their lives and replaying part of a game that had passed into baseball limbo, the famous game on July 2 when Umpire Bill Klem made the only error in his life—at least the only error in which he was caught. Klem failed to call an infield fly with two on base, the Cards protested, and the game which the Cubs won, 7 to 4, was ordered replayed from the point just before the error occurred.

And so, at two P.M. today the two teams took the field exactly as they had been on that afternoon of July 2. English was on second base, Billy Herman was on third, Babe Herman was at bat, and Paul Dean was pitching. I wonder if Dean felt the import of the situation? Or if Frankie Frisch did? Because never was fate and the sequence of things so deliberately thwarted as this afternoon. In the original game Babe Herman smashed a single, scoring two runs. Today Dean lazily and with complete deliberation threw four wide, high balls, and Babe Herman trotted to first base with a walk. The Cardinals took no chances that Herman would repeat his single. The Babe couldn't have reached that ball with a broom.

I liked that. I thought it was a thrilling moment. Here were the Cards with a chance to do something over again that they wished they hadn't done. They took no chances. They might be making a NEW mistake by passing Herman, but THEY WEREN'T MAKING THE SAME MISTAKE AGAIN.

In the original game, after Herman singled, Jim Mooney replaced Dean, and Kiki Cuyler was purposely passed, filling the bases. Gabby Hartnett flied to Rothrock, and so did Don Hurst. In the replay the setup was different in that two were out instead of one. With the bases full, Dean pitched to Cuyler and got him on an easy grounder and three were out with the score 5 to 1 instead of 7 to 1. That much, at least, the little maggots who crawl the face of this globe were permitted to tamper with the cosmic design. It struck me as a great concession and momentous event.

What wouldn't you give to have a Boxing Commission rule that Tunney got a long count, that he must place himself against the ropes hands down and let Dempsey hit him eight punches, lefts and rights to the chin, and have the count begin immediately his pants hit the deck? [*The reference is to the boxing match on September 22, 1927, in Chicago, in which, aided by a so-called "long count," in the seventh round, Gene Tunney defended his heavy-weight championship against Jack Dempsey.*]

Both sides thereafter played fate for even money. It is the sheerest bumptiousness to imagine that the director of the scheme of things was sufficiently interested in maintaining at least a part of the original score of that game. But the final score DID end up at 7 to 1 because in the Cub half of the new eighth, instead of two strikeouts, a double, and a ground-out, the Cubs scored two runs. Whether by cosmic orders or not, the Cubs had their seven runs.

The Cards batted once more in the ninth, but by this time fate was bored, and Medwick, Collins, and DeLancey were easy outs. The replayed game was over. Twenty-two minutes had been snatched from the unreclaimable past. It was the sort of thing people dream about. If only we could do this or that over again. How differently we would do it. I wonder whether we would—whether we would walk Babe Herman or pitch to him again. And what I really wonder is whether it would make any difference WHAT we did if we had another chance. It didn't today.

Paul Gallico, New York *Daily News*

◦ *Thursday, August 2* ◦

[*On August 1, in Chicago, the Cardinals won, 4–0. Winning pitcher, Paul Dean; losing pitcher, Jim Weaver. Cardinals' standing: 56 wins, 40 losses, in third place.*]

"Paul's good pitching—she is because him pitch to the hitters," Coach Mike Gonzalez explained. "He pitch outside, inside, low, high, not try to blow by the pitch. Blow by the pitch is stupid when she has hitters like this Cubs. Paul smart feller. Mike tell Paul how to pitch, Frank tell Paul how to pitch—Paul remember. Smart boy, great pitcher. Paul win plenty game. He can do."

It is easy to agree with Coach Miguel Gonzalez. Paul does remember. He welcomes advice, and because he has taken advice and pitched as advised, he has won a dozen games while losing four, his twelfth victory coming yesterday, a four-hit shutout masterpiece.

J. Roy Stockton, *St. Louis Post-Dispatch*

Somewhere upon the walls of each major league ball park is a warning that gambling is not permitted within the premises. The signs were placed to reassure a public badly let down by certain revelations of 1920 and shocked anew in 1924. [*In 1920, Commissioner Landis banished from baseball eight members of the Chicago White Sox for allegedly conspiring to "throw" the 1919 World Series, the famous "Black Sox" scandal. In 1924, a Giant utility player, twenty-three-year-old Jimmy O'Connell, was similarly expelled for a remark, probably made in jest, to shortstop Heinie Sand of the Phillies to "go easy" on the Giants, who, along with Brooklyn and Pittsburgh, were in a three-team battle for the pennant.*]

Recently I've been trying to discover whether those conspicuously located "Thou shalt nots" mean what they say. I find that they do not. I believe there is as much betting done daily upon baseball as upon poker, that other great National Game.

Anybody can make a bet. You don't have to wander down the third base line or into the reserved seat section in back of first base (where the most eminent performers sit). [*In this instance, the reference is to Yankee Stadium.*] If you show some slight sign of prosperity or of having taken six easy lessons in how to play bridge, you're apt to be visited in your seat by some person who will inform you in hoarse tones above a whisper what the latest odds are. If you display interest, the voice that comes from the corner of a mouth will add that he's ready to take care of any investment ranging from $1 to $100.

The average bet is $5. You can bet on almost anything. Bets on the result of the game are most popular, but shutouts, inning scores, home runs, the outcome of a series, how many innings a pitcher will last, also are well supported.

The money is passed back and forth freely, with little or no attempt at concealment of the transaction. Of course you have to use cash.

A somewhat diligent effort is made to prevent betting at Yankee Stadium, but the stadium is so large that gentlemen who wish to gamble merely avoid congregating around third base, as they do at the Polo Grounds and Ebbets Field. By shifting to a different location each day they avoid the attentions of a lad called "The Greek," who operates as a "spotter" for stadium police.

Known gamblers are barred from all three local parks, but false whiskers and dark glasses have been effective disguises in the midst of a crowd.

Hugh Bradley, *New York Post*

○ *Friday, August 3* ○

[*On August 2, in Chicago, the Cardinals lost, 6–2. Winning pitcher, Bill Lee; losing pitcher, Bill Hallahan. Cardinals' standing: 56 wins, 41 losses, in third place.*]

HITLER BECOMES ABSOLUTE DICTATOR,
SEIZES FULL POWER BY SUDDEN COUP
—front-page headline, Pittsburgh *Post-Gazette*

The Cardinals are trying to compete for the pennant with less manpower than other teams have. The Cubs and Giants have 23 men, but the Cardinals struggle along with 21, and in bitterly contested games that is not enough.

Yesterday, for instance, Frisch, in his eagerness to overcome a Chicago lead, used up the men he had, and when the ninth inning rolled around Jess Haines, leading off, had to bat for himself. A single and two walks followed, and a pinch-hitter for Haines might have changed the complexion of the game. But Chick Fullis, Pat Crawford, Bill DeLancey, Francis Healey, and Burgess Whitehead had been used, and nobody was left.

J. Roy Stockton, *St. Louis Post-Dispatch*

○ *Saturday, August 4* ○

[*On August 3, in St. Louis, the Cardinals defeated Pittsburgh, 9–3. Winning pitcher, Dizzy Dean; losing pitcher, Waite Hoyt. Cardinals' standing: 57 wins, 41 losses, in third place.*]

Jerome Herman has his nineteenth victory safely tucked away. Paul has a dozen, and with 56 more games to play it seems certain that the dazzling Deans will more than make good on their spring prediction to register 40 or 45 victories. If the Dean boys continue at their pace, they will have 46 triumphs when the race is run, and considering their splendid record thus far, it should not be surprising if they exceeded that total.

Dizzy has his heart set on being the first pitcher to win 30 games in the National League since Grover Cleveland Alexander. [*Pitching for the Phillies, Alexander had three consecutive 30-game seasons, 1915–17. The most recent American Leaguer to win 30 games had been Lefty Grove, of the Athletics, with 31 wins and 4 losses in 1931.*] With this in mind, Dean will be eager to work frequently and may even go the hill every fourth day. He could thus appear in at least 14 more games. Dizzy would have to win 11 out of 14 to reach the 30 mark, but it is not unreasonable to visualize Jerome Herman achieving his objective.

Dizzy was back in his best form yesterday as he avenged his defeat of last Saturday. The Pirates made 11 hits, but 8 were in the last three innings, when the Great Man had a comfortable lead.

J. Roy Stockton, *St. Louis Post-Dispatch*

° *Sunday, August 5* °

[*On August 4, in St. Louis, the Cardinals defeated Pittsburgh, 6–4. Winning pitcher, Tex Carleton; losing pitcher, Larry French. Cardinals' standing: 58 wins, 41 losses, in third place.*]

Tex Carleton, fragile cowboy from Comanche, Tex., registered his twelfth victory yesterday, but the triumph required the ubiquitous Jerome Herman Dean, the people's choice for anything, to appear once more in the hero's role. Carleton had a four-run lead in the sixth inning, but the slender Texan began to weaken in the seventh, and in the eighth the St. Louis lead was reduced to one run, a situation fraught with perilous potentialities for the forces of Frankie Frisch.

With two men out and Tommy Thevenow on second carrying the tying run, Manager Frisch decided that a weary Carleton was not the man to protect a slim advantage.

Dizzy the Great had been warming up, and when the boys and girls in the left field stand saw the great hero they began to chant, "We want Dean. We want Dean." Well, Frisch gave them Dean, the elder Dean, the Jerome Herman (nee Jay Hanner) Dean who only the day before had pitched nine victorious innings. [*As noted earlier, Dean's middle name was not Hannah or Hanner, but Hanna.*]

The boys and girls were glad to see Jerome Herman, but not the Pirates. Earl Grace, the batter, didn't like him at all. Dizzy gave Grace a slow strike that cut the outside corner, and then a blow torch past the Pirate catcher for strike No. 2, also called. Then Dizzy moved Grace a little nearer the plate by putting the ball just outside the strike zone which set the stage for the next pitch, a crackling curve inside, at which Grace swung with tremendous force and profound futility.

That was the ball game for the boys and girls and a victory for Tex Carleton, who can thank Dizzy Dean for saving it for him.

J. Roy Stockton, *St. Louis Post-Dispatch*

° *Monday, August 6* °

[*On August 5, in St. Louis, the Cardinals lost a doubleheader to Pittsburgh, 6–4 and 7–2. Winning pitchers, Larry French and Waite Hoyt; losing pitchers, Paul Dean and Bill Hallahan. Cardinals' standing: 58 wins, 43 losses, in third place.*]

Frankie Frisch and his Cardinals, who have talked in terms of the margins separating them from second and first place, today nursed their wounds, smoothed bedraggled plumage, and furtively cast eyes in the other direction to note the danger of falling.

Perhaps it would be well to forget about first and second place margins and accept the Redbirds as outstanding candidates for third money. Perhaps smouldering embers of championship hope still linger in the stouter Cardinal hearts, but the Pirates' double victory yesterday convinced most of the 13,500 customers and undoubtedly many St. Louis players that no important checks would be mailed by Judge Landis in October to employees of Sam Breadon. The Giants increased their lead over the Cards to 6½ games, and they seem to be "going away."

One of the many misfortunes yesterday was the fifth defeat of the year for Paul Dean, who could have marched off with his thirteenth victory if the Cardinals had displayed more skill afield and had been more alert at critical times. Three Pirate runs were gifts.

The second game was a mess. Lloyd Waner singled, Paul Waner doubled, and Fred Lindstrom doubled in the first inning, and the Pirates went in front to stay. Bill Hallahan walked two men in the second, and Frisch replaced him with Bill Walker. Before Walker could end the inning, the Pirates had two more runs, and the Cards received much jeering and cruel razzing.

One positive note was sounded in the sixth inning of the first game when Leo Durocher hit a line drive home run into the left field seats, a smash that would have done credit to a Foxx or a Simmons. [*This may have been the longest and most powerful of the twenty-four home runs that Leo Durocher hit in his major league career.*]

J. Roy Stockton, *St. Louis Post-Dispatch*

Pasadena—Donkey baseball, which has gained a wide following in Southern California, today suffered its first fatality. William Beck, a Pasadena policeman, fell to the ground, fatally injured, in the midst of a game last night. He died at a hospital of a cerebral hemorrhage.

In donkey baseball the batter knocks the ball afield and then tries to reach first base on the donkey ahead of the throw from the fielders, also mounted on the desert beasts.

Beck was thrown from his mount three times but managed to make first base. The fourth time he was thrown his spine was fractured near his skull. [*Not surprisingly, donkey baseball flourished only in Southern California.*]

St. Louis *Globe-Democrat*

NATIONAL LEAGUE STANDINGS

	W	L	PCT	GB		W	L	PCT	GB
New York	66	38	.635	—	Pittsburgh	48	51	.485	15½
Chicago	62	40	.608	3	Brooklyn	43	57	.430	21
St. Louis	58	43	.574	6½	Philadelphia	43	60	.417	22½
Boston	52	52	.500	14	Cincinnati	35	66	.347	29½

° *Tuesday, August 7* °

[*On August 6, the Cardinals were not scheduled to play.*]

New York—The fans will miss Babe Ruth next year, but his brother ball tossers will miss him far more. When Babe passes, high salaries will pass with him. [*This would be Ruth's last season with the Yankees. In 1935, his career would end after he had appeared in twenty-eight games with the Boston Braves and compiled a batting average of .181.*]

A major league official said clubs already are planning drastic cuts for next season, and if the hired hands don't like it they will have to find more lucrative fields for their talents. And, he added, it is doubtful if truck driving pays better than ball playing.

"I'll admit," said the official, "that Ruth has always been underpaid even at $80,000, but I'm equally sure many others have been overpaid.

"Major league salaries are now almost at their peak. They average around $8,000, which is about twice what the average was when Ruth began packing ball parks. Some clubs must make drastic retrenchments or sink. Therefore you may hear some awful wails of anguish from the poor, downtrodden wage slave of the diamond who can hardly afford to devote a couple of hours an afternoon for six months for 10 or 12 thousand dollars, and who not only has his expenses paid for several weeks each spring but also for half the season when his team is on the road.

"But wails or no wails, when Ruth goes, those high salaries will go with him, and it will be a long time before they come back."

St. Louis Post-Dispatch

The gutta percha baseball with which they are playing in the National League this year has been, as expected, a boon to bat swingers. It's been a hitter's year.

Yet, strangely enough, only a few pitchers and none of the good ones are complaining. Now that they've had time to check the returns, they have adopted a most complacent attitude.

They've found out that the new ball, instead of handicapping pitchers, has actually permitted them to complete more impressive records. The good ones are winning more consistently than ever.

The latest records prove it. Earned-run statistics aren't so flattering as they were a year ago, but highly impressive won-and-lost records are being compiled. There are likely to be ten or a dozen 20-game winners. And for a decade almost, the 20-game pitcher has been a baseball rarity. Carl Hubbell's name headed a list of four last year, and the season before only two. [*And in 1931, there was not even one 20-game winner in the National League.*]

This year "Dizzy" Dean may even achieve 30, and 25 is within reach of Hal Schumacher and Hubbell of the Giants, Curt Davis of the Phillies, and Lon Warneke of the Cubs.

What is the explanation? Schumacher advances one, and it seems to cover the situation.

"There aren't nearly so many close games this year," he said. "Most of the games are easier to win. I've yielded more runs than last year, been hit harder, but the Giants have scored many more runs for me. Where last year I would win 2 to 0 and 3 to 1, I now win 8 to 4."

Good pitchers thus enjoy an advantage. They can hold the batters in some restraint, whereas the second stringers are mauled by the new ball. Most anybody could pitch a three-or-four run game in 1933. Now only the good ones can, and they win consistently.

Garry Schumacher, New York Evening Journal

∘ *Wednesday, August 8* ∘

[*On August 7, in Cincinnati, the Cardinals split a doubleheader, winning 2–0 and losing 9–2. Winning pitchers, Dizzy Dean and Allyn Stout; losing pitchers, Si Johnson and Bill Hallahan. Cardinals' standing: 59 wins, 44 losses, in third place.*]

The Reds were completely baffled by Dizzy Dean in the first game of the double-header yesterday. But they came back strong in the second game to trounce Wild Bill Hallahan.

Dizzy, pitching his twentieth victory of the year, was so tough that 6 hits and 4 bases on balls could not be converted into a single tally. The Reds were hypnotized by Dizzy.

Our boys showed quite plainly in the second game that the Deans are the Cardinals' mainstay. They slammed Wild Bill with utmost freedom, scoring almost at will. Manager Frisch figured his team had no chance and left Wild Bill for the entire game to take his beating. With Dizzy done for the day and Paul not ready for another attempt, there was nothing to do but let Wild Bill stand the gaff.

Jack Ryder, Cincinnati Enquirer

Cincinnati—Several thousand women were in the stands, and they took pleasure in handing Dizzy the raspberry in soprano, contralto, and alto, but the Great One merely grinned at his would-be tormentors.

St. Louis Globe-Democrat

[The author of the following piece was twenty-six years old and was with the Giants for part of the season, during which time he appeared in thirty-one games as an outfielder-pinch hitter.]

The parents are to blame.

I say that unhesitatingly as a Jewish boy who had to overcome months of parental objection before I received my father's and mother's permission to earn my living in professional baseball.

My people love the game. Just stand at the turnstiles some big Sunday or holiday, and you'll see a big percentage of the crowds will be young Hebrews eager and rabid in their rooting. Here, you would say, is a great breeding ground for future players, but Jewish mothers don't want their sons to be ball players. They dream of professional men and successful businessmen. To them baseball isn't much of a business.

"But mama," protests the boy who doesn't want to go into a dull office, "look at the money Babe Ruth makes."

"Just one in a million," sniffs his mother. [*Of the 184 men named to baseball's Hall of Fame by mid-1983, 2 have been Jewish, Hank Greenberg and Sandy Koufax.*]

Phil Weintraub, New York Post

∘ *Thursday, August 9* ∘

[On August 8, in Cincinnati, the Cardinals, in 12 innings, won, 10–4. Winning pitcher, Dizzy Dean; losing pitcher, Don Brennan. Cardinals' standing: 60 wins, 44 losses, in third place.]

If it isn't one Dean its the other, and yesterday it was both of them. It was Paul's turn, but Jerome Herman, hero of Tuesday's shutout triumph, finally emerged victorious.

Jesse Haines was on his way to his second victory of the year, but the old veteran couldn't quite negotiate nine innings. He held the Reds to four hits in seven innings, but he weakened, and with the Cardinals leading 4 to 2 it was evident that it was time to make a change.

Manager Frisch called on the reserves always summoned when a game must be saved. When there is a lead, with only a couple of innings to go, it is business for the Deans, and so Frank wig-wagged to the bullpen and Paul Dean walked to the hill.

The greatest pitchers, even the Deans, have their wild moments, and it was one of Paul's, the young man having had scant time to warm up. And so two more runs came over the plate to tie the score.

Paul worked one more inning and did a good job, and was then withdrawn for a pinch hitter. That is how Brother Jerome Herman broke into the game.

Jerome went to the hill in the tenth, and for three innings he mowed down the enemy. In the twelfth, Cincinnati's morale plainly bogged down, and six runners crossed the plate.

"This country may have needed a good five-cent cigar," said Dizzy as he stirred his coffee this morning. "But what the Cardinals need is more Deans." [*Thomas Riley Marshall, for eight years Woodrow Wilson's Vice-President, is remembered for nothing but his statement, "What this country needs is a good five-cent cigar."*]

J. Roy Stockton, *St. Louis Post-Dispatch*

In the twelfth inning yesterday with the score tied, Ripper Collins doubled. Chick Fullis then shot a single into right field. Collins raced toward the plate as outfielder Adam Comorosky came in fast and fired the ball in. Captain Leo Durocher, next Cardinal batter, rushed down the third base line and yelled, "Slide, slide, get down and slide. It's going to be close."

Collins, however, came in standing up and beat the play by a fraction of a second. Durocher fumed and fussed, and after he had batted he went into the dugout and tore into Collins for failing to slide.

Collins resented Durocher's outburst, adding fuel to the fire.

"You're trying to show me up!" he shouted.

"I'm just trying to win games for the Cardinals," Durocher shot back, "and I think you deserve a severe reprimand for not sliding."

Collins contended that he knew he could beat the throw and decided not to take any chances of getting injured. This brought a rebuff from Durocher and further argument from Collins. Finally Frankie Frisch said, "I give Durocher my wholehearted approval. Ripper, you should have slid, and you know it."

Ray J. Gillespie, St. Louis *Star-Times*

Followers of the Cardinals have been pleading for "another Dean," and their requests were granted today, the St. Louis National League office announcing the "purchase" of Elmer Dean, elder brother of Dizzy and Paul.

Elmer, for the past year and a half with the Houston club of the Texas

League, where Dizzy and Paul got their starts, is reported to be strong in a department which is not believed to be up to previous Cardinal standards, though official figures are not available.

Elmer will be thrown into the breach immediately on his scheduled arrival tomorrow, thus seeing his first major league action while the strong Chicago Cubs are furnishing the opposition.

Credit for scouting Elmer is being taken by Blake Harper, head of Sportsman's Park concessions.

Elmer won't be seen on the pitching mound or in the infield or outfield. His talent lies in another direction.

Elmer will sell peanuts!

Elmer was given an opportunity to prove himself "greater than Dizzy or Paul." He turned up with the Houston club in 1933, and Fred Ankenman, president of the club, held his breath as the youngster was given a trial. Much to the chagrin of his brothers, Elmer couldn't hit, field, run, throw, or slide. However, he seems to have all the color of a Dean, and Ankenman signed him up for the concession department. And today he is a champion peanut vendor, attracting much more attention than the players. He's a typical Dean.

St. Louis Post-Dispatch

Many claim that ladies' day at ball parks pays handsome dividends in the purchase of lemonade, hot dogs, and such.

Arch Ward, Chicago *Tribune*

Night baseball is rapidly gaining no favor. One or two major league magnates were willing to give it a trial a year ago, but arc-light baseball is losing ground in the minors, and major league magnates, with some relief, are about to call it a dead issue. The general conclusion is that baseball needs more than a touch of the sun to keep it in good health.

John Kieran, *The New York Times*

∘ *Friday, August 10* ∘

[*On August 9, the Cardinals were not scheduled to play.*]

Upholding the reputation and traditions of the Deans, the elder brother of Dizzy and Paul "jumped" the club today.

Just when baseball followers were wringing their hands with glee at the prospect of another Dean performing at Sportsman's Park, someone shouted, "Where's Elmer?"

Elmer, who was supposed to report for duty at the Cardinals-Cubs game today as a peanut vendor, upheld the legend surrounding his name. He just wasn't! He told his brothers last night that he had left Father Dean at home in Houston alone. This, the three Deans decided, was not the humane thing to do. So Elmer caught a bus for Houston to rejoin his dad.

St. Louis Star-Times

"What's wrong with the Cardinals?" Many fans have asked me this question during the past few days.

What's wrong with the Cardinals? Erratic pitching. Bill Hallahan's flop tells the story.

Hallahan is the team's mystery man. Something has happened to the little southpaw. He has 4 victories and 12 defeats and failed to finish in 14 of 21 games he has started. At this time in 1933 he had a 14–7 record.

When a ball club skids, stories circulate regarding dissension. Are members of Frisch's cast at odds with their manager? Frankie laughs at that. And the players reply, "Who me? I should say not."

I do not subscribe to the belief that the Cardinals have faded because of dissatisfaction among the players. It is just possible that the team's talent does not measure up to a championship standard and that no amount of managerial masterminding can compensate for this.

I cannot understand the attitude of Sam Breadon and Branch Rickey. They have made no serious attempt to strengthen the Redbirds. When the Cardinals started sliding in June and July, Breadon and Rickey should have called upon their farm clubs to assist the parent club, especially since the roster is 2 under the limit of 23 players.

It is not too late to engineer a few deals to perk up the Cardinals. The Redbirds are only 6½ games behind the Giants.

Sid Keener, St. Louis Star-Times

◦ *Saturday, August 11* ◦

[*On August 10, in St. Louis, the Cardinals defeated the Cubs, 17–3. Winning pitcher, Tex Carleton; losing pitcher, Lon Warneke. Cardinals' standing: 61 wins, 44 losses, in third place.*]

St. Louis—The Cubs, who came to this tropical city snorting pennant threats, were whirled back to their hotel more severely lacerated than they have been in the memory of observers.

The Cards made 21 hits, including Rip Collins' twenty-fourth homer. They doubtless could have made many more, but a thermometer on the field registered 120 degrees, and Manager Frisch, who retired after making four straight hits, warned his lads not to run around any more than they had to.

Edward Burns, Chicago Tribune

∘ *Sunday, August 12* ∘

[*On August 11, in St. Louis, the Cardinals beat the Cubs, 6–4. Winning pitcher, Bill Walker; losing pitcher, Bill Lee. Cardinals' standing: 62 wins, 44 losses, in third place.*]

Frankie Frisch's Cardinals showed the qualities of a championship contender yesterday. They saw the Cubs of Charley Grimm take a three-run lead in the first two innings and then courageously went to work, overcame the advantage, and scored their second straight victory over the sluggers from Chicago.

Bill Walker pitched the victory and was brilliant after a wobbly start. However, it was a team triumph, the Cardinals performing with a brilliance that squelched Chicago rallies. Leo Durocher was a demon at shortstop, showing an uncanny knowledge of where hitters were going to drive the ball.

J. Roy Stockton, St. Louis Post-Dispatch

∘ *Monday, August 13* ∘

[*On August 12, in St. Louis, the Cardinals lost a doubleheader to Chicago, 7–2 and 6–4. Winning pitchers, Jim Weaver and Pat Malone; losing pitchers, Paul Dean and Dizzy Dean. Cardinals' standing: 62 wins, 46 losses, in third place.*]

What's the matter with the Cardinals? You can get the answer from 36,073 cash customers who crowded Sportsman's Park yesterday and saw the Cubs win a double-header. Paul Dean suffered his sixth reverse of the season in the first game, and Dizzy took his fifth loss in the second contest, but it was not bad pitching that caused the downfall.

Paul was not as effective as in previous games, but it was a break in the defense that caused his retirement after five innings, and Dizzy easily could have journeyed to a triumph but for the same defensive flaw—failure to throw out a base stealer.

In Paul's game the runner was given a stolen base and the runs scored against him recorded as earned. But in Dizzy's contest four unearned tallies drifted over the plate after Durocher dropped a throw on an attempted steal, and the runs made the difference between Jerome Herman's twenty-second victory and his fifth defeat.

The Cardinal fielding was ragged, erratic, and nonchalant, and so the Cubs are 3½ games ahead of St. Louis, and the Giants' first place margin over Frisch's team is 7½ games.

J. Roy Stockton, *St. Louis Post-Dispatch*

No such enthusiasm has been displayed anywhere this year as was turned on by those folks at St. Louis over every move Dizzy Dean made yesterday. Every ball he pitched brought a gale of response from those areas of white-shirted humanity packed like popcorn on every inch of the grandstand. The fellow has magnetism, leadership, dramatic instinct.

Ralph Cannon, Chicago *Daily News*

Houston—Take it from Elmer Dean, the big show "Ain't what it's cracked up to be."

Elmer was back at Buffalo Stadium last night doing a land office business after his flying trip to St. Louis. Elmer said he didn't "like the looks of St. Louis."

St. Louis *Globe-Democrat*

NATIONAL LEAGUE STANDINGS

	W	L	PCT	GB		W	L	PCT	GB
New York	70	39	.642	—	Pittsburgh	52	54	.491	16½
Chicago	66	43	.606	4	Brooklyn	45	60	.429	23
St. Louis	62	46	.574	7½	Philadelphia	44	63	.411	25
Boston	54	54	.500	15½	Cincinnati	37	71	.343	32½

∘ *Tuesday, August 14* ∘

[*On August 13, the Cardinals played an exhibition game in Detroit against the Tigers. The first entry below was published in the morning; the second entry appeared in the afternoon.*]

What disciplinary action, if any, is taken against the Dean brothers for not making the trip to Detroit with the Cardinals for an exhibition game yesterday will be decided today. Sam Breadon, club president, stated that he understood the Deans were slated to accompany the team, "but whether Manager Frisch excused them from the trip is something I do not know. If they were not excused, it will be up to Frank to handle the case as he sees fit."

Dizzy Dean declares that he and Paul just decided not to make the trip. Asked if he had been given permission to remain in St. Louis, he replied, "We did not have our coats or bags with us at Sportsman's Park, so we figured we'd stay in St. Louis. The team left right after Sunday's second game and we came back to our hotel. I did not see any reason to make the trip. Besides, I hurt my arm Sunday. That's why I lost my fast ball.

"I pulled something loose in my right elbow in the fourth inning. I didn't have my stuff after that." Dizzy said he may not be able to pitch for several weeks because of the sore arm.

"I'm not going to pitch again until the arm is healed," he said. "Other pitchers don't work if they have sore arms, and I'm not going to, either. If I went out there, I might ruin my career."

It would be a strange birthday gift were Paul fined or suspended, for this happens to be Paul's twenty-first birthday.

"I hurried out of the clubhouse Saturday after the game," Paul said, "without reading the notice about the trip to Detroit. Then I went to the park Sunday morning without a coat or grip. I returned to the hotel for them after the double-header and waited around, thinking Jerome would pick me up.

"He did not show up, and when I called the station they told me the train had left. I'm not passing the buck to Jerome, 'cause I'm not sorry I stayed in St. Louis. I was really tired and needed a rest. I pitched part of the first game Sunday and warmed up in the bull pen in the second. My ankle is still bothering me.

"The ankle has not been right since I sprained it a month ago. When we went from Philadelphia to New York, and I was hobbling on crutches, I had to get along the best I could when I got off the train. The hotel was several blocks from the station, and I had to hobble all the way."

If Frisch did not sanction the Dean brothers' stay in St. Louis, it appears they may face a fine or suspension.

Martin J. Haley, St. Louis *Globe-Democrat*

Dizzy Dean and his brother Paul were disciplined by Manager Frankie Frisch this morning, following a conference with President Sam Breadon, for failing to make the trip to Detroit. Dizzy was fined $100, and Paul was fined $50.

"There must be discipline on a ball club," Frisch said. "I played 18 innings on Sunday, and so did the other regulars. Paul pitched 5 innings and Dizzy 7⅔. So they didn't do as much work as lots of others.

"When the Yankees schedule an exhibition game, Babe Ruth is always present. So I see no reason why the Dean brothers should not be on hand when the Cardinals play an exhibition.

"That was a great show at Detroit, and it should have meant a lot to the players. The park was crowded with boys and girls, future customers, and the ball player owes something to a crowd like that.

"There's no hardship in a train ride. People pay money to take train rides. Baseball is our business, and the mere fact that we worked Sunday is no excuse for running out on a Monday game just because it's an exhibition."

J. Roy Stockton, *St. Louis Post-Dispatch*

° *Wednesday, August 15* °

[*On August 14, in St. Louis, the Cardinals won against Philadelphia, 5–1. Winning pitcher, Jesse Haines; losing pitcher, Euel Moore. Cardinals' standing: 63 wins, 46 losses, in third place.*]

The latest rebellion of the Dean boys may turn out to be the best thing that could have happened to Frankie Frisch and his Cardinals.

Out of the mess a new team spirit has been born. The team morale and allegiance to Manager Frisch reached a new high yesterday.

"There are only 19 of us left, including Frank," the boys in the dugout announced, "but the 18 of us will fight with everything we have to show Frank we're for him."

The boys weren't talking through their hats. They took the field with grim determination, and they took the Phillies. The Cards went after seemingly impossible plays without a suspicion that they could not be executed.

Dazzy Vance and Jess Haines pitched with speed and cunning that belied their years.

J. Roy Stockton, *St. Louis Post-Dispatch*

Dizzy and Paul Dean have been suspended without pay by Manager Frisch, but they are free to rejoin the team whenever they see fit, Frisch said yesterday shortly after the suspensions were dished out.

The Deans really suspended themselves. Frisch had fined Dizzy $100 and Paul $50 for failing to accompany the team to Detroit. The Deans reported to the Cardinal clubhouse yesterday and donned uniforms.

Dizzy asked Frisch, "Do those fines stick, Frank?"

"Sure they stick," Frisch replied.

"Well, then, we'll take off our uniforms," Diz retorted.

"Yeh, we'll take 'em off," Paul echoed.

"All right, then, you're suspended," Frisch declared.

"We've got to have discipline," Frisch stated. "One set of rules applies to all the players. The Deans had no excuse for not going to Detroit, so I fined them, and after they wouldn't play I suspended them. They can put on their uniforms any time they care to, but the fines stick."

Sam Breadon explained that Dizzy was fined more than Paul because he is older and receives more salary. Besides, this is Paul's first offense, and Breadon feels that he was influenced by Dizzy.

Shortly after yesterday's game started, the brothers came up to the press box, Diz in a white shirt and bluish gray trousers, Paul in blue shirt and brown trousers. Dizzy's wife joined them later.

"It sure looks different from up here," exclaimed Dizzy.

"Yes, sir," added Paul.

About the fourth inning Mrs. Dean got up from her chair and said, "Come on, Diz, let's go."

"Where are you going?" they were asked.

"To Florida," said Diz.

Martin J. Haley, St. Louis *Globe-Democrat*

Fined, suspended, paid off in full, and removed from the Cardinal pay roll, the Dean brothers announced they have quit the club. However, they have altered their plans for the immediate future. Instead of leaving St. Louis on a long tour of the south, as they had planned this morning, they will remain here until the Giants call at Sportsman's Park, August 23, for a three-game series.

"Then we figure," Dizzy explained, "the Cards will ask us to rejoin the club. Now, while they're playing the Phillies, they don't have to worry about us. Anybody can beat the Phils. But it'll be different when the Giants come to town. It takes Diz and Paul to stop the Giants, and the Cards know it!"

This announcement was made after the pair had visited the office of Treasurer William O. De Witt to receive their pay checks. Prior to this, Dizzy had presented an ultimatum to the management, demanding that their fines be remitted and also that they be returned at once to good standing without being "docked" for being out of uniform yesterday.

Manager Frankie Frisch replied negatively and instructed De Witt to deduct from their checks the amounts he had prescribed. Thus Dizzy, fined $100, lost an additional $100, representing his approximate salary of $50 a day, while Paul, fined $50, lost an additional $40, representing his salary of $20 a day. De Witt explained that the pay checks, issued on the fifteenth of each month, include that day's salary.

President Sam Breadon, while announcing that the Cardinals have adopted a stand-pat policy on the matter, stated that Dizzy was charged $36 for two uniforms he destroyed during a fit of rage in the clubhouse yesterday.

Frisch was as stern today as he was yesterday.

"Those fines will stick," he said. "I appreciate the fine pitching the Deans have done, but that doesn't give them the privilege to do as they please. Even if it costs me my job, I'm standing pat. I won't give in because that would be unfair to others who have been fined and have taken it like men."

Frisch then said that 40,000 youngsters had attended Monday's game in Detroit in hopes of seeing an advertised feature—the Dean boys coaching on opposite coaching lines. They were disappointed, he said, when the colorful hurlers failed to appear.

"I'm certainly pleased with the attitude of the others," Frisch went on. "Yesterday my players gathered around me and gave me a vote of confidence and said they'd give the best they have."

Frisch and Breadon agreed upon fining the Dean boys at a conference yesterday. Then the manager went to the dressing room, where the Cardinals were donning their uniforms.

The subject of the "Deanless" exhibition game came up, and Dizzy took the stump, announcing that "he had purposely missed the train to Detroit, was glad he didn't go, and what of it?"

When told that he and Paul had been fined, Dizzy pranced up and down, announcing, "They'll take those fines off, or the Cardinals will finish the season without us."

The bell rang for batting practice, and most of the players left for the field. Dizzy, lounging on a rubbing table in the trainer's quarters, refused to move. Paul sat nearby, half dressed. Manager Frisch returned to the clubhouse and said, "Come on, boys, this is a big league ball club. Let's go."

"We're not a-goin' out on the field!" Dizzy replied defiantly.

"You're not?" Frisch shouted. "Well then, take off those uniforms. You're both suspended!"

Dizzy leaped to his feet, shouting, cursing, and announcing to one and all that he would never pitch again for the Cardinals.

"This will be the end of my Cardinal uniforms!" he yelled as he tore his white "home" shirt and his traveling gray paraphernalia to shreds and scattered them over the floor. [*For decades, every major league player was issued two uniforms, a white one for home games and a gray one for playing on the road.*]

Cooler heads tried to intervene. Tex Carleton and Ripper Collins warned the boys that they would be sorry later for whatever hasty action they might take. But Dizzy and Paul only stamped up and down the clubhouse, kicking benches, throwing cushions, and upsetting the place in general.

Up the steps they marched to the press-box from where they viewed the game, aided by a pair of binoculars belonging to one of the telegraphers.

"You'll be back in uniform by Thursday," a writer told Dizzy.

"Here's ten bucks that says I won't," the pitcher shot back as he whipped out two five-dollar bills.

Ray J. Gillespie, St. Louis *Star-Times*

∘ *Thursday, August 16* ∘

[*On August 15, in St. Louis, the Cardinals' scheduled game with Philadelphia was postponed because of rain.*]

A peace conference with "striking" Dean brothers failed to accomplish its purpose, and, after an hour of wrangling between the two players and executives of the Cardinals, Manager Frankie Frisch announced that the two pitchers had been "suspended indefinitely" and would not be back with the Redbirds until they met his terms.

"It's all up to them now," said Frisch. "Either they accept the fines or we don't want them on the club."

When Dizzy and Paul entered Mr. Breadon's office, Dizzy addressed the officials as follows:

"You want to win the pennant, don't you?"

"Of course we do," Frisch said.

"Well, take off those fines, and restore the wages for the days we missed, and Paul and I will be back out there to help you," Dizzy said.

"Those fines stay," Frisch shot back. "Take it or leave it. Go to Florida if you want and stay there. I don't want you back unless you meet my terms."

When the Deans announced they would leave for Florida immediately, Vice President Rickey offered to pay their transportation.

The conference ended, and the Deans hurried away without accepting Rickey's offer.

Dizzy, in an optimistic mood, hoped that President Breadon and the Cardinals would refund his $36 for the two uniforms he destroyed.

"I think I can get them patched up," he volunteered.

Meanwhile offers from avaricious promoters poured in on the Dean boys. One promoter wanted either brother to pitch for him Sunday, for which the player would receive $500.

Ray J. Gillespie, St. Louis *Star-Times*

About all the Deans can expect from their uprising is the loss of salary for all idle days, the price of two uniforms, fines for their rebellion against authority, and, worst of all, loss of respect of their teammates.

The Deans' most recent ebullition has crystallized the club's determination to settle once and for all whether the Deans or the owners are running the club.

Ball players have been referred to as chattels. They are, in a sense, tied to the soil, like serfs of old. They cannot change their club affiliations of their own volition or seek employment from the highest bidder.

The contract that binds them has been, on one occasion at least, pronounced not binding. Players, however, know that if they could not be bound to one club baseball could not continue. They therefore consent to be bound. They never take their contracts to court.

Players understand that absolute control by club owners is what makes possible the amazing salaries drawn by some players.

The Deans don't seem to realize that failing to live up to their contract hurts not only themselves and the owners, but their 19 teammates as well. The Cardinals are in third place. Should the Deans remain obstinate, the team will hardly remain there. It might even slip out of the first division. That would mean the loss to 19 members of the Cardinal club of about $15,000, representing a third place share of the World Series money. With the Deans working, they might still capture second place, which last year paid $21,000.

It must take a mighty ego to produce a frame of mind where, for no particular reason, a man can cause 20 others to suffer such a loss.

John E. Wray, *St. Louis Post-Dispatch*

St. Louis (UP)—Mrs. Jerome Herman "Dizzy" Dean predicted both Diz and Paul would be back with the Cardinals "in a day or two."

"Diz will never admit it," Mrs. Dean told the United Press, "but the reason he didn't go to Detroit was that he was heart-broken over that double-header Sunday.

"Diz was so disgusted he simply didn't want to see anyone. He wouldn't even have a soda with me after the game.

"Diz hates to lose. It hurts his pride. If he had won, he could have gone to Detroit a hero, but losing, he felt he would be a heel.

"It was expensive, $100 for a day's vacation, but I feel that if he wanted the vacation he should accept the fine and go back to the club. He wasn't trying to flaunt any rules; he was just heart-broken."

Mrs. Dean was asked if Dizzy didn't appreciate he couldn't win every game.

"That's just it," she replied. "He believes he should win every game, and I hope he never gets to the point where he doesn't feel that way, for then he would be letting down."

Perhaps this was her most convincing reason why Dizzy and Paul will be back on the job soon: "The Dean family needs the money."

Chicago *Daily News*

Manager Frankie Frisch announced that John Leonard Martin would be given a chance as a pitcher. Martin always has had ambitions to be a hurler, and with an emergency created by the suspension of the Deans, he may appear soon as a starting pitcher.

"Martin has been working on his curve," Frisch said, "and he always had a good fast ball. He has pitched in batting practice and has shown fairly good control. Injuries have kept him out of action, and we won't be breaking up the team to try him as a pitcher. Pepper thinks he can stop hitters with his high fast ball, and I'll give him the chance." [*Martin had never pitched in a major league game, but in 1924–26 he had appeared as a pitcher in 24 minor league games, with a record of 4 wins and 4 losses and 43 strikeouts.*]

J. Roy Stockton, St. Louis Post-Dispatch

While it has been a custom for fans to retain balls hit into the stands, apparently under the impression that the price of admission entitles them to possess all spheres on which they can get their hands, we do not believe such action is fair.

Baseballs cost money. The outlay for unreturned balls is a heavy item. Spectators should be honest enough to return them even though it seems to be an old American custom not to do so. [*Interestingly, in no American sport but baseball do the fans insist on the right to retain balls that happen to fall into their hands.*]

The Sporting News

° *Friday, August 17* °

[*On August 16, the Cardinals won a doubleheader from Philadelphia, 4–3 (in 11 innings) and 7–2. Winning pitchers, Jesse Haines and Bill Walker; losing pitchers, Syl Johnson and Phil Collins. Cardinals' standing: 65 wins, 46 losses, in third place.*]

Tex Carleton and Bill Walker held the Quakers in tow, and the Deanless Cardinals won both ends of a twin bill. The Dean boys were spectators.

The first game Ol' Jesse Haines gained the decision, going to the mound to finish up when Carleton was taken out for a pinch-hitter in the ninth. The Redbirds won this one in the eleventh on a pass to Ripper Collins, a sacrifice by Haines, and Durocher's long double off the right field wall.

Philadelphia Inquirer

Kenesaw M. Landis, baseball commissioner, has called a hearing in the Dizzy vs. Cardinals case to be held in St. Louis Monday morning. This was the latest step in the controversy that has aroused unusual interest throughout the baseball world.

Landis announced the showdown conference in a long-distance call to President Sam Breadon of the Cardinals following a personal visit to his office in Chicago by none other than Dizzy.

All parties involved have been ordered by Landis to attend the conference. President Breadon, Vice President Branch Rickey, Manager Frisch, and Dizzy will present their evidence in the muddled affair.

Dizzy sprang a surprise when he arrived in Chicago this morning and visited the commissioner's offices in the Straus Building.

"Sit down, young man," said Landis.

Diz accepted the invitation and unfolded his story—that he was "being persecuted by the Cardinals' management."

"Well," said Landis, "we'll straighten out this whole matter. You go back to St. Louis and be at the Park Plaza Hotel at 10 o'clock on Monday morning. And when I say '10 o'clock' I don't mean 'one minute after 10.'"

President Breadon said he was more than pleased to have a showdown conference.

"We feel that we have been extremely lenient with the Dean boys," said Breadon. "We did not bring on the controversy. They are responsible for their suspensions. The Cardinal management will not tolerate flagrant disobedience of club regulations."

A player's right to appeal to Commissioner Landis is covered in Rule 13 of Major League Rules: "A player suspended by a club has the right to appeal to Commissioner Landis, who has authority to order his reinstatement and afford him adequate redress if he holds that the punishment is excessive or not merited."

Ray J. Gillespie, St. Louis *Star-Times*

Dizzy Dean sent this letter to the *Post-Dispatch:*
As a favor to me I want you to print this letter. I want to present my side of this argument. I realize I made a mistake in not making the trip to Detroit. Had I known what the game was all about I would not have disappointed those kids for anything in the world. But I was so disgusted about losing that double-header Sunday that I didn't care if I never saw another game or not.

You know how bad I hate to lose. And when Paul and I both lost before that crowd of loyal St. Louis people I was downhearted. It's bad enough to lose when I am away from home, but to go out there and pitch my heart out in that hot sun and still lose—well, you can imagine just how I felt.

Then, Tuesday, when the team came home I went out to the park expecting a fine. I realized I had made a mistake. When I went into the clubhouse I expected Frank to call me over and tell me I was fined. But it seems as though everybody on the team had been told about it before I was. So when they all, from the bat boy up, got through telling me I was fined I wasn't in any frame of mind to be jumped on. So I blew up. One word brought on another, and when the storm was over I had torn up my uniforms.

The ball club announced I was suspended until I would accept the fines and that I could return when I was ready to. I wanted to return today, and I agreed to take the fines, suspension for two days without pay, and to pay for the uniforms. But after I agreed to do that, the "powers that be" informed me that I would get an extra ten days' suspension, because Paul does not care to return. Paul is 21 years old and a man with his own mind.

I have apologized and admitted I was wrong, and I want to go back to work now, not ten days from now. I'll leave it up to you and all the sports fans, what else can I do?

Sincerely,
"DIZZY" DEAN

St. Louis Post-Dispatch

Paul Dean, junior member of the firm of Dean & Dean, was reinstated by the Cardinals following a conference with club officials this afternoon. The confab was attended by President Sam Breadon, Vice President Branch Rickey, Manager Frankie Frisch, and young Paul.

Young Dean was locked in the private chambers of Breadon for half an hour, and then Breadon issued this statement:

"Paul Dean has been reinstated by the Cardinals. He admitted that he had erred in failing to make the trip to Detroit and in refusing to return to the team. The boy apologized to Manager Frisch and begged to be given another chance.

"He accepted the terms of the club, agreeing to pay the $50 fine imposed on him and forfeited three days' salary. His financial loss will amount to approximately $120."

The following statement was issued by Dean:

Mr. Sam Breadon
President, St. Louis Cardinals

Dear Sir: I regret very much the unfortunate misunderstanding between myself and Manager Frisch. I had said to several people that I knew I was in the wrong when I refused to go to Detroit and again when I refused to go on the field when asked to do so by Manager Frisch.

I do not want you to think I am ungrateful for past favors, and I do not want Manager Frisch to think that I am unmindful of his consideration this spring when, after looking bad in my first three or four games, he continued to use me regularly. He has always treated me kindly, and I think I understand his position in this difficulty, and I am ready to accept the fine and loss of salary during the time of my suspension.

I would like to be reinstated immediately, first, because I want to make up as much as I can for my mistake, and I also want to make more money next year. But above all I want to help keep the Cardinals in the pennant race. I certainly do not want the players to think that I am throwing them down, and I do not want the St. Louis public to think that I am throwing them down.

I assure you that I will apologize to the team for my action which occasioned all this trouble.

Yours very truly,
PAUL DEAN

St. Louis *Star-Times*

Jerome H. "Dizzy" Dean is not only cutting out a dizzy pace for National League pitchers, but also leading the baseball goofy league in all departments. The goofy league of the national pastime is taking plenty of leading this year, too. But "Diz" is thoroughly capable of handling the job.

This has been the dizziest baseball season in twenty years. There have been mysterious disappearances, strikes, fist fights, walkouts, lockouts, near riots, riots, high record crowds, low record crowds; in short, just about everything you can think of. And through it all the Dizzy Dean Freres have held their place at the top.

Kid brother Paul has been reduced to the role of stooge. Where "Diz" goes "Daz" goes, whether he wants to or not. He is in a fair way of becoming the greatest yes-man on record.

The current strike, however, won't last long. As Mrs. "Dizzy" Dean so pertinently pointed out, the Deans must eat. Even so, it will be hard to wrest the goofy league pennant from Jerome. He's tops even among the squirrels.

Bill Corum, New York *Evening Journal*

Add baseball slang: "Two o'clock hitter"—one who hits line drives during batting practice but pops up during the game. [*At this time, the usual starting time for games was three o'clock.*]

Al Abrams, Pittsburgh *Post-Gazette*

° *Saturday, August 18* °

[*On August 17, in St. Louis, the Cardinals defeated Philadelphia, 12–2. Winning pitcher, Paul Dean; losing pitcher, Euel Moore. Cardinals' standing: 66 wins, 46 losses, in third place.*]

Paul Dean, who made a separate peace with Manager Frisch and Sam Breadon, quickly profited by his return to good standing. When Jim Mooney, the starting pitcher, was knocked out, and Dazzy Vance, his relief man, was withdrawn in the second inning for a pinch hitter, Paul went to the hill with a 4–2 lead and was credited with his thirteenth victory when the Cardinals overwhelmed the enemy.

Paul pitched effectively, and the Cardinals collected 17 safeties, including Jimmy Collins' twenty-eighth home run of the season. The Ripper had a perfect day at the plate, with the homer, two doubles, and a single.

Leo Durocher, who has become "Captain Slug," also had a large afternoon. Leo made three hits in four times at bat and drew an intentional pass.

The Cardinals accepted Paul Dean's return without fanfare or wisecracks. They were polite and sympathetic. In a late inning when Paul's hands were wet with sweat and he was having difficulty gripping the ball, Tex Carleton ran out with a towel to wait on the juvenile member of the staff.

When it was evident that Vance would be withdrawn for a pinch hitter, Carleton, who had worked nine innings the day before, went into action in the bull pen. That has been the spirit of the Cardinals during the Dean controversy. The boys have felt that Manager Frisch was put in an embarrassing position and they have volunteered to work in and out of turn— every day if necessary.

When Paul Dean appeared, and Carleton's chance to pick up a fourteenth victory was taken away, Tex accepted the situation gracefully.

J. Roy Stockton, *St. Louis Post-Dispatch*

"I am glad to see Paul back with us," Sam Breadon commented today. "This is the first time we have had trouble with him. Dizzy, however, has been a source of worry on each of the teams he has been with since joining our organization."

Asked if the Cardinals might sell or trade Dizzy, Breadon declared, "We would not sell him for $500,000. How could we trade him? We could not get his value in return. No, he stays with the Cardinals, and I believe he'll be a good boy after this latest affair."

St. Louis *Globe-Democrat*

○ *Sunday, August 19* ○

[*On August 18, in St. Louis, the Cardinals defeated Boston, 15–0. Winning pitcher, Bill Hallahan; losing pitcher, Ben Cantwell. Cardinals' standing: 67 wins, 46 losses, in third place.*]

William Anthony Hallahan, whose failure on the hurling mound has been one of the mysteries of 1934, returned to the pitching technique of his great years, and with the Cardinals lambasting three Boston pitchers for 20 safeties, Wild Bill pitched the Redbirds to their fifth straight victory.

Hallahan was so pleased at finding his old form he did not relax with a commanding lead. He pitched in the ninth as in the first inning, and it probably was his happiest afternoon of the season.

Several Cardinals distinguished themselves as batsmen. Captain "Slug" Durocher was the outstanding walloper, with a home run and two doubles, but Manager Frisch had a perfect day at bat with three singles and a sacrifice. Also, Joe Medwick had two doubles and a single, Chick Fullis four singles in four times at bat, and Jack Rothrock drove in four runs with a home run and a double.

J. Roy Stockton, *St. Louis Post-Dispatch*

Dizzy Dean, back from Chicago, where he asked Commissioner Landis to review his case, was turned down when he asked Sam Breadon to place him on the pay roll.

Breadon informed Dizzy that the Cardinals desired to await the Landis meeting.

"You've placed this in Landis' hands," Breadon told him, "and now we'll let it go until Monday."

St. Louis *Globe-Democrat*

° *Monday, August 20* °

[*On August 19, in St. Louis, the Cardinals split a doubleheader with Boston, losing the first game, 10–9, and winning the second, 3–1. Winning pitchers, Huck Betts and Bill Walker; losing pitchers, Paul Dean and Flint Rhem. Cardinals' standing: 68 wins, 47 losses, in third place.*]

Leo Durocher lost a pop fly in the first inning of the first game yesterday, and that gave the Braves three runs. Carleton lost control in the second frame and was sent to the showers, and before the game was finally lost, Haines, Mooney, Pepper Martin, Vance, and Paul Dean served on the hill.

After four innings the Braves led, 7 to 0, but the Cardinals fought back and finally tied the score, 9 to 9, in the eighth. Paul Dean went to the hill then, and it looked like a great chance for him to pick up an easy victory. But he walked Baxter Jordan, the first man he faced. Berger doubled, Jordan scored, and Paul accepted his seventh defeat.

Joe Medwick did some thoughtless base-running. He opened the fourth inning with a single and reached third on Collins' double. Spud Davis walked, filling the bases. Then Fullis popped to second baseman Les Mallon, not far behind the infield, and Medwick tried to score. It might have been good baseball if the score had been tied. But the Braves were leading, 7 to 0. One run could do no good. It wasn't daring base-running. It was reckless and stupid. Medwick was out, and he could have scored a moment later on Durocher's long fly.

John Leonard Martin made his debut as a pitcher under handicaps. He was suffering from a wrenched muscle in his side, and Manager Frisch had decided to postpone Pepper's pitching inaugural. But an emergency developed when Mooney, the third pitcher, couldn't get anybody out, so with the bases filled Martin went to the hill in the fourth inning.

Johnny made it a great show while it lasted. He threw "high hard ones," baffling knuckle balls, a side-armed slow curve, and he displayed unexpectedly good control. He didn't walk a man. The first man he faced flied to Medwick, and the next hit into a double play.

Martin then went to the bull pen to warm up some more and almost tore Francis Healey's glove from his hand. In the fifth Pepper retired the side without the ball being hit out of the infield, but he injured his right elbow. This was too much even for the cast-iron Martin, and he was relieved by Vance. [*Only once again as a major leaguer, in 1936, would Pepper Martin appear in a game as a pitcher.*]

In the second game, the Cardinals needed only one pitcher, Bill Walker, who scattered seven singles. The game was won in the very first inning with home runs by Medwick and Collins.

J. Roy Stockton, *St. Louis Post-Dispatch*

Baseball's highest court, Commissioner K. M. Landis, ruled at a special hearing at the Park Plaza Hotel today that the Cardinal baseball club acted within its rights in fining and suspending Dizzy Dean. Landis stated that the fine and suspension were not excessive.

The meeting lasted four hours and five minutes and ended when Landis passed out his ruling. Immediately, Vice President Rickey suggested that the ten days' suspension be cut to eight, whereupon Sam Breadon said, "I don't want to be hard on Dizzy. I'll cut it to seven and make Dean eligible to return to uniform tomorrow if this meets with Manager Frisch's approval."

Frisch nodded his consent, but Dizzy, apparently heart-broken, told a *Star-Times* representative, "I got a raw deal. It was unfair, but what can I do? I'm whipped."

"Will you go through with your promise to put on a uniform tomorrow?" Dizzy was asked.

"Positively," he replied. "I can't afford to lose any more money. It costs me $50 a day to be idle, and so far I've lost $486—a $100 fine, $36 for two uniforms I destroyed, and $350 for seven days under suspension."

Members of the press were not admitted to the hearing, but an open transom proved a handy outlet to the words exchanged.

At times the hearing became heated. On one occasion Breadon shouted, "Don't you call me a liar, Dizzy!"

To which Dizzy replied, "Well, then, don't you call me a liar."

Rickey presented the Cardinals' case and examined Pitcher Jesse Haines, Shortstop Leo Durocher, Coaches Clyde Wares and Mike Gonzalez, Team Trainer Dr. Harrison J. Weaver, and Secretary Clarence F. Lloyd. He attempted to convince Landis that Dean could contract an alleged sore arm on the least provocation.

During the club's second trip to New York this summer, Dean was accused of telling several players that he would be unable to pitch because of a sore arm. Yet evidence was brought in to show that Dean with his lame arm whipped the Giants.

"Tell us what you know about Dean's clubhouse actions," Rickey asked Durocher.

"He came in storming," replied Durocher. "I told him he put himself in a fine mess by not going to Detroit, and I offered to bet him $20 that he would be fined."

Frisch was asked by the commissioner to tell what he knew about Dean's peace-offering and his plea for reinstatement.

"I was called to the club's offices last Thursday, Judge, shortly before we were to play the Phillies in a double-header," Frisch said. "Mr. Breadon was with Dizzy and Paul. Diz said he would be willing to return if the club would pay him his salary for the two days he was not on the field. I told Diz I was too busy to take up his case at the moment because I had to rush out on the field. I told him to come back the next morning and I'd talk it over with him. I told him that as far as I was concerned he was suspended for ten days."

"Yes, but Mr. Breadon said I'd be reinstated if I'd agree to bring Paul back with me," said Dizzy. "But Paul said he didn't want to go back, and I was forced to remain suspended."

Dizzy appeared to be gaining an advantage with his testimony until brother Paul informed Landis of his failure to go to Detroit.

"It happened like this," said Paul. "When I got ready to leave the club-house after the Sunday double-header, I told the clubhouse boy to take my auto over to the garage. I then went to my hotel and waited for Dizzy, expecting him to pick me up and we'd go to Detroit.

"Dizzy didn't appear, so I forgot about going to Detroit. That's how I missed out, Judge."

Dizzy was then invited to explain why he failed to make the Detroit trip.

"I ain't got no excuse, Judge," said Dizzy. "I was feeling sore when we lost those two games to the Cubs. I realized that if we had beaten them, we'd have been right up in the race. We lost, and I didn't want to look at another ball game. I was disgusted. That's the truth. I decided I wouldn't go to Detroit. I can't defend myself, Judge. I was wrong, and I know it."

"You two boys have been almost inseparable," said Landis. "I can hardly believe that you, Paul, didn't know that Dizzy wasn't going to Detroit, you Dizzy—that you didn't know that Paul wasn't going.

"Ball players owe their public an obligation. You two boys owed the city of Detroit, the management of the Tigers, and the management of the Cardinals something.

"You were disgusted, Dizzy, you said, because you lost to the Cubs. Paul, you said you sat at your hotel waiting for Dizzy to drive you to the station. This is too deep for me. It is difficult for me to accept your statements about not knowing that the other one would not go to Detroit.

"You boys owe it to your profession to show yourselves on the field at all times. People pay to see you, and you threw down baseball in this instance.

"Then, when you were informed by your manager of your fines, you got huffy and wanted to quit, and you failed to obey your manager by not going onto the field. You were not going to do this or that. After listening to all of the evidence, I do not feel that the management of the Cardinals was unreasonable. I support them fully."

President Breadon then commented on Dizzy's attitude.

"Dizzy has the wrong idea about this business," said Breadon. "He goes around knocking the owners, the manager, and the club. When he does that, he's knocking his own business. He says we're cheap. Well, last year our pay-roll was the second highest in the National League. I believe we're no lower than third this season. Does that look like we're cheap, Dizzy?

"This is the seventh day of Dizzy's suspension. I'm willing to call it seven days and let it go at that."

The hearing then came to a close. It was noted that there was no hand-shaking between Dizzy and Frisch or Dizzy and Breadon.

Ray J. Gillespie, St. Louis *Star-Times*

After hearing testimony of all parties involved in the Dean vs. Cardinals controversy, I am more impressed by the remarks of Frankie Frisch than by all evidence submitted by others in the case. Frisch brought up this point: "There are ten million people out of work in this country, yet Dizzy Dean is willing to sacrifice a daily income of approximately $50 to fill the role of a play-boy."

There's one, Dizzy, that you can't shake off! Your pay averages $50 a day from mid-April until late September whether or not you turn a single chore on the field!

"Baseball may be considered an amusement by the fans," continued Frisch, "but with us it's a business. It gives us our livelihood and nets us a comfortable income. Now we come to Dizzy's flare for causing a rumpus. He refused to abide the club decision and decided to go on a strike that cost him $50 for each day he is out of uniform. He's too deep for me to solve."

While commenting on Dizzy's case, Frisch brought out some interesting figures on the boy's pitching this season.

"He's a great one," said Frisch. "I can't take that away from him. But we've given him considerable support. Dizzy feels that he's the only one who wins his games. In fact, we have scored 114 runs for him in 16 of his full-time victories. That's an average of 7 per game. That's giving your pitcher a lot of assistance.

"Dean won a game from the Reds, 3 to 0. In that game Jimmy Collins and Burgess Whitehead turned plays that prevented the Reds from scoring at least four runs. So you'll see that while the box score gave Diz credit for the game, some of the other boys helped. That's baseball—a pitcher can't do it all by himself."

President Breadon plans to curb Dizzy's bits of comedy. "I've been at the head of this club more than ten years," said Breadon, "and we've had more trouble with Dizzy than with all our other ball players. I am going to put an end to his capers. He will obey the rules, or I'm afraid he will have a short career in baseball.

"I'm not saying that we are always right, and Dizzy is always wrong. But we have been extremely lenient and generous with him. We developed him from a raw rookie to a great pitcher by putting him through our system of development. I am not saying we are entirely responsible for making Dizzy what he is, but we have gone a long way in bringing him around."

And there the case rests—to await Dizzy's next move.

Sid Keener, St. Louis *Star-Times*

Chicago—A photographer aroused the ire of Cubs' Manager Charley Grimm in the eighth inning of today's game with the Phillies. With the bases full, one of Curt Davis' pitches got away from Catcher Al Todd of the Phils. As Stan Hack started for home, the photographer tosses the ball to the Phillies' catcher, forcing Hack to scamper back to third. The young man got a good bawling out from the Cub manager.

Philadelphia *Inquirer*

NATIONAL LEAGUE STANDINGS

	W	L	PCT	GB		W	L	PCT	GB
New York	75	41	.647	—	Pittsburgh	54	59	.478	19½
Chicago	70	46	.603	5	Brooklyn	49	63	.437	24
St. Louis	68	47	.591	6½	Philadelphia	44	70	.386	30
Boston	58	57	.504	16½	Cincinnati	40	75	.348	34½

○ *Tuesday, August 21* ○

[On August 20, the Cardinals were not scheduled to play.]

At yesterday's hearing before Judge Landis, Branch Rickey at one point asked Diz about a radio broadcast he made last Thursday night. Rickey accused him of stating, in answer to a question, "Yes, I'll be glad to pitch for the St. Louis fans—but not for the Cardinals."

"Yes," admitted Dizzy, "I said that, but I was sore at the time, and I'm sorry about it."

At another point in the hearing, Secretary Lloyd described an "act" put on in the clubhouse by Dizzy. According to Lloyd, Dizzy ranted around, tearing his hair and giving an imitation of how Rickey tried to talk the Detroit club out of the Cardinals' $3,800 guarantee for the exhibition game there.

When, a little later, Rickey disclosed testimony to show that the Cardinal organization had had trouble with Dean in St. Joseph, Mo. [*for whom he had played in 1930, his first year in organized baseball*], and Houston, Dizzy countered with a statement that when he was sick several years ago the Cards put him up at the home of one of the Cards' minor league officials.

"They charged me $80 or $100 a month to stay there," Diz said, "and I could have stayed at some other place for $35 a month."

When Rickey was interrogating one witness from the Cards' office force, Dizzy yelled, "Sure, they'll say what you want. They'd be a fool if they didn't."

When Landis finally handed down his opinion, Dizzy was flabbergasted. His facial expression indicated he could not believe what he had heard. He had the appearance of a great pitcher who had been tagged for a home run with the bases loaded by the weakest hitter in baseball. It seemed as if he felt that his best friend had turned against him. He had asked Landis to hear his case, and baseball's highest authority had ruled against him.

Dizzy sat sullenly for ten minutes as newspaper photographers "shot" him in group poses with Landis, Breadon, and Frisch. They asked him to smile and be cheerful, but not the slightest smile creased Dizzy's countenance.

Just how Dizzy and Manager Frisch and the other members of the Cardinal team who testified will "hit it off" as a result of the meeting, is a point at question. Diz showed no inclination to shake hands with Frisch for a "picture" when asked to do so. Frisch said he was willing, but Dean shook his head. That was too much.

Martin J. Haley, St. Louis *Globe-Democrat*

∘ *Wednesday, August 22* ∘

[*On August 21, in St. Louis, the Cardinals defeated Boston, 6–2. Winning pitcher, Rex Carleton; losing pitcher, Bob Brown. Cardinals' standing: 69 wins, 47 losses, in third place.*]

Tex Carleton gave an excellent exhibition of control as he scored his fourteenth victory of the season yesterday and pitched the Redbirds to their seventh triumph in the last eight games.

J. Roy Stockton, *St. Louis Post-Dispatch*

The incident involving Brother Elmer, peanut vendor of Houston, was brought into Monday's hearing, and Dizzy held his ground for a moment while he criticized Branch Rickey.

"How did you treat my brother?" snapped Dizzy. "You told me you'd get him a job at Sportsman's Park, and what kind of a job did you pick for him—selling peanuts."

"Yes, but wasn't it at your invitation that the club brought Elmer from Texas?" said Rickey. "You knew he wasn't making much money in Houston, and you asked us to see what could be done for him."

"Don't give the impression that you're taking care of Elmer," Dizzy cut in. "You're hardly taking care of me and Paul."

"Hardly taking care of you?" asked Rickey. "Your salary is $7,500, a pretty good salary, I would say, for a young man only 23 years of age."

Dizzy was stopped by Rickey's reply, apparently feeling he had done pretty good for himself by coming up from the semi-pro lots and within three years advancing to a salary of $7,500. [*On February 19, 1983, a labor arbitrator made a binding ruling that an annual salary of one million dollars should be paid to Fernando Valenzuela, a twenty-two-year-old pitcher for the Los Angeles Dodgers with two years of major league experience.*]

Sid Keener, St. Louis *Star-Times*

◦ *Thursday, August 23* ◦

[*On August 22, the Cardinals were not scheduled to play.*]

The feeling of the Cardinal players toward the Deans has dropped from the freezing point to ten degrees below zero since the latest rebellion. Some of the fellows, including Captain Durocher, especially resent the use of the term "bushers" as applied to them by Paul, a first-year man.

Sid Keener, St. Louis Star-Times

Most major league magnates have evaded the subject of night baseball as though it were contaminating.

The chief argument against night baseball is that it is unnatural, that the game is essentially a daylight diversion. This may be true, but times are changing, and baseball must keep step with the transformations. The trend is toward shorter work weeks, which means more leisure week-ends, but less time for diversion in the daytime during the rest of the week. Men won't quit their tasks during the week to go to ball games, but a vast majority would welcome a place to go in the evening to relax. The picture palaces have had their vogue, but their entertainment is indoors, and people prefer outdoor diversion in the summer. Moreover, the current decency crusade is threatening movie attendance. As is apparent from the crowds drawn to softball, the ball park would exercise a natural attraction on warm nights. [*In 1934, the Production Code Administration was established in Hollywood with the power to award or deny a seal of approval to motion pictures. Only films that observed the Code's moral restrictions received the seal, without which a motion picture could not be distributed. This practice continued for about thirty years.*]

The Sporting News is not waging a campaign for night baseball in the majors. It simply is presenting the facts, believing that they merit more study than hidebound prejudice has heretofore accorded them, and offers the suggestion as one that might help fill the stands on days when they are empty. [*Within a year the first major league night baseball game would be played, on May 24, 1935, in Cincinnati.*]

The Sporting News

Mr. Joe Cambria, the Baltimore laundryman who owns the Albany club [*in the International League*] has come out strongly against arguments with umpires in night games. He likes players to protest against close decisions in the daytime, but at night Mr. Cambria wants no unnecessary conversation until such time as electric light is as free to consumers as sunlight.

The New York Times

∘ *Friday, August 24* ∘

[*On August 23, in St. Louis, the Cardinals lost to New York, 5–3. Winning pitcher, Dolf Luque; losing pitcher, Paul Dean. Cardinals' standing: 69 wins, 48 losses, in third place.*]

Joe Moore's home run to the right field pavilion roof with two out in the ninth inning drove in three runs and enabled the Giants to win the epic ball game of the season.

In addition to being epic in its particulars, the game is generally looked upon by cognoscenti of the national pastime as the clincher in the current pennant race. Taken in combination with the conquest of the Chicago Cubs by the dear old Brooklyn Dodgers, it drops the Giants' closest competitors, the Cubs and Cardinals, safely behind. Chicago now has 6½ games to make up, and St. Louis, 7.

Bill Terry brought to bear every resource of strategy and manpower. Eighteen players, including five pitchers, three pinch hitters, a pinch base runner, and a spare catcher, were brought into the fray. When it was over the Giants, ordinarily an unemotional matter-of-fact set of ball players, jumped around and congratulated each other like giddy collegians. They had won at the last possible moment, and they had beaten Paul "Daffy" Dean on one of his good days, the Giants' first victory of the year over either of the Dean brothers.

Stanley Woodward, New York *Herald-Tribune*

∘ *Saturday, August 25* ∘

[*On August 24, in St. Louis, the Cardinals defeated New York, 5–0. Winning pitcher, Dizzy Dean; losing pitcher, Joe Bowman. Cardinals' standing: 70 wins, 48 losses, in second place.*]

They tell only the simple truth when they say that Jerome Herman, the celebrated "Dizzy" Dean, is baseball's most colorful character.

He has that trick of creating interest in everything he says or does. No other player, save only Babe Ruth, can so dramatize the action on the diamond, paint it in such vivid colors. And none is able to inject the humor and laughs with which "Dizzy" lightens his effects.

Yesterday his gift for showmanship was so heavily emphasized as to win a deeper appreciation when, as the repentant prodigal son, he took up the Cardinals' pitching burden. It was the best baseball show of the year. He recognized that the crowd had come out to see him, expected something unusual—and he didn't miss a cue.

That he pitched a shutout is only half the story. The score merely expressed his pitching skill. He went farther than that, made of the game a one-man show—a show for which he wrote the scenario, directed start to finish, and acted the hero's role.

He acted a part the whole way. Sensing that the situation demanded a chastened and subdued hero, a prodigal who was truly repentant, he assumed that character as the game began. He allowed his shoulders to slump and hung his head, focusing his eyes on the ground as though anxious to avoid the gaze of the crowd. Whenever Manager Frisch offered a word of advice he listened with studied attention. The crowd got the impression he wanted them to get—that here was a man sorry for his sins and anxious to make amends.

As the game progressed, and his pitching won storms of approval, his attitude changed. He straightened his shoulders, became his old aggressive, assertive self. He began to talk to the Giant batters, taunt them as they came to the plate. The crowd caught the spirit and with "Dizzy" they laughed at the futile efforts of the New Yorkers.

And then to top off the performance, give it one extra bit of punch, "Dizzy" stole a base. And he did it in a manner to suggest the greatest base runner in the game. While pitcher Al Smith was concentrating on the batter, "Dizzy" sneaked off to a big lead, "broke" perfectly, and completed the steal ahead of Gus Mancuso's accurate throw with a perfect hook slide. [*Accomplished with none out, this was Dean's first (and last) stolen base of the 1934 season. His one previous major league stolen base had come in 1933.*]

Yes sir, it was "Dizzy's" day, his show. If St. Louis didn't kill the fatted calf in his honor last night, it is truly ungrateful.

Garry Schumacher, New York *Evening Journal*

° *Sunday, August 26* °

[*On August 25, in St. Louis, the Cardinals lost to New York, 7–6. Winning pitcher, Hal Schumacher; losing pitcher, Dizzy Dean. Cardinals' standing: 70 wins, 49 losses, in third place.*]

A cracking single from the bat of Travis Jackson pulled the Giants from the depths to the heights in as exciting a struggle as the Giants have weathered under the leadership of Bill Terry.

Jackson's blow climaxed a bitter uphill struggle which saw the Giants come from five runs behind. It came in the eighth inning with the bases loaded, two out, the Giants trailing, 6 to 5, and Dizzy Dean on the mound. Dean had just intentionally walked Mel Ott to get a crack at Jackson, who waved aside this gesture by chasing home the runs that meant precious victory.

The win kept the Giants 6½ games ahead of the Cubs, and the Cardinals skidded from second position to third. More, it shattered the bugaboo that the dizzier of the Dean boys has cast over the Giants. Today the Terrymen scored their first victory over Dizzy in six starts this year.

Dizzy was rushed to the rescue in the seventh when Bill Walker was shelled off the mound and a five-run lead the Cardinals had acquired in the fourth inning was fast disappearing. Back for his second time in as many days, it was asking too much of even the great Dizzy to deliver. The Giants leaped upon him for 6 hits and 4 runs in the three innings he worked.

James P. Dawson, *The New York Times*

The Cubs this year installed a public address system for the first time. Charley Grimm opposed it and withdrew his opposition only after he was assured that music records would not be played during pre-game practice as is done in many parks, including Wrigley Field, Los Angeles, where the Cubs do much of their spring training.

Grimm contends that miscellaneous records would clash with the rhythm of baseball procedure and that records would not be selected to meet the tempo of the varying movements in practice workouts.

Ruth Reynolds, New York *Daily News*

○ *Monday, August 27* ○

[*On August 26, in St. Louis, the Cardinals split a doubleheader with Brooklyn, losing 11–5 and winning 7–2. Winning pitchers, Dutch Leonard and Bill Hallahan; losing pitchers, Tex Carleton and Les Munns. Cardinals' standing: 71 wins, 51 losses, in third place.*]

Yesterday in the first game of a double-header Brooklyn's big Belgian relief pitcher "Dutch" Leonard was called to the peak when the Cardinals were batting Van Mungo all over the premises. Dutch stepped in and for 5⅓ innings gave no runs and two hits. Truly a great performance for a lad rated as the team's eighth pitcher at the start of the campaign and but a month's experience away from a class B league.

Les "Nemo" Munns didn't pitch bad ball in the nightcap, but he couldn't get past that one bad inning habit of his. In the seventh the Redbirds found him for all the runs they needed.

Stan Lomax, New York *Evening Journal*

NATIONAL LEAGUE STANDINGS

	W	L	PCT	GB		W	L	PCT	GB
New York	78	44	.639	—	Pittsburgh	57	62	.479	19½
Chicago	72	49	.595	5½	Brooklyn	53	66	.445	23½
St. Louis	71	50	.587	6½	Philadelphia	46	74	.383	31
Boston	62	58	.517	15	Cincinnati	43	79	.352	35

○ *Tuesday, August 28* ○

[*On August 27, in St. Louis, the Cardinals lost to Brooklyn, 10–1. Winning pitcher, Tom Zachary; losing pitcher, Tex Carleton. Cardinals' standing: 71 wins, 51 losses, in third place.*]

Old Tom Zachary, 17 of whose 37 years have been spent in the major leagues, yielded one scratch run yesterday as Brooklyn's batters hammered a parade of Cardinal hurlers into submission.

Manager Casey Stengel, short on starting flingers, named Zachary, hoping that Old Tom might have a good day. Stengel's hopes materialized, and Zachary shut out the Birds after their first two batters, Whitehead and Rothrock, scored a run at the outset of the first frame by sandwiching a stolen base between two scratch hits.

Martin J. Haley, St. Louis *Globe-Democrat*

The Deans may have been squelched and humiliated in their recent insurrection against law and order as Sam Breadon sees fit to administer it, but the spanking they received hasn't hurt their popularity with the St. Louis knothole gang.

Three thousand youngsters out in left field in Sportsman's Park started the well-known familiar chant that burns up the rest of the Cardinal pitchers when Tex Carleton was being bumped around by the Dodgers in the fourth inning yesterday.

"We want Dean! We want Dean! We want Dean!" over and over again in a rising crescendo as Carleton fidgeted in the box, trying to get the enemy out, and Dazzy Vance, once the most noted pitcher in baseball, warmed up. Jesse Haines got the same war cry later on, and when Mooney, instead of Paul or Dizzy, came in to relieve, the youngsters booed him at every step.

Tommy Holmes, Brooklyn *Eagle*

Giant Manager Bill Terry thinks the background of white shirts in Wrigley Field's center field bleachers has dimmed his men's batting eye. [*The Giants had just lost to the Cubs, 1–0.*]

"I swear I can't see the ball," says Memphis Bill [*who batted well enough to compile an average of .401 in 1930*]. "I'm not afraid of the Cubs. I'm afraid of their park."

Lefty O'Doul says, "If that ball coming out of those white shirts ever hit you, it would knock you silly." [*With the single exception of the 1962 All-Star game, baseball fans have been prohibited from sitting in the center field bleachers in Wrigley Field since 1952.*]

Harold Burr, *New York Post*

Colored semi-pro ball players stick together. They have to, a cynic might say, or they'd be sunk. Fortunately, bigots are an unknown species in this quarter of semi-pro activity, and the strong ties among colored clubs and players are due to common interests and friendship rather than sheer necessity.

For example, take a look through the colored publication edited by that bright young man Nat Trammell, whose paper records the doings of every dusky nine on the circuit.

The editor takes up the ever present question, "Why aren't colored players permitted to play in the big leagues?"

Trammell proceeds on the premise that there must be some logical basis for this exclusion. Can it be lack of ability? He proceeds to recall several exhibition games in which colored clubs trimmed white major league outfits.

Trammell then swung around to Bill Holland, star pitcher of the Black Yankees. Holland, he says, has a very impressive record against white opponents. One winter, playing in Cuba, Holland won a $500 cash prize for the best pitching record in the Cuban Winter League. He won this against competition which included Fred Fitzsimmons, Jakie May, and Jess Petty. [*As major league pitchers, Petty won 67 games, May won 72, and Fitzsimmons won 217.*]

Editor Trammell told the writer recently that he was thankful for the opportunity semi-pro ball gives to his people.

"We're developing great stars," he said, "and some day, if we stick together and succeed in our fight to reach the big leagues, the colored big leaguers will be all the better because of the training they got in semi-pro games." [*In Ebbets Field on the opening day of the 1947 season, Brooklyn beat Boston, and Jackie Robinson became the first black man to play in a major league baseball game. This occurred eighty-four years after the Emancipation Proclamation, but organized baseball was not at the end of the line. When Robinson signed his first contract with Branch Rickey, there were no blacks in the National Football League, and it was not until 1950 that a black player was signed to a National Basketball Association contract, nor until 1955 that a black singer, Marian Anderson, was permitted to perform with the Metropolitan Opera Company.*]

Irwin N. Rosee, Brooklyn *Times-Union*

∘ *Monday, August 29* ∘

[*On August 28, in St. Louis, the Cardinals defeated Brooklyn, 2–0. Winning pitcher, Paul Dean; losing pitcher, Ray Benge. Cardinals' standing: 72 wins, 51 losses, in third place.*]

Pitching perfect ball for six out of eight innings and allowing only a base on balls in another, Ray Benge still went down to defeat due to one unlucky session. After retiring the Cardinals in rapid-fire order for 5⅓ innings, Benge was reached for four straight hits, and it cost him his duel with Paul Dean.

Leo Durocher sent a fast hopper through the right side of the infield and ended Benge's bid for no-hit fame. Dean then caught a curve on the end of his bat and shot one down the right-field line, a foot inside the boundary, sending Durocher to third. Burgess Whitehead looped a drive behind second and a strong wind carried it beyond Jimmy Jordan's reach, and Durocher scored. Jack Rothrock then hit a lazy wind-blown fly toward left field which dropped for a double and scored Dean. Benge then retired Frisch and Medwick and resumed his white-washing, but it was too late.

Dean was hit often but was sturdy in the pinches and was helped by poor Dodger base running.

Arthur E. Patterson, New York Herald-Tribune

∘ *Thursday, August 30* ∘

[*On August 29, in St. Louis, the Cardinals defeated Brooklyn, 4–1. Winning pitcher, Bill Walker; losing pitcher, Johnny Babich. Cardinals' standing: 73 wins, 51 losses, in third place.*]

Southpaw Bill Walker received congratulations from teammates after five-hit pitching netted his seventh win of the year, and he modestly admitted that he "had his stuff."

The triumph was described by President Sam Breadon as "the best game the Cardinals played all year."

"They played heads-up, interesting baseball," the club owner remarked.

The Cards' clever work on the bases, coupled with Dodger stupidity, contributed to the St. Louis victory. The prize plays came in the eighth when DeLancey fell asleep and the Brooklyn infield snored with him.

One was out. DeLancey was on second and Ernie Orsatti on first when Burgess Whitehead shot a grounder to Third Baseman Tony Cuccinello, whose throw forced Orsatti. DeLancey, figuring three were out, strolled leisurely toward third as the Dodgers tossed the ball to First Baseman Sam Leslie, who nonchalantly prepared to give it to the pitcher. Suddenly informed by the frantic Cuban, Señor Coach Miguel Gonzalez, that only two were out, DeLancey took out for third as though the entire Cuban Army was at his heels. Leslie, noting this, tossed the ball to third but it was too late, and a moment later DeLancey redeemed himself, at least partially, by stealing home to complete his half of a double steal.

The game marked the return of Pepper Martin to third base after an absence of several weeks due to a side injury, a bruised arm, an ailing right elbow, and several other things.

Ray J. Gillespie, St. Louis *Star-Times*

◦ *Saturday, September 1* ◦

[*On August 30, the Cardinals were not scheduled to play. On August 31, the first day of their final road trip, in Chicago, the Cardinals won, 3–1. Winning pitcher, Dizzy Dean; losing pitcher, Guy Bush. Cardinals' standing: 74 wins, 51 losses, tied with Chicago for second place.*]

Dizzy Dean yesterday had the extreme satisfaction of hanging up his twenty-second victory of the year, the first time in eight starts that he has defeated the Cubs.

Dean pitched a much more leisurely game than usual, bearing down only when his sangfroid got him into minor jams. The Cubs had two runners on with two out in the sixth, two on with one out in the seventh, and two on with none out in the eighth. On these occasions Dean bore down, with the result that the gents who rushed up to supply the big punch were utterly helpless.

Edward Burns, Chicago *Tribune*

◦ *Sunday, September 2* ◦

[*On September 1, in Chicago, the Cardinals won, 7–1. Winning pitcher, Bill Hallahan; losing pitcher, Bill Lee. Cardinals' standing: 75 wins, 51 losses, in second place.*]

The Cubs, at one time favorites to win first or second place in the final standings of the National League, yesterday suffered a severe whipping from the Cardinals of St. Louis. The Chicagoans pounded home a run off William Hallahan in the ninth inning, but this splendid uprising did not keep them from plunking into third place, a game behind their adversaries and 6½ games behind the Giants.

William Lee, a handsome young man from Louisiana, was the first of three pitchers employed by the home team and was withdrawn in the third inning after James Collins stroked his thirty-first home run of the season and William DeLancey knocked his eleventh home run of the season. The St. Louis players knocked 15 hits, 4 of which were made by Burgess Whitehead, the Cardinals' substitute shortstop. [*During this season, Whitehead was an extremely handy utility infielder: he appeared in 48 games at second base, 29 at shortstop, and 28 at third base.*]

Edward Burns, Chicago *Tribune*

∘ *Monday, September 3* ∘

[*On September 2, in Chicago, the Cardinals' scheduled game was postponed because of rain.*]

NATIONAL LEAGUE STANDINGS

	W	L	PCT	GB		W	L	PCT	GB
New York	81	47	.633	—	Pittsburgh	60	65	.480	19½
St. Louis	75	51	.595	5	Brooklyn	55	70	.440	24½
Chicago	74	52	.587	6	Philadelphia	47	77	.379	32
Boston	65	61	.516	15	Cincinnati	46	80	.365	34

∘ *Tuesday, September 4* ∘

[*On September 3, Labor Day, in Pittsburgh, the Cardinals lost a doubleheader, 12–2 and 6–5. Winning pitchers, Larry French and Heinie Meine; losing pitchers, Paul Dean and Dizzy Dean. Cardinals' standing: 75 wins, 53 losses, tied with Chicago for second place.*]

Hailed as conquering heroes a fortnight ago, our Cardinals today would be willing to give themselves up if properly encouraged.

It's not the prospect of opening a series with the hapless Dodgers tomorrow in Brooklyn that causes the Redbirds to drop their chins sadly on their chests; it's the double loss suffered in Pittsburgh yesterday while the Giants were idle. The two defeats virtually eliminated St. Louis from the 1934 pennant scramble.

However, Frankie Frisch, the master optimist, refuses to relinquish hope.

"Give up, Frankie?" he was asked.

"Never, not until we're counted out officially," he fired back. "No team of mine will give up. We're in this race until we're out of it, and, believe me, we'll fight to the last ditch. When I played under John McGraw, I was taught to fight to the finish, and you can bet your last dollar that every man playing for me will do the same."

There was no comforting of the Dean brothers, who played leading roles in providing a holiday celebration for Pittsburgh fans yesterday.

Paul was merely a batting practice pitcher in the opening game, and an eight-run uprising sent Junior rushing through the exits in favor of Dazzy Vance in the third inning.

In the afterpiece, with two on base in the ninth and the Cards trailing, 3–2, Pepper Martin crashed out a long triple and later scored on Joe Medwick's fly, giving the Birds a 5–3 advantage. But when Dizzy Dean, pitching in relief of Bill Walker, permitted Pinch-Hitter Grace to single, followed by a base hit by Lloyd Waner and Freddie Lindstrom's double, the margin was cut to 5–4. Bill Hallahan was called in and pitched to Shortstop Vaughan, whose long fly scored L. Waner with the tying run. Traynor then singled over Frisch's head that drove in the winning run.

Two blunders ultimately spelled defeat. In the sixth, Medwick, on first base, stopped half way between the bases and refused to run when Paul Waner lost Collins' fly in the sun, staggered around, picked it up and threw to second in time to catch the jogging Joe. The Cards made two runs but might have made several more had Medwick been awake.

Then in the seventh the Pirates scored a run after Martin failed to cover third base as Collins caught a pop fly off Pitcher Hoyt's bat. Thevenow, on third, could have been trapped off the bag by 20 feet as he faltered, slipped, fell, got up, and returned in plenty of time.

Ray J. Gillespie, St. Louis *Star-Times*

Dizzy Dean is up to his pranks again.

The eccentric Cardinal pitcher added a new wrinkle to his list of oddities. He refused to pass up an exhibition game, as ordered by Manager Frankie Frisch, missed a train for New York, and remained in Pittsburgh last night so as to be on hand at Greensburg, Pa., where the club was to play today.

Secretary Clarence Lloyd was instructed by Manager Frisch to send Dizzy and his wife on to New York ahead of the club, but at 10:35, 25 minutes before train time last night, Mrs. Dean was rushing frantically about the Hotel Schenley seeking Frisch.

"I must find Frankie," she said. "Dizzy refuses to go to New York. He's upstairs in a card game with several players and positively won't accompany me to the station."

That brings up the question: If the Cardinals fined Dizzy $100 for failing to go to Detroit for an exhibition game, what will be the penalty—or bonus—for insisting on going to an exhibition game at Greensburg after the team management had excused him from so doing? [*Greensburg was one of six small Pennsylvania towns with teams in the Pennsylvania State Association, a Class D league then in its first year of existence. The Greensburg team, part of the Cardinals' extensive system of farm clubs, won the league pennant in 1934. The league's last year of operation was 1942, when it became a war casualty.*]

Ray J. Gillespie, St. Louis Star-Times

° *Wednesday, September 5* °

[*On September 4, the Cardinals played an exhibition game in Greensburg, Pennsylvania.*]

Two Labor Day defeats for the Cardinals and the Giants' two victories yesterday have increased the margin over the Redbirds to seven games, and it is almost time to recognize William "What's-in-it-for-me" Terry as the man who equalled Gabby Street's record of winning pennants in his first two years as a major league manager. [*The Cardinals won pennants in 1930 and 1931, Gabby Street's first two years as a manager in the major leagues. Terry had managed the Giants for a major part of 1932, when he succeeded John McGraw, but his first full year on the job was 1933.*]

It is still possible to take a pencil and paper and figure how the Cardinals and Cubs could win, but it is necessary to have a good imagination, with visions of train wrecks, broken arms, and paralysis of the Giants' optic nerves.

The Giants have only 24 games remaining, with 20 of them in the friendly shadows of Coogan's Bluff; they are to be excused for window-shopping with their prospective World Series checks. [*Coogan's Bluff was a hill overlooking the Polo Grounds, from which it was possible to catch a glimpse of the field.*]

All right, what happened? What caused the Cardinals' failure? Here are some reasons they are not winning the pennant:

Virgil Davis, a .349 batter in 1933, is hitting only .297, and the catching has not been comparable to what it was when Jimmy Wilson did the bulk of it. [*Wilson was the Cardinals' regular catcher for six years, 1928–33, during which time the team won three pennants.*]

Joe Medwick, after a fine start, when he was among the league's leading batters, has been in a bad slump for more than a month. In the last 12 games he has batted .213. Due to inexperience and other things, Joe has to hit .350 to be valuable to the team.

Center field has been a problem all year. [*Ernie Orsatti and Chick Fullis shared the position, with Orsatti appearing in 90 games and Fullis playing in 69 after his trade, early in the season, from the Phillies.*]

Pepper Martin has missed 44 games because of a multitude of injuries.

Tex Carleton has had long stretches of ineffectiveness.

Last but not least, the club has tried to compete on even terms with the Giants and Cubs with only 21 men. This has caused team morale to bog down and has forced pitchers to bat for themselves in late innings of close games that might have been won if pinch hitters had been available.

On the bright side of the picture have been the fine work of Jack Rothrock [*probably the most underrated player on the team*], the pitching of the Dean boys, and the greatly improved batting and fielding of Ripper Collins, factors which have enabled the team to put up a stubborn fight.

Second place is still open to the Cardinals, but the Giants' seven-game margin virtually silences the old pennant bee. It is practically impossible for the Cardinals or Cubs to win.

J. Roy Stockton, *St. Louis Post-Dispatch*

Today the Giants are intrenched behind a SEVEN GAME lead over the Cubs and Cardinals.

"I guess we couldn't ask for much more," Bill Terry said. And indeed his club's lead insures them fully against anything in the way of breaks or bad luck. The Giants can be overtaken, but it's a million-to-one shot.

Garry Schumacher, New York *Evening Journal*

∘ *Thursday, September 6* ∘

[*On September 5, in Brooklyn, the Cardinals won, 2–1. Winning pitcher, Dizzy Dean; losing pitcher, Dutch Leonard. Cardinals' standing: 76 wins, 53 losses, in second place.*]

Branch Rickey, in the course of his career as director of the Cardinal organization, during which he has catalogued thousands of young ball players, has waxed oratorically grandiloquent about many an athlete who has turned out to be what the trade inelegantly calls "just a bum." But he knew what he was talking about last spring when he said that Bill DeLancey could move into the first-string catching job on almost any ball club.

Bill is still young in experience. [*He was twenty-two years old and in his first year in the major leagues.*] He calls for an occasional "fat one" at critical times, and he has much to learn about shifting to stop potential wild pitches.

But Bill DeLancey today looks like one of the coming catchers of major league baseball, and when the great minds of the Cardinal organization get together in the early season, DeLancey will be one Redbird to give solace to the disappointed and comfort for the next pennant race.

Bill has hit a dozen home runs, and they have been important blows. He hit his twelfth yesterday, and it paired with Ripper Collins' thirty-second of the campaign to give Jerome Herman Dean his twenty-fourth victory of the season and the Cardinals undivided possession of second place.

With a batting average of .300 and steady improvement behind the plate, DeLancey has become the first string catcher. Bill has no glaring fault. He can travel a long way for a pop foul. He has a powerful arm, which will be more valuable when he acquires confidence in himself. He is a long-distance hitter and fast for a big man. And when the star rookies of the league are named, Bill should be near the head of the list.

Yesterday DeLancey went to bat in the ninth inning with the score tied, 1–1, and got the full force of his powerful swing into his bat and lifted a low strike high over the screen about the right field wall, a sky-scraping fly that was a home run in any park.

Dizzy pitched a brilliant game to make the homers of Collins and De-Lancey enough for a victory, holding the Dodgers to three hits.

[*Following the 1935 season, DeLancey became a victim of tuberculosis, which ended his career at the age of twenty-three.*]

J. Roy Stockton, *St. Louis Post-Dispatch*

° *Friday, September 7* °

[*On September 6, in Brooklyn, the Cardinals won, 7–5. Winning pitcher, Tex Carleton; losing pitcher, Tom Zachary. Cardinals' standing: 77 wins, 53 losses, in second place.*]

The Cardinals may not win the pennant, but with the help of the hapless Dodgers, may get second place sugar. While the Giants were knocking off the Cubs, Mr. Frisch's noble lads knocked off Mr. Stengel's lalapaloosas.

Brooklyn has been a little gift from Heaven to several other clubs in the circuit, and they seem to be bent on assisting the Cardinals to pad up their bank rolls.

Tom Zachary, who is older than General Robert E. Lee, tried to tame St. Louis with his crippled fast ball. It has worked well on other occasions, but it was a flop yesterday. Tex Carleton pitched for the Cards and ran into lots of trouble in the last inning, but managed to struggle through without losing the game.

One surprise of the day was that Leo Durocher cracked out a couple of hits, including a double. Leo goes in for fancy clothes and jockeying the opposition, but hits are very rare in his life.

Jack Kofoed, New York *Evening Journal*

When winter comes with snow and sleet, the pitching firm of Dizzy and Daffy Dean will let you know that they'll never put on a Cardinal uniform again unless they "draw the salary that great pitchers are supposed to get."

"We've forgotten all about this summer insofar as a rise in salary is concerned," said Dizzy last night. "Of course we're going to win as many games as we can. I am out to bag 29, and Paul should bag 4 more, and that'll give him 19 for the season. Pretty good for a first year man, eh what!

"But we'll be well compensated for the work we're doing now or else refuse to pitch in the big leagues next summer. We haven't decided yet on what our demands will be, but we'll try to be as fair with the Cardinals as we can.

"It might interest the public to know that we know of one pitcher who gets more than both of us combined who can't hold Paul's glove, let alone mine." [*Dean may have been referring to Bill Hallahan, who in fact was being paid more than the combined salaries of Dizzy and Paul.*]

"It also might interest the public to know that I was offered $15,000 a year for four years to pitch three games a week for an industrial team in the

Middle West, and the same concern was willing to give Paul $10,000 a year, with jobs calling for $75 per week when our baseball careers end.

"We're in demand all right. I know for a fact that the St. Louis club was offered $100,000 and a few players for me, and several teams have been trying to buy Paul for $50,000. I don't care where I pitch so long as I get the salary I'm entitled to. And that goes for Paul, too.

"The St. Louis club advertised Paul and me to pitch a double-header against the Cubs. They ballyhooed us all week, and nearly 39,000 fans, the largest in the history of St. Louis, came out to see us. The people know class when they see it, and I'm not kidding when I say Paul and I have it."

The feeling persists around the league that Dizzy will demand $20,000 for himself and advise Paul to remain adamant unless he gets a $10,000 stipend.

Dizzy said that no batter in particular is hard for him, claiming that when he's in stride they are all pushovers. Once in a while, he says, he lets up and some "busher" will get a base hit.

Dizzy also says that he doesn't like publicity. He maintains that they can't keep him out of the headlines. He claims he's just a bashful boy from Oklahoma whom the big town sports pages thrive on because without a Dizzy to write about they would pass out of existence.

Bill McCullough, Brooklyn *Times-Union*

There's going to be a Negro World Series at Yankee Stadium on Sunday. The Black Yankees will play the Chicago American Giants, and the Pittsburgh Crawfords will meet the Philadelphia Stars.

Negro baseball has enjoyed a great comeback here in the last two years. Back in the days before legalized Sunday ball in New York [*that is, before 1919*], Negro players held the center of the stage on the Sabbath. The famous Lincoln Giants, with the great John Henry Lloyd and Cannonball Williams, made Negro diamond history at Olympic Field, in Harlem, where they met major leaguers in exhibition games and comported themselves well enough to win the admiration of John J. McGraw and Christy Mathewson.

In those days Cannonball Williams was rated the grandest Negro pitcher of all time. But we are told that Satchel Paige, of the Crawfords, is an even more adroit master of the hurling art. It was no tremendous effort for Williams to fan 15 or 16 batsmen, but Paige this year has whiffed as many as 18 in one game.

Negro fans say that Paige is another Dizzy Dean. Paige affects some of the quaint mannerisms of Stepin Fetchit of the movies—until he heaves that ball. Then he is all pitcher. [*Finally, in 1948, when he was at least forty-three years old, Paige was allowed to enter the major leagues, and he helped the Cleveland Indians win the pennant with 6 wins and 1 loss and an ERA of 2.47. Stepin Fetchit was the first black person to earn a million dollars from the films. He has been strongly criticized because his role was always that of the stereotypical servile, sycophantic Negro, but in fairness to Stepin Fetchit it should be noted that his roles were created by filmmakers who were white (and male), and that a protest by him would have ended his motion picture career. Many years later he said that by putting his foot in Hollywood's door he made it possible for that door eventually to open all the way for such performers as Cicely Tyson and Sidney Poitier.*]

Before Sunday baseball was legalized, it was our pleasure to watch the Lincoln Giants nearly every Sabbath they were at home. Their greatest player was Lloyd, an infielder, a sort of black Honus Wagner [*the Pittsburgh Pirates' shortstop from 1900 until 1917, Honus Wagner is universally regarded as the best infielder of all time, and, along with Ty Cobb and Babe Ruth, as one of baseball's three greatest players.*] At 56, Lloyd is still playing. [*Twelve years after his death, in 1977, Lloyd was named to baseball's Hall of Fame.*]

"If we could bleach this Lloyd boy, we would show the National League a new phenomenon," said McGraw one afternoon. Mac spent many a Sunday watching the Lincoln Giants and got a tremendous kick out of their skill and their antics. A Negro ball game is not a staid and stolid demonstration of fielding and hitting. It embodies comic relief impossible in white games because no Caucasian can play baseball with the rhythmic quality inherent in the black race.

McGraw once tried to run a Negro into the National League. He was an infielder named Monroe, who was light skinned. When McGraw became manager of Baltimore in the American League [*in 1901*], he attempted to use Monroe under another name, and announced that he had a new Indian star. But the wily Ban Johnson was on Mac's neck. [*Ban Johnson, president of the newly formed American League, along with virtually every other official in organized baseball for the next forty-five years, was strongly dedicated to the proposition that America's national pastime was forever to be kept off limits to members of the black race. According to Albert "Happy" Chandler, baseball's second commissioner, when Branch Rickey signed Jackie Robinson for the 1946 season, his action was bitterly opposed by the owners of all the other major league clubs.*]

When the Negroes played an All-Star game at Comiskey Park in Chicago a few weeks ago, they drew 35,000 despite the counter-attraction of the Cubs and Giants.

Dan Daniel, New York *World-Telegram*

∘ *Saturday, September 8* ∘

[*On September 7, in Brooklyn, the Cardinals' scheduled game with Brooklyn was postponed because of rain.*]

It is quite generally accepted that it would take a baseball holocaust to prevent a World Series between the Giants and the Tigers.

Dan Daniel, New York *World-Telegram*

∘ *Monday, September 10* ∘

[*On September 8, in Brooklyn, the Cardinals' scheduled doubleheader was postponed because of rain. On September 9, in Philadelphia, the Cardinals won a doubleheader, 7–3 and 4–1. Winning pitchers, Paul Dean and Bill Walker; losing pitchers, Euel Moore and Curt Davis. Cardinals' standing: 79 wins, 53 losses, in second place.*]

For a few minutes in the dusky gloom of evening it appeared the Phillies had found their batting medium. They looked like champion ghost hitters.

The Phils were experiencing the new sensation of playing against time. The Cardinals had already beaten them, and now time had them licked. They were far behind, and at 7 o'clock the game must end. They had not time enough to win, even if they could produce the punch.

It was the first Sunday double-header in Philadelphia's big league history, and under the law play had to halt at 6 o'clock standard time, 7 o'clock daylight time.

In the eighth inning it looked as if the Phils would start hitting. Ethan Allen cracked out a double. Johnny Moore swished a single to center. And 7 o'clock was drawing nearer. If the Phils kept it up, the game would be called before the inning could be completed, and the whole frame would be tossed into discard because the visiting team was ahead. And these hits would be ghost safeties never to be recorded.

But even that feeble spark flickered and vanished as Ernie Orsatti caught Jimmy Wilson's fly for the final out just before the clock reached the hour.

After all, everything counted, and another chapter was added to local big league baseball, the two-for-one on Sunday, a feature in other cities for years. Now the Sunday double bill is sure to become a regular.

When the law was passed permitting Sunday baseball, both clubs decided that double headers were out of the question. Then Gerry Nugent [*owner of the Phillies*] decided to take a chance. Contrary to most expectations, it was proved a double bill could be played to a decisive conclusion. When it was finished, only one inning had been lopped off, and there was no doubt of the proper winner in the minds of the spectators.

It might be a good idea to put a time limit on all double headers. The boys hustled through their chores, and there was no loafing.

Harry Robert, Philadelphia *Evening Bulletin*

NATIONAL LEAGUE STANDINGS

	W	L	PCT	GB		W	L	PCT	GB
New York	85	49	.634	—	Pittsburgh	65	65	.500	18
St. Louis	79	53	.598	5	Brooklyn	57	75	.432	27
Chicago	77	56	.579	7½	Philadelphia	48	81	.372	34½
Boston	69	64	.519	15½	Cincinnati	47	84	.359	36½

○ *Tuesday, September 11* ○

[*On September 10, in Philadelphia, the Cardinals won, 4–1. Winning pitcher, Dizzy Dean; losing pitcher, Phil Collins. Cardinals' standing: 80 wins, 53 losses, in second place.*]

Chalk up Number 25 for Jerome "Dizzy" Dean.

The Cardinal clown, a jester on the field but a Solomon on the pitching peak, handed the Phillies a lacing yesterday. He permitted the Jimmy Wilson men 5 hits, fanned 7, and was master of the situation at all times.

Phil Collins, Dean's mound opponent, pitched well enough to win 9 out of 10 tilts. But that is never good enough for Dean—he is always the tenth occasion.

Leo Durocher, not a power but a pest at the bat, started Collins' downfall in the third inning by working him for a pass. Dean, a hitter not to be ridiculed, smacked a safety to left. Martin quickly clipped a hit to right which scored Durocher, and when Rothrock sliced a single to the same pasture, Dean made a picturesque slide across home plate for the second tally. The slide was not necessary—no play was made on him—but Dean gave it to the cash customers just the same, to give them their money's worth.

Stan Baumgartner, Philadelphia *Inquirer*

∘ *Wednesday, September 12* ∘

[*On September 11, in Philadelphia, the Cardinals split a doubleheader, losing 5–0 and winning 6–4. Winning pitchers, Syl Johnson and Bill Hallahan; losing pitchers, Tex Carleton and Roy Hansen. Cardinals' standing: 81 wins, 55 losses, in second place.*]

Red Miller Day was "red letter" day at the Phillies Ball Park. Not only did the Wilsonmen pay tribute to their trainer with gifts, but they also handed the Frischmen a defeat in the first game and forced Dizzy Dean to come to the mound to save the second.

The setback in the opening contest was a bitter one for the visitors to swallow, for it cost them valuable ground in their hysterical efforts to overtake the Giants.

Stan Baumgartner, Philadelphia *Inquirer*

∘ *Thursday, September 13* ∘

[*On September 12, in Philadelphia, the Cardinals lost, 3–1. Winning pitcher, Roy Hansen; losing pitcher, Dazzy Vance. Cardinals' standing: 81 wins, 55 losses, in second place.*]

Pennants are mostly won in June, July, and August. It is therefore a nine-day wonder when a team comes along and gets tough in September. Thus the St. Louis Cardinals, a two-pitcher outfit, is needlessly exciting the National League with a phoney bid for the flag.

Yesterday the Cards said farewell to the Phils and departed hindmost down the back stairs. It was no way for a pennant bidder to exit. That's what makes this observer feel strongly that the Redbirds are pretenders, joshing the public, the Giants, and themselves above all.

You can't win pennants when pitchers like Dazzy Vance have to drive in the runs. Poor old Dazzy—kind of felt sympathy for the once blazing bomber. [*In his heyday—in the early and middle twenties—Vance probably pitched the most powerful fastball in baseball.*] Kind of pushed around, the old boy has been, now that the flame has died down on the fast one. Still a right pert pitcher, given some runs to make him comfortable. Still a smart head with nice control. Still pretty tough for lads like Dolf Camilli and Lou Chiozza, Bucky Walters and the other kids. Knows too much. Fools 'em with that old change of pace—slow and then slower. Good curve left, too.

But Dazzy wasn't to win yesterday. Up to the eighth we thought he'd scrape through, although the Cards looked sick against just fair pitching by Roy "Snipe" Hansen. The Cards, we may say, looked sick against all the Phil pitchers. If they think they're on a pennant drive with such hitting, they should have new works put in their thinkers.

The Dazzler took it easy, blanking his opposition for seven rounds. In the second he slapped into a pitch and drove it far over the left field sward, clearing the bleacher screen. [*This was the first home run Vance hit since 1925, and it was the seventh, and last, of his major league career.*]

Well, one run is better than none, and when the Phils came up in the eighth, the Dazzler had to keep the status just quo. But the Dazz was tired. When you've been tossing up bird shot for so long, the old arm begins to wear through, and Charles Arthur Vance was born on March 4, 1893, making him 41. [*Vance actually was 43, having been born in the village of Orient, Iowa, on March 4, 1891.*] Yes, Vance has been on that mound a long time, and when the score is 1–0 in the eighth, we may understand that his old arm was tired.

Jimmy Wilson, who doesn't pause for sentiment about such things, led off the eighth with a single, then let Andy High swing instead of bunting. Andy helped Dazz by rapping into a twin killing, and it looked as if the fisherman of Homosassa Springs, Fla., would land his quarry. But George Davis slapped a two base hit into center, and Dick Bartell singled home the tying run.

It was still Dazzy's contest, but when Chiozza got another base hit, the Cards' board of strategy suggested Dazzy retire, and they called in Dizzy Dean, who usually stops the Phils by wafting his glove to the peak. This time the Phils wafted Dizzy.

He passed Moore, and then Ethan Allen raised a high, short fly behind second. Orsatti rushed in, young Whitehead dashed out, and the ball fell safe, giving the Phils two more tallies and the game.

If Frank Frisch had been playing, which he wasn't because of a stomach ache or something, he would have captured that fly and the game gone into added innings. The Phils may yet have won, but Dazzy wouldn't have lost.

This game shows how futile is this bid of the Cards. They can't go far when nobody makes a run but the pitcher. They didn't deserve to win. They are not to be taken seriously for the pennant—and since New York won while they were losing, increasing the Giant lead to 5½ games, we may as well forget all about it.

Cy Peterman, Philadelphia *Evening Bulletin*

Back in March, when there was a furore over the Cubs and Chuck Klein [*who had just been traded by the Phillies to the Cubs*], we sat fanning with Bill Terry in Miami Beach. "The Cardinals will be the boys to beat," vociferated the Giant pilot. "Klein won't bat the Cubs into the World Series. But Frankie Frisch has the pitching, the manpower. We'll beat him through spirit and fight."

Terry certainly had his situation well doped. The St. Louis club has had the man power, but it seems destined to be overcome by a superior mental attitude. The St. Louis club, having lost $100,000 in 1933, had to cut salaries. This sent the players off on the wrong foot mentally. In Florida the Cards suffered the chagrin of hearing jockeys of other teams shout, "Cheap coolie labor!"

On top of the financial situation came a certain amount of internal dissatisfaction. Some Cardinals were slow in getting over resentment born of Frisch's promotion and Gabby Street's banishment. Some pitchers did not like the "Great I Am" conversation which Dizzy Dean spilled through Florida. "I will take 25 and Paul 20, and that will leave only 50 for the other pitchers to win," said the not so goofy Dizzy. The other slingers got sore. Tex Carleton, for one, was reported to have received the Dean pronunciamento with considerable acerbity. [*Partly because of his antagonistic feelings toward Dizzy Dean, Carleton would be traded to the Cubs in the winter*]. And the other hurlers seem to have permitted their resentment to hamper their arms.

It is our impression that if Dizzy hadn't organized that series of strikes he would have had an excellent chance to pass the 30 mark in victories and perhaps win the pennant for Sam Breadon. "We have the best club in the league," Frisch told the writer recently. "But we cannot win a pennant with a strike popping up every week."

Thus we find Dizzy is a paradox. While he has kept the Cardinals in the fight, he also very likely has cost them the pennant.

Dizzy's rise has reacted badly on other members of Frisch's firing squad.

One of the hardest working pitchers in the majors is Bill Hallahan. Once when Dizzy developed a sore arm after being advertised to pitch, the announcer shouted to the customers, "We wish to apologize for pitching Hallahan." Imagine the feelings of the ever willing Bill!

While Dizzy was under suspension, he went to the press coop at Sportsman's Park and made divers announcements about certain Cardinals. Leo Durocher, who testified against Dizzy in the Landis hearing, was Dizzy's pet peeve.

Taking it by and large, it is not one big, happy family. That's why the Cards, with pitchers and man power, are chasing the Giants, with fight and esprit de corps.

Dan Daniel, New York *World-Telegram*

The National League pennant situation came under complete control at the Polo Grounds yesterday [*when the Giants won while the Cardinals were losing*]. The world's champions put the finishing touches to reinforcing their position until it was generally accepted as practically impregnable.

John Drebinger, *The New York Times*

◦ *Friday, September 14* ◦

[*On September 13, in New York, the Cardinals, in 12 innings, won, 2–0. Winning pitcher, Paul Dean; losing pitcher, Freddie Fitzsimmons. Cardinals' standing: 82 wins, 55 losses, in second place.*]

It's just as well for the Giants their name is Dean—D-E-A-N—and not Dionne! [*The highly publicized Dionne quintuplets had been born in Callander, Ontario, on May 28, 1934.*]

The two of them, Jerome Herman and Pesty Paul, are bad enough. Imagine what would happen if they used the French spelling and were quintuplets! Bill Terry wouldn't have to worry about the whereabouts of the Dodgers. His Giants would be down there with them.

If the Giants succeed in carrying their pennant lead to the October finish—they're still 4½ games in front—it won't be the fault of the Texas pitching titans. Between 'em they've toppled the Giants ten times this year, and they haven't yet pitched their last game at the Polo Grounds.

It is something to marvel at, the Deans' absolute mastery over the Giants. All either of the Deans has to do, seemingly, is to step onto the mound. Automatically handcuffs are fitted to the Giants' wrists. They're helpless, and what is worse, they know it.

Heretofore it seemed as though "Dizzy" was the more effective of the two, but there's reason today to doubt that. Paul has stepped into the shutout class himself, and just to give the performance conviction he spread the whitewash over 12 innings. [*To whitewash a team means to hold it scoreless.*]

It was a day to pitch, and the Giants' fleshy Frederick Fitzsimmons also sponsored a masterpiece. Heavy clouds hung over the ball park and shrouded it in gloom. The visibility was bad. Under the circumstances it would have been impossible to follow any pitcher's fast ball.

But that doesn't explain it all. Dean was all pitcher, and pretty much man, too. The Giants had chances to beat him. Jo Jo Moore reached third base with one out in the first inning, and in the eighth the Giants jammed the bases. Each time the junior Dean faced the power of the batting list—Terry, Ott, and Travis Jackson. He faced them, and he beat them down. There was no taint attached to his victory. It was gloriously won. In every crisis he compelled the Giant bat swinger to dribble weakly to a Cardinal infielder, usually Frisch, and that's always a mistake.

Well, today is another day and another Dean. Jerome Herman. "Dizzy," in person. Hal Schumacher will try to beat him. He should be warned to bring a couple of runs along with him.

Garry Schumacher, New York *Evening Journal*

Chicago (AP)—Commissioner Kenesaw Mountain Landis and representatives of five cities which still hope to get into the big fall show made final arrangements for the 1934 World Series.

For the first time in the fall classic's history, radio broadcasting rights were sold. The Ford Motor Company purchased exclusive radio privileges for $100,000, a sum to be divided among participating players, clubs, the commissioner, and players on teams finishing second, third, and fourth in the major league races. [*World Series games had been broadcast since 1923, but prior to 1934 they could be aired freely by any station or network.*]

It was estimated that each player on the winning team would receive $1,000 extra from the radio, the losers getting about $600.

Ticket prices will be the same as usual: box seats, $6.60; grandstand reserved, $5.50; general admission, $3.30; and bleachers, $1.10. [*For the Cardinals' most recent World Series appearance, in 1982, tickets for box seats* cost $24, for reserved grandstand seats $18. The cost of most goods and services increased from ten to twelve times between 1934 and 1982.]

The New York Times

∘ *Friday, September 15* ∘

[*On September 14, in New York, the Cardinals lost, 4–1. Winning pitcher, Hal Schumacher; losing pitcher, Bill Walker. Cardinals' standing: 82 wins, 56 losses, in second place.*]

The scholarly Hal Schumacher [*a graduate of St. Lawrence University*], who is very serious-minded on and off a baseball field, injected himself with great energy into the pennant race yesterday and promptly ended these foolish fears of recent date that perhaps another World Series will not be staged on the west bank of the Harlem this fall.

By spinning a brilliant performance and aiding the cause with a loud home-run wallop that probably was heard around both circuits, the young collegian pitched his twenty-second triumph of the campaign.

This result, widely acclaimed by a ladies' day crowd of 15,000, virtually doomed whatever lingering hopes Frankie Frisch and his crew may have entertained of snatching the pennant from the Giants.

John Drebinger, *The New York Times*

New York (AP)—At 5:16 this evening [*September 14*] a small triangular navy blue flag was run up to the top of the staff above the clock on top of the clubhouse in center field at the Polo Grounds. It told travelers on the elevated trains that the Giants had won. It is an old Harlem custom.

St. Louis *Globe-Democrat*

Bill Terry began to groom Hal Schumacher for the opening game of the World Series. The pilot of the Polo Grounders threw off all restraint and admitted that he planned to open fire on the American League champions with the St. Lawrence College alumnus.

Dan Daniel, New York *World-Telegram*

° *Sunday, September 16* °

[*On September 15, in New York, the Cardinals' scheduled game was postponed because of rain.*]

"There's only a couple of us good pitchers left," said Jerome Hanner Dean, Dizzy to you, between poker hands yesterday, "so I'm going to make 'em pay next season. I'll be the biggest, brightest, toughest holdout you ever seen. They just gotta pay me."

Dizzy had been fussy all afternoon because of the rain which had washed away the day's game. He had borrowed a fourth dollar from brother Paul and was losing it to Jesse Haines, Tex Carleton, and a couple of other Cardinals as fast as he could throw dimes into the pot.

"Look at it this way," he said. "I bring 'em into the parks, and I win games. So far I've won 25 and lost 7. Those 7 was unlucky. I expect to win 2 more and maybe lose 1. I can't see any chance of winning 30 with only 16 to play.

"When we started the season Paul and me says, 'We'll win 40 games.' We've won 41 so far and maybe it will be 45.

"The Giants are in. There's no use kidding ourselves. Paul and I will beat them tomorrow, but after that it don't matter.

"Next season? Well, like I said, I'll have to get a lot more money or I won't pitch. Another thing: I don't play if Frank Frisch don't manage. He's the greatest manager that ever was. Nobody else could of done what he done this year with a pitching staff like ours. We got two pitchers, Paul and me, but nobody else that can last five innings."

"You're up a dime," said Haines.

"I'm getting $7,500 now," said the Diz. "I'm worth $100,000 or more in a trade or a sale. If we don't get good dough next season, there will be a walkout that will make Rhode Island laugh theirselves sick.

"The four best pitchers in the National League? Warneke, Hubbell, Schumacher, and me."

"You should have named Dizzy Dean first," said the guest.

"Yeh, I should of," said Dizzy Dean.

Richard L. Tobin, New York *Herald-Tribune*

◦ *Monday, September 17* ◦

[*On September 16, in New York, before the largest crowd in the history of the National League, the Cardinals won a doubleheader, 5–3 and 3–1. Winning pitchers, Dizzy Dean and Paul Dean; losing pitchers, Hal Schumacher and Carl Hubbell. Cardinals' standing: 84 wins, 56 losses, in second place.*]

The Cardinals are gone to Boston, loaded with poignant regrets that they had not pulled together more spiritedly, that there had not been deleterious divertissements like the Dean strikes, and that they had not been able to cash in more thoroughly on their undoubted power and superlative pitching.

The Cardinals won a double-header from the Giants and made it 3 out of 4 in the final series and 13 out of 22 for the season. But with New York 3½ games in front, and only 12 more to be played, Frankie Frisch bade a sad adieu, not only to Harlem, but to the 1934 World Series as well.

For the Cardinals, those last appearances at the Polo Grounds were heartbreaking despite their success. The St. Louis players realized that their lack of cohesion and team spirit tossed the pennant into the laps of the Giants.

The outstanding feature at the Polo Grounds yesterday was not Dizzy Dean's twenty-sixth victory of the season in the first game. As a matter of fact, Dizzy left under fire and let Tex Carleton save his triumph for him.

It wasn't Paul Dean's second success of the series in extra innings in the nightcap, in which he beat Carl Hubbell in the eleventh. Since Paul pitched the opening victory, 2 to 0, in 12 rounds, in 23 innings against the younger Dean, within a space of four days, the champions of the world scored one run!

The grand feature was the crowd, the largest turnout in the history of the National League. Jim Tierney, secretary of the Giants, announced that 62,573 persons witnessed the thrillers. The Giants never before had played to more than 55,000 at the Polo Grounds.

As the Harlem plant has less than 52,000 seats, one may imagine how the 10,500 extras disposed themselves. They jammed the aisles, crowded two in a seat, and clung precariously to rafters. They stood at points from which only the home plate was visible.

At 2:30 the Fire Department ordered all gates locked. At that time more than 15,000 were trying to fight their way into the park.

When one recollects that 77,000 persons, with 25,000 turned away, saw a recent double-header between the Yankees and Tigers at the stadium, it becomes evident that New York is in the grip of its strongest baseball mania, and that the old game is making an amazing rise out of the financial slough into which it was thrown by the depression.

But for the cloudy, threatening weather, the situation would have been far more serious for police and fire officials. A hard shower drenched the park just before game time, but thousands kept crowding through all entrances.

Every element of baseball drama was jammed into the program, which wound up in the murk at seven o'clock. It was perhaps the darkest finish seen at the Polo Grounds in 20 years. At the close of the tenth inning of the nightcap, Umpire Bill Klem seemed in favor of calling it a draw, but he allowed another inning of play.

To open the eleventh, Pepper Martin crashed a home run into the lower right field stand, and Hubbell's hope for his twenty-first victory went aglimmering. The Cards then yielded the plate to the Giants. In the gathering gloom, Paul Dean's fast ball was altogether too much for them, and they were retired in order.

It was Hubbell's fourth defeat in five decisions against the Cardinals this season, and it was Paul's sixth victory over the Giants. Between them, the Dean brothers have taken 12 decisions from the New Yorks.

Dan Daniel, New York World-Telegram

Ramblings of a fascinated onlooker at the Polo Grounds yesterday: Look at that little man with the big nose in the gray suit with the red birds on the chest. Name of Martin on the scorecard. Nickname, Pepper. I remember when he was a hero. Big hero. Capital H Hero. Won a World Series single-handed. Or, rather, single-footed, when he stole the Philadelphia Athletics into a state bordering on nervous breakdown. For several days headlines five inches high shrieked "Martin," and thereafter he was never heard from again. He became just a feller playing with the St. Louis Cardinals. I suppose there ought to be a lethal chamber for heroes to repair after having performed their deeds, received their praise and acclamation, and be decently chloroformed. [*This was written before the end of the second game, which, as was noted in the preceding entry, was won by the Cardinals when Martin hit a home run in the eleventh inning.*]

Dizzy Dean is a strange-looking fellow. He has high Slavonic cheekbones and a large, big-lipped mouth which is never quite closed. He never seems to change his expression. He chews no gum or tobacco. He spits often. When he walks to the dugout after the inning is over, no one speaks to him on the way. He speaks to no one, but trudges with his eyes on the ground and his mouth open. Dizzy was interviewed before the game. He was asked what he thought of Frankie Frisch. He said, "I think Frisch is the most wonderful manager in the world."

The reporter asked, "Why, Diz?"

"Because," replied Dizzy, "he's the only man who could keep a club in a pennant fight with only two pitchers."

"Who are the two pitchers, Dizzy?"

"Me and Paul."

Three other Cardinal pitchers were standing beside him when he made this earnest statement. Maybe that is why he must pitch surrounded only by his own thoughts.

Paul Gallico, New York *Daily News*

Jerome Dean has a distorted sense of humor. It's all right to steal a rabbit's foot or tamper with a luck piece or cut the case leaf off a four-leaf clover, but when you introduce a black cat into an enemy ball park and flaunt it in front of the enemy bench, you're carrying the joke too far.

Dean is guilty on all counts. On Friday he invaded the Giant dugout with this cat, a particularly black and sinister beast. He added insult to injury by pointing its nose at second baseman Hughie Critz, an impressionable little fellow from Mississippi, and making all kinds of hex signs and mumbo passes in Hughie's direction.

"Cat, get Critz," said Mr. Dean. "Critz, get jinxed. Zmmmmm."

Mr. Critz looked around for the nearest exit and vanished into the clubhouse.

Mr. Dean seemed satisfied. "That got him," he said. "This will get 'em all."

Then Diz proceeded to walk the cat up and down the dugout in full view of the fans. Fortunately, the maneuvers of this cloddish person were in vain. Lightning did not strike the Polo Grounds, the Giants won the game, and Mr. Critz performed prodigies at bat and afield.

It seems evident that Dizzy is a psychical ignoramus, trifling with matters beyond the reach of his understanding. It might be a good idea, though, to keep him away from the Giant bench next season just in case he happens to stumble across the right word and the right cat.

John Lardner, *New York Post*

So the broadcast of the World Series has been turned into a commercial! It was a fine stroke of business for Judge Kenesaw M. Landis to sell the sponsorship to a motor company for $100,000, of which he magnanimously promised $42,000 to the players' kitty. The Judge is jubilant, the club owners are glad, though slightly sour over Landis' lavish provision for the hired men, and the players are more than elated.

The fan is skeptical about the amount of automobile palaver he will have to take with his baseball. He hopes that the sales talk will not be too long winded or obtrusive, and he wants it to be restrained.

When you listen to the radio almost any night in the week and hear gush about your Java and your gums, your neighbor's car and your neighbor's wife's furs, you wonder what the air will bring out of the Polo Grounds and Navin Field [*the Detroit ball park*]. Will automobile sales talk cut in on description of the crowd picture and discussion of strategy and technique? That is the sponsor's problem.

Meanwhile the players are tickled that each winning share will carry an added bonus of about $1,000. They vision tremendous possibilities in the future.

While players glimpse happily into the years to come, the owners no doubt are getting ready to put the clamps on the boys. The magnates believe that the players have been getting too much World Series dough, and at the joint meeting in December some owners are sure to holler for the whole air kitty.

Dan Daniel, New York *World-Telegram*

NATIONAL LEAGUE STANDINGS

	W	L	PCT	GB		W	L	PCT	GB
New York	88	53	.624	—	Pittsburgh	68	67	.504	17
St. Louis	84	56	.600	3½	Brooklyn	61	77	.442	25½
Chicago	80	58	.580	6½	Philadelphia	50	85	.370	35
Boston	71	68	.511	16	Cincinnati	50	88	.362	36½

° *Tuesday, September 18* °

[*On September 17, the Cardinals were not scheduled to play.*]

Last Sunday afternoon in the Polo Grounds there was a Frank Merriwell hero act in which a little man named Pepper Martin was at particular pains to make a bum out of me for writing that he had done with the hero business. He heroed the Giants smack out of the final game when he lined the ball into the right field stands in the eleventh inning. That was no lucky fly. That home run was hit! [*Frank Merriwell was created by Burt Standish and was a popular figure in early-twentieth-century light fiction. He was a Yale University athlete who was famous for last-minute, game-winning heroics, and so when a game of any kind was won with a spectacular play at the end it was often called a "Frank Merriwell finish."*]

And that second game was pure baseball drama, with two great pitchers, Paul Dean and Carl Hubbell, holding on to the game grimly, controlling hungry batters. Hubbell's one-run lead looked like ten. At every graceful wave of his arm enemy batsmen retired to the dugout, gnashing their teeth and looking sourly at the umpire and Hubbell. Then, suddenly Ripper Collins laced a ball on a line into the right field stands, the score was tied, the raven of darkness spread its wings over the field, and still the pitchers refused to let go.

Somehow, nothing makes the soul so sore and the brain so tired as trying to root home your team in baseball. It grew darker and darker, and the ball was growing more and more difficult to see. Dean, big and lanky, seemed to be getting stronger every minute. We cursed him helplessly. Hubbell was just as good until the gloom was suddenly split by a white streak off the end of Pepper Martin's bat, and we all simply shriveled up inside to see that ball whistle into the grandstand. THERE is the most helpless feeling. There's just nothing you can do. There was the game, except for the miracle performed in the gloom by Ducky Medwick, who went up against a sign in left field and just got his glove between the billposter and Terry's liner. What a game!

Paul Gallico, New York *Daily News*

Both St. Louis ball clubs are on the market, which is good for the game. The owners blame it on the town, but I think it would be nearer the truth if the town blamed it on the owners. Take the case of the Dean boys. Instead of being encouraged to outdo themselves as they probably would if shown the least bit of consideration, they are underpaid and treated like striking mill hands whenever the flagrant injustice of their case leads them to register a protest.

Any other club would recognize the value of this colorful brother act and pay them at least twice as much as the Cards. But the nickel-nursing Cardinal owners only look at it from the angle of how much they can save by underpaying the brothers. This case is typical of the policy followed by the two St. Louis clubs for years until they have almost succeeded in killing off baseball interest in what used to be one of the game's strongholds.

Dan Parker, New York *Daily Mirror*

∘ *Wednesday, September 19* ∘

[*On September 18, in Boston, the Cardinals' scheduled game was postponed because of threatening weather. In New York, the Giants split a doubleheader with Cincinnati.*]

New York (UP)—A proposed triple-header between St. Louis and Boston, sought by Manager Frankie Frisch, will not be allowed. The request was turned down by President John Heydler of the National League, who said his ruling was in behalf of the players.

St. Louis was rained out in Boston today and yesterday, and with 14 games to go, Frisch was anxious to get in all scheduled games in the desperate effort to overtake the Giants. The Cards play the Braves a doubleheader tomorrow and the Dodgers two games in Brooklyn Friday.

Three triple-headers have been played in the National League, the last one on October 2, 1920, between Pittsburgh and Cincinnati. The first one was held on September 1, 1890, between Brooklyn and Pittsburgh, and the other one on September 7, 1896, with Baltimore and Louisville as foes.

St. Louis *Star-Times*

The old breach between the Dean brothers and the Cardinal management has been healed. A telegram of congratulations received yesterday by Paul Dean from President Sam Breadon turned the trick. The young man read the wire, showed it to Dizzy, and the pair spent most of the day singing the praise of Breadon, Frankie Frisch, and the Cardinal organization in general.

The message read: "Congratulations on your performance in New York. A remarkable performance for a first-year pitcher. Remember me to Dizzy."

"We've had our misunderstanding," Paul said, "but, after all, Mr. Breadon is a business man, and he is grateful when you deliver. I'll bet there aren't many players who can show such telegrams from their boss."

Dizzy pranced up and down the hotel lobby, showing Paul's telegram to such pals as Burgess Whitehead, Coach Mike Gonzalez, and Frisch.

"He's a real fellow after all, that Breadon," said Dizzy.

Ray J. Gillespie, St. Louis *Star-Times*

° Thursday, September 20 °

[*On September 19, in Boston, the Cardinals' scheduled doubleheader with Boston was postponed because of rain. In New York, the Giants defeated Cincinnati.*]

Giants President Horace Stoneham and Secretary Jim Tierney are accepting ticket applications for the World Series.

Garry Schumacher, New York *Evening Journal*

° Friday, September 21 °

[*On September 20, in Boston, the Cardinals won a doubleheader, 4–1 and 1–0. Winning pitchers, Tex Carleton and Bill Walker; losing pitchers, Ed Brandt and Fred Frankhouse. Cardinals' standing: 86 wins, 56 losses, in second place. In New York, the Giants beat Cincinnati.*]

The St. Louis Cardinals maintained its slim mathematical possibility of winning the pennant by taking a double-header from the Braves behind the fine left-handed pitching of Tex Carleton and Bill Walker, who between them allowed 1 run and 12 hits in 18 innings.

The spirit and enthusiasm of the Cardinals were remarkable. Frisch had himself ejected, and there was considerable "popping off" in the dugout, not a little of it by Dizzy Dean.

Harold Kaese, Boston *Evening Transcript*

Bill Terry announced a change in his plans for the World Series after watching Carl Hubbell hang up his twenty-first victory against the Reds yesterday. Terry shifted from Hal Schumacher to Hubbell as his pitching choice for the opening game of the classic in Detroit on October 3.

Dan Daniel, New York *World-Telegram*

° Saturday, September 22 °

[*On September 21, in Brooklyn, the Cardinals won a doubleheader, 13–0 and 3–0. Winning pitchers, Dizzy Dean and Paul Dean; losing pitchers, Tom Zachary and Ray Benge. Cardinals' standing: 88 wins, 56 losses, in second place. New York won one game from Boston.*]

Those highly publicized Dean brothers lived up to every advance notice as they hurled the Cardinals to a double victory over the Dodgers at Ebbets Field yesterday. In the opener Dizzy allowed three safeties, the first coming in the eighth inning, as the Cards won 13 to 0.

Good as Dizzy was, he went into eclipse behind the extraordinary feat of his brother, who gave 18,000 fans the thrill of a lifetime, a no-hit game.

Paul's work was one point short of perfection. He issued a pass to Len Koenecke in the first inning after two were out, but thereafter the Stengel athletes marched to the plate and back again with monotonous regularity.

By taking two games while the Giants were winning one from the Braves, the Cardinals advanced to within three games of the New Yorkers.

The tension on the Cardinal bench and among the fans could almost be felt in the ninth inning of the second game. Thousands of fans rose to their feet and leaned forward to watch every move, while two or three Cardinals in the dugout could be seen holding their fingers crossed.

Stengel gave Paul no break. Casey had Jimmy Bucher, a dangerous southpaw hitter, bat for Al Lopez, and he cut viciously at the first pitch. But Paul slipped both the second and third strikes across the outside corner of the plate, and cheers cascaded from the stands.

Then Johnny McCarthy, another portside swinger, went in to bat for Ray Benge. He connected hard with the ball, and for a split second the fans held their breath. But the ball went high in the air and nestled in Frankie Frisch's glove.

Now only Ralph Boyle stood between Paul and his goal, and Buzz [*Boyle's nickname*] came close to spoiling everything. He drove a slashing grounder toward short that sizzled into Durocher's glove on the short hop, and Leo couldn't hold it. But he pounced on the ball like a cat, and his lightning throw just beat Boyle to end the game.

As Umpire Bill Sears waved high to signify the out, thousands of fans swarmed onto the field and engulfed the young pitcher. But Dizzy and several park policemen were there first and managed to clear a way for him off the field.

In winning his twenty-seventh game, Dizzy broke a mark established by Cy Young in 1899 as a Cardinal hurler to win the most games in a season. Cy won 26 and lost 15. Dizzy has lost 7.

When Paul won the nightcap it was his eighteenth victory and thus made good Dizzy's boast in the spring that "Paul and I will win 45 games."

The dizziest prophecy of all was voiced in the Cardinals' hotel yesterday morning when Dizzy said, "Zachary and Benge will be pitching against one-hit Dean and no-hit Dean today." Dizzy fell down only by allowing three hits instead of one.

Roscoe McGowen, *The New York Times*

Paul Dean, who entered baseball's hall of fame by pitching a no-hit game, was never excited or flustrated over the prospects of accomplishing the feat, he said. [*The term "hall of fame" is used here figuratively. The Hall of Fame in Cooperstown, New York, was founded in 1936. Six members of the 1934 Cardinals have been named to the Hall of Fame: Frank Frisch, Dizzy Dean, Joe Medwick, Jesse Haines, Dazzy Vance, and General Manager Branch Rickey.*]

"When did I first think about it? After the third out in the first inning," Paul said. "I said to myself as I went to the dugout, 'Well, no hits so far,' and after the second inning I said the same thing.

"Then after a couple more innings I started to talk to DeLancey about it. We're roommates, and I think a lot of him, and we told each other after each inning that there wasn't no hits yet.

"After six innings I said to Dee that if we could bear down just a little bit longer, we'd have a no-hit game for the room. Dee thought it was a good idea, and we both cut the pie at each other when Medwick goes out near the bleacher wall in the seventh and comes up with Leslie's fly, which was well rickety-cacked.

"I've hear tell that you jinx a no-hit game by talking about it, but I think that's all bunk, because somebody's sure to think about it and what's going to happen is going to happen. I never was excited about nothing. But I was pouring that ball through there in the late innings. How did you like them strikes I throwed to Bucher in the ninth inning? He ain't never saw anything I thrun."

Paul was asked if he wasn't just a little excited when McCarthy's fly settled in Frisch's glove for the second out in the ninth, and there was only one more out for a no-hit game. How would he have felt if Boyle had hit safely at that point?

"It wouldn't have bothered me none," Paul replied. "Course I was thinking it would be kinda nice to have the no-hitter, but if Boyle had been man enough to sock one I'd have taken it without crying. I wouldn't have been the first one to go that far and have somebody hit." [*On August 5, 1932, pitching against Washington, Tommy Bridges, in Detroit, had a perfect game until two were out in the ninth, when pinch hitter Dave Harris singled for the only Washington hit. On April 15, 1983, another Detroit pitcher, Milt*

Wilcox, pitched a perfect game against the Chicago White Sox for 8⅔ innings, and then he allowed a single to pinch hitter Jerry Hairston.]

Did he have more stuff than usual?

"My curve was breaking good, and as the game went along I felt looser and better. I got faster as I went along, and the funniest thing was that I wasn't a bit tired when it was over. I didn't feel like I'd done no work at all. The other fellows acted like they'd been under a great strain, and they kept a-sighing and heaving that they was glad it was over. But I didn't feel none of that. I felt like I could have pitched a couple more games. I guess my arm was just right."

What was the biggest thrill of the game?

"I got the biggest kick out of my hitting. I guess those two hits I got will knock Dizz off for a while. Did I hit those or didn't I? I never hit so good in my life. That single to right was good, but that double I larruped out there to left-center was what I got a big kick out of. Yes, sir, I guess Dizz won't talk about his hittin' for a while after those two wallops." [*This last paragraph contains just one of about ninety-seven arguments that could be leveled against that peculiar creation the designated hitter.*]

J. Roy Stockton, St. Louis Post-Dispatch

Eighteen thousand saw the Deans pitch a week-day double-header. And more than 62,000—a league record—saw the Deans win a double-header at the Polo Grounds Sunday.

And the combined salary of the Deans is still $10,500. The holdout act that Dizzy and Paul are due to stage in the spring will be what Signor Durante would call colossal. [*The reference is to Jimmy Durante, who was then at the height of his popularity, with a weekly radio show in addition to motion pictures.*]

After the firing had died down, Al Lopez put it very well in the Dodger clubhouse.

"If," he said, "there is such a thing as getting a kick out of losing, I got it today. I think we were all up there with our mouths open in admiration of the stuff those two were throwing."

"I know I was," said left fielder Johnny Frederick. "I'll swear that Paul struck me out with a fast ball that hopped a foot."

Tommy Holmes, Brooklyn Eagle

Encyclopedias listing the Seven Wonders of the World mention the pyramids of Egypt, the Hanging Gardens of Babylon, the Temple of Diana, the statue of Zeus, the mausoleum at Halicarnassus, the Colossus of Rhodes, and the Pharos of Alexander.

But not one word about the Brothers Dean.

This obvious oversight will doubtless be corrected by the next printing.

Jerry Mitchell, *New York Post*

Dizzy Dean's wife sat behind the St. Louis dugout yesterday, modestly attired in a flaming red dress. She chewed vigorously on a wad of gum throughout the double-header. Whenever her crackpot spouse got on base, he would clown around for her private amusement, and she would throw him the softest goo-goo eyes you ever did see and wave encouragement with a cigarette in her hand. Her little finger was always stuck out when she did this, proving she knows her etiquette. [*The term "goo-goo eyes," which means to look at someone lovingly, came from a popular song of 1923, "Barney Google," whose refrain was "Barney Google, with the goo-goo-googly eyes." Barney Google was the hero of a popular comic strip.*]

Dan Parker, New York *Daily Mirror*

∘ *Sunday, September 23* ∘

[*On September 22, in Cincinnati, the Cardinals' scheduled game was postponed because of rain. New York lost to Boston, reducing its lead to 2½ games.*]

"What we're trying to do is win every game possible. There won't be a letdown so long as we have the slightest chance to win. Anything can happen in baseball, and if the wind should miraculously blow our way, we'll have our sails set."

Thus spoke Frank Frisch, once known as the Fordham Flash, whose St. Louis Cardinals are still pennant-hunting. Frisch is a tough battler and a hard loser, and he has inspired his men with his own high spirit.

Frank was earnest in his praise of the remarkable work of the Dean brothers.

"Some people may think that these boys are a little erratic," he said. "But they are really as sincere, ambitious, and hard-working as any players I have ever known. Both would rather pitch than do anything else, and they are not only willing but anxious to go in out of turn to help out at any time. They are terribly hard losers, too, and I admire them for that. Too many present-day players dig up excuses and alibis when their team loses and laugh off a defeat as if it didn't mean very much. But Dizzy and Paul would rather lose a week's salary than a ball game. If all players had their winning disposition, baseball would be even better than it is."

Frisch said that only two balls were hit hard off Paul in his no-hitter. Joe Medwick made one fine catch of a hard drive, but the younger Dean needed little assistance. Dizzy might also have had a no-hit game if the Cards had not had such a big lead. He did not allow a hit for the first seven innings and would very likely have held the Stengel outfit hitless for the last two innings if he had to bear down.

The Cardinal manager says that pitching is by far the most important part of the game.

"Most critics make pitching about 70 percent of the game," he said, "but I believe it is fully 90 percent. I don't care how many good hitters and fielders are on a club, it can't win if its pitchers are knocked around every day. Give me the two Deans, Warneke, Hubbell, Schumacher, and Parmelee, and I'll be up there even if the rest of the team is second rate." [*In 1930, the Phillies had a remarkably high team batting average, .315, but because only two of their pitchers won more than seven games they finished in last place, forty games behind the league-leading Cardinals.*]

Jack Ryder, Cincinnati *Enquirer*

∘ *Monday, September 24* ∘

[*On September 23, in Cincinnati, the Cardinals split a doubleheader, winning 9–7 and losing 4–3. Winning pitchers, Jesse Haines and Paul Derringer; losing pitchers, Benny Frey and Paul Dean. Cardinals' standing: 89 wins, 57 losses, in second place. The Giants also split a doubleheader with the Braves, to remain 2½ games in the lead.*]

If Bill Terry's Giants top off the season with four straight victories, two over the Phillies and two over the Dodgers, they will win the pennant, even if the Cardinals win seven straight. And if this happens, the Redbirds will look back for many a moon at Sunday, Sept. 23, as the day they lost the flag in the second game of a double-header.

Paul Dean will tell in many a fanning bee [*an informal conversation on baseball*] how Umpire Ernest Quigley was blind, stone blind. So blind that he couldn't see a perfect third strike that Paul threw to Adam Comorosky.

A slick curve that cut through a goodly segment of the plate, a curve with such a fancy break that Comorosky was fooled absolutely. [*On this pitch Comorosky walked and later scored the tying run.*]

Other Cardinals may whisper that if Ripper Collins had made a better throw to the plate, or Frisch had made a better throw to DeLancey, or if Collins had caught a foul fly, or Durocher had handled a grounder hit straight at him, on Sunday, Sept. 23, the Cardinals might have the championship.

But the true story is one of buck ague. Once upon a time the writer was hidden on an Ozark hillside on a cold December morning. It was the first day of the turkey season, and Buddy Jimerson of Sligo, Mo., had scattered a flock of turkeys the night before, and he stationed us at strategic points and told us to be very quiet.

"Don't even move to spit," he warned us. "If you have to spit, spit on your chin. But don't move a head, ear, or whisker."

We sat until dawn, and there coming down the hollow was a turkey that looked as big as a giraffe. The writer tried to place the lip of his turkey caller on the resin-rubbed stock of his gun. The turkey caller flipped out of his hands and dropped 20 feet away. The writer had buck ague, turkey ague, or what you will.

And so it was yesterday. An enormous turkey, the championship of the National League, was strolling down the hollow that is the baseball diamond at Redland Field, and the Cardinals had a bad case of buck ague, or turkey ague.

J. Roy Stockton, *St. Louis Post-Dispatch*

The crowd of more than 13,000 yesterday got to look over both of the celebrated Deans.

Dizzy finished both games. He took up the burden in the opener after the Reds had filled the bases off Jesse Haines in the last half of the ninth, with one out, and got the side in plenty of time.

Paul broke into the picture in the second game when the Reds got too familiar with Tex Carleton in the sixth round. They tied the count, and Paul undertook to stop them, and did so capably until the ninth. Then Dizzy made his second appearance, so the afternoon was quite full of Deans, a condition which was perfectly satisfactory to the fans.

Jack Ryder, Cincinnati *Enquirer*

GIANTS REST UP FOR WORLD SERIES
Headline in *New York Post*

Two hours after they lost the second game of a double-header to Boston the Giants learned that they had been spared the brand which would condemn them as the largest flops baseball has ever known.

Last night in a Boston hotel the Giants learned that they had been kicked upstairs into the World Series. A telephone message from President Stoneham to Bill Terry, carrying the news that the Cardinals had been defeated, miraculously put $5,000 into the pockets of a couple of dozen nervous wrecks.

So the Giants are resting and preparing for the Tigers. Although the Cardinals are the best team in the National League right now, the Giants will play Detroit because they cannot possibly blow the pennant no matter how hard they try.

Stanley Frank, *New York Post*

NATIONAL LEAGUE STANDINGS

	W	L	PCT	GB		W	L	PCT	GB
New York	93	56	.624	—	Pittsburgh	72	72	.500	18½
St. Louis	89	57	.610	2½	Brooklyn	66	80	.452	25½
Chicago	82	63	.566	9	Philadelphia	54	87	.383	33
Boston	73	72	.503	18	Cincinnati	52	94	.356	37½

○ *Tuesday, September 25* ○

[*On September 24, in Chicago, the Cardinals won, 3–1. Winning pitcher, Bill Walker; losing pitcher, Lon Warneke. Cardinals' standing: 90 wins, 57 losses, in second place. The Giants did not play.*]

The National League pennant is still a possibility for the Cardinals, who trail the Giants by two games.

If the Cardinals win their remaining six games and the Giants lose one of their four contests, the race will end in a tie, and it will be necessary to play a three-game series for the championship. [*This would be the first time a play-off would decide the pennant winner in either major league. In 1908, the Giants and Cubs played their final game after the season had formally come to a close, but this was not a play-off, only the replaying of a game that had ended earlier in a tie.*]

Bill Walker turned in a brilliantly pitched game yesterday for the Cardinals' seventeenth victory of the trip against six defeats. Walker scattered 7 hits and struck out 7. The co-hero was John Leonard Martin. The Wild Horse of the Osage blasted a sky-rocket home run into the faraway jury-box bleachers in left-center in the third inning, after Leo Durocher had doubled and the two runs produced the Redbirds' margin of victory. [*After the 1931 World Series, when he ran wild and stole five bases, Martin acquired his second nickname, "The Wild Horse of the Osage." The name is actually a misnomer since Martin was born and raised in Temple, Oklahoma, which is far to the south, near Texas, and the Osage country is on the northern border of the state.*]

J. Roy Stockton, St. Louis Post-Dispatch

Little did Bill Terry think when he made his epic remark about the Dodgers that the pennant race might be decided during a New York-Brooklyn series. Yet yesterday's victory for the Cardinals virtually assured that importance to the two-game interborough rivalry which will end the Polo Grounds' season Saturday and Sunday.

"The Dodgers? Are they still in the league?" Brooklyn fans by the thousands will pour these words at Terry and his teammates unless the Cardinals fold up entirely, and with the Deans ready to go to work against the Pirates today and tomorrow not even the Giants hold out much hope of that.

Arthur E. Patterson, New York Herald-Tribune

∘ *Wednesday, September 26* ∘

[*On September 25, in St. Louis, the Cardinals defeated Pittsburgh, 3–2. Winning pitcher, Dizzy Dean; losing pitcher, Larry French. In Philadelphia, the Giants lost to the Phillies, reducing their lead over the Cardinals to one game.*]

Dizzy Dean's victory yesterday, coupled with the defeat of the Giants by Philadelphia, place the Cardinals only one game behind the world champions, and teams are tied on the losing side of the standings. The Cardinals can gain a tie if they win their remaining five games regardless of what the New Yorkers do in their contests.

Jerome Herman's triumph was a thriller, on its own merits and because so much was at stake.

Just as the game started, the scoreboard flashed the news that the Giants had suffered a defeat, meaning that the Cardinals could drive on to a pennant on their own power.

Dizzy was the right man for the assignment. He didn't feel at his best. The excitement of the pennant hunt has his nerves on edge, and before the game he said he felt ragged. But he said nothing to Frisch about it, and there was no indication of nervousness or weariness as he mowed down the enemy.

In the very first inning the Redbirds gave Dean the winning runs. With one out Rothrock grounded to short and was safe on Arkie Vaughan's wild throw. Frisch lived up to his reputation as a great money player by slamming a double to right-center, moving Rothrock to third. Joe Medwick singled to center, sending Rothrock home and Frisch to third. Then came a big break. Ripper Collins tried to draw back his bat after starting to offer at an outside pitch. The ball hit the back and sailed over first baseman Gus Suhr's head for a pop double, scoring Frisch and sending Medwick to third. Virgil Davis' long fly scored Medwick with the third run. Those runs were enough to give Dizzy his twenty-eighth win.

J. Roy Stockton, St. Louis Post-Dispatch

The Giants are in a sea of trouble—and their boat has sprung a leak!

Unhappily the Giants have little with which to win their remaining three games. They're tired and worn, their spirit has sagged. They can't hit, and their pitchers have yielded to physical weariness.

Their collapse is a baseball story unlike anything in the annals of the game. No team in major league history ever went into September with a seven-game lead and lost it. The Giants haven't done that yet, but it now appears inevitable.

Garry Schumacher, New York Evening Journal

If St. Louis wins the pennant it will be largely the fault of the New York management. It happened this way. On September 7 and 8 the Cardinals were rained out of games in Brooklyn, and as no future meetings were scheduled between the teams it looked as though the games were off the schedule. However the Phillies offered to play the Dodgers on September 20 [*instead of September 21, when the game was scheduled to be played*], leaving the next day as an open date on Brooklyn's schedule. The Cardinals having that day off, too, could play the games it had lost with Brooklyn.

The members of the league had to pass on the proposal unanimously The Giants were given the first vote and agreed to the proposal. The other teams were willing to see the games played if the Giants were, so St. Louis stopped in Brooklyn on September 21, and the Dean brothers hurled a pair of victories. Thus the Giants practically voted a full game to their closest rivals.

The Giants' motives in this matter are something to think about. Probably the New York front office thought its team was "in" and to refuse the request would be considered "small potatoes." It was a generous gesture but may have an ironic ending. Can we guess the thoughts of the Giants' players if they lose at least $3,000 each in World Series money because of the owners' decision.

Harold Kaese, Boston Evening Transcript

Leo Durocher, captain and shortstop of the Cardinals, was married today to Mrs. Grace Dozier. The ceremony was performed by Judge Edward E. Butler of the Court of Criminal Correction in the judge's office at the Municipal Courts Building.

Ernie Orsatti of the Cardinals was best man, and Miss Barbara Abner was bridesmaid. Mr. and Mrs. Carl Dubinsky took the bridal party to the court building. Spectators gathered in the judge's office were entertained by Orsatti, who juggled the small box which contained the wedding ring. Mrs. Dozier, who is a style designer, wore a black tailored gown and white ermine cape.

Both Durocher and his bride have been divorced. His former wife obtained her decree last spring on the charges of cruelty. Mrs. Dozier obtained a divorce from Vernon Dozier on Monday, charging nonsupport and desertion. They were married in 1918 and separated ten years later. [*Leo Durocher was currently twenty-nine years old.*]

St. Louis Post-Dispatch

◦ *Thursday, September 27* ◦

[*On September 26, in St. Louis, the Cardinals lost to Pittsburgh, 3–0. Winning pitcher, Waite Hoyt; losing pitcher, Paul Dean. The Giants also lost to the Phillies and maintained their one-game lead.*]

Jimmy Wilson's Phils opened the door for the Cardinals, but Pie Traynor's Buccaneers slammed it shut by blanking the Birds after Philadelphia had again beaten New York.

Even so, the Cards can reopen the door today and tomorrow if they win twice from Cincinnati, as the Giants do not play again until Saturday. St.

Louis is one game back of New York. Each has lost 58 games, but New York has won 93, the Cards 91. Therefore, if the Birds win twice they will be wrapped up in an absolute deadlock on the eve of the last two days of the bitter campaign.

Yesterday the Cardinals were restricted to two hits by Waite Hoyt, who has been pitching professional baseball since 1916, and who did not allow a Redbird to reach third base.

Paul Dean, shooting for his nineteenth decision, was erratic during his six innings on duty. He struck out seven, but twice when he appeared to have the Pirates killed off he was solved for runs.

Six hits were all the Pirates collected, as Bill Hallahan baffled them completely after Paul Dean was withdrawn for a pinch hitter in the sixth. Half of the hits were gathered by Arkie Vaughan. The Pirate shortstop gave Dizzy Dean a close call by blasting a bull's eye with a man on base in the ninth inning of Tuesday's struggle. He came right back yesterday with a single, followed by a loud double and a homer to the right field pavilion roof with Paul Waner on base, his fourth straight hit against the Deans.

Hallahan finally stopped Vaughan, but it was too late. Waite Hoyt gave no quarter. The two hits off him were fashioned by Jack Rothrock, who singled in the first and in the fourth.

Martin J. Haley, St. Louis *Globe-Democrat*

Who shuffled the Cards? Not Frankie Frisch. All he does is lead his aces. He's playing with something more potent than deuces wild, the Deans.

That, gentlemen, explains why the Cards are hot. That's why everybody asks, "How did the Cards come out today?" And next, "Who pitched?" The Deans have the public by the ears.

To many, the World Series will be an anti-climax if this stretch drive fails. Mickey Cochrane [*manager of the Detroit Tigers*] has nailed down his pennant, and so he is forgotten. Now it's Dean, Dean, Dean.

It's one of the greatest stretch drives in history. Great races are traditional in the National League, but few have equaled this. And around it all, the buzzing of the fans. Yes, they're pulling for the Cards. They want to see the Deans pitch their team to a pennant and then fire at the Tigers in the Series.

Harry Robert, Philadelphia *Evening Bulletin*

Dizzy Dean is the game's greatest showman since Babe Ruth. Has two names—Jerome Herman and Jay Hanner—in two different *Who's Who in Baseball*. It's his sense of humor. That's Dizzy. People expect him to break out in a rash of silly things when they meet him, but he's a well-behaved young man. On the Cardinals' recent trip East, three Brooklyn reporters went to him, one by one, for interviews. Very obliging, he gave each a different birthday and birthplace. Explained he wanted each to have a scoop, so he might get a salary increase. [*In point of fact, as already pointed out, he was born Jay Hanna Dean on January 16, 1911, in Lucas, Arkansas.*] He's good company. Sees a joke before it's half told, and his contagious laughter makes the joke better. He's a great mimic—can imitate all the big shots of the Cardinal organization and gives frequent one-man shows for his comrades.

He's never too busy to chat with hotel lobby fans and will give autographs anywhere at any time. He's just beginning to learn about clothes. The awkward figure of his rookie days is being transformed into a slender dude by the art of tailoring. He's also learning about money. In the old days he would buy an $80 overcoat from a fly-by-night peddler in a hotel lobby. Now the only persons he insults are those trying to make gyp sales to ball players.

If Jerome Herman had had an education, he'd have made good at anything. He's generous to a fault. If a small boy wants an autograph and has no paper, Dizz will tear off a cuff. He's quick as a trigger in the exchange of wise-cracks, has a fine co-ordination between mind and muscle, and he always has a sense of humor.

J.G. Taylor Spink, *The Sporting News*

∘ *Friday, September 28* ∘

[*On September 27, in St. Louis, the Cardinals defeated Cincinnati, 8–5. Winning pitcher, Bill Walker; losing pitcher, Paul Derringer. The Giants, idle, lead by half a game.*]

Another victory over Cincinnati this afternoon would boost the Cardinals into a deadlock with the Giants for first place.

Yesterday the Birds were outhit 13 to 7, but they profited by Cincy's mistakes and grouped their hits to better advantage. Off to a five-run lead in the first inning, when they dovetailed three hits with three errors by shortstop Gordon Slade, the Cardinals were never overtaken.

Martin J. Haley, St. Louis *Globe-Democrat*

Democracy and one man's chances being as good as another in this free country, the first thing a young man learns about the time he is scraping the fuzz off his upper lip, if he is lucky to find someone to tell him, is— never kick the office boy in the shins. You never can tell when you will come to work some morning and find him sitting at the Vice President's desk with three telephones and a beautiful blond secretary. Before the start of the current baseball season, which is winding up in the biggest thrill-finish in years, Master Will Terry, the Franken-honest man of the Giants, let fall a disparaging remark about the Brooklyn Baseball Club. The Brooklyn team was mentioned in Terry's presence, and our Will said: Brooklyn . . . Brooklyn . . . are they still in the league? The assembled reporters, with whoops of anticipatory glee, leaped into cabs and subways and made for their offices to get it into the papers.

Immediately a gentleman named Robert Quinn, business manager of the Brooklyns, began calling up newspapers, demanding retractions, demanding Terry's scalp, threatening all sorts of things. For a while it looked as though Mr. Quinn might challenge Mr. Terry to a duel. I believe he even contemplated suing Terry. We were all delighted because it looked like a swell controversy and did our best to steam it up, but it sort of died out. But Brooklyn never forgot.

Tomorrow and Sunday, New York must face Brooklyn in the final games of the year. To win or tie for the pennant, New York probably must win both. Can you see every Brooklyn batter coming to bat waving his bludgeon, mutter, "So you want to know whether Brooklyn is still in the league, do you? When we get through with you, YOU won't be in the pennant race. Bang!"

For this auspicious occasion, Master Casey Stengel has reserved Van Lingle Mungo and Ray Benge, his two best pitchers. If the Brooklyns can knock the Giants off in these games it will be the sweetest revenge for a cutting remark that any one ever heard of. Those games at the Polo Grounds will probably be two of the greatest ever played. Here is the best baseball story of the year. Of course a good deal depends on what the Cards do with Cincinnati, but if the Cards keep winning, the Giants will have to beat Brooklyn or be sunk forever. Will that be a story, or won't it?

The World Series will be an anti-climax to those two brawls at the Polo Grounds. The most rabid, vituperative, hysterical rooter in the world, the Brooklyn fan, will troop across the bridge by the thousands, bringing cowbells, sirens, razzberries, whistles. [*A razzberry is a small rubber instrument with a mouthpiece which when blown creates a sound of obvious contempt and ridicule.*] A pennant and thousands of dollars will hang on every pitch, every hit, every error, every putout. The Giants are faltering, and the

Brooklyns are frantic to get even. The big iron trough beneath Coogan's Bluff will be an absolute bughouse. Oh no, my friends, we can't miss that.

Baseball has never looked more honest than in these last few days. The Phils, seventh in the standings, with no place to go, beat the Giants out of two games, the last one a thriller won in the ninth inning. The Phils might have eased up on the Giants or put in less capable pitchers, and no one would have been the wiser. Jimmy Wilson, manager of the Phils, hates Frank Frisch and has no love for the Cards. He was doing the Cards a favor when he beat the Giants. And I never saw a team try harder to win than those Philadelphia boys.

Waite Hoyt has no love for Bill Terry. Hoyt faced Ducky Medwick, the last man up, with two on and two out the other day. Was he tempted to deviate an infinitesimal but lethal fraction of an inch in his pitch and slide one down Medwick's groove? Who would ever know? And if the Cards won, that would fix Terry. Hoyt struck Medwick out.

Boston is supposed to be a Giant farm, more or less, friendly to the Giants. But the best the Giants could do in the last series was break even with Boston. Slade's three errors in the first inning at St. Louis yesterday might look suspicious if you didn't know that Slade is a Cardinal castoff who hates Breadon and the whole St. Louis outfit and would give his eyeteeth to beat them.

You get a lot of confidence in the game when it winds up in a dog-fight like this, and the players put personal likes and grudges aside and play the best they possibly can and a little bit better.

Paul Gallico, New York *Daily News*

Casey Stengel will apply his sternest pressure to humble Mr. Terry's Giants tomorrow and Sunday. This is a personal matter with Mr. Stengel.

Probably no pair of games ever played in major league baseball could mean so much to a manager who has not enjoyed a salubrious season. In these two games, Stengel can provide an almost satisfactory substitute for a winning team. Next to the Dodgers winning the pennant, what is dearest to a Flatbusher's heart? Beating the Giants out of a pennant, of course. If Stengel can do this, all will be forgiven. Two birds with one brick, too. A jolting answer it would be to Mr. Bill Terry's scornful quip concerning the fair prestige of Brooklyn baseball.

The World Series for Brooklyn and Casey Stengel will be staged tomorrow and Sunday at the Polo Grounds.

Ed Hughes, Brooklyn *Eagle*

Times have changed for John Leonard Martin.

It seems but a few months ago, after the 1931 World Series, that the key to the city of St. Louis was turned over to the Pepper Kid. And why not? No other World Series performer had ever topped Pepper's performance. It was Martin versus the Athletics. [*Perhaps there was just one greater performance, that of the Giants' Christy Mathewson, who, in the five-game 1905 World Series, pitched three shutouts against the Athletics.*]

Martin was flooded with theatrical offers. He turned actor, and the public satisfied its desire to see him. He received huge sacks of fan mail. He could name his own fee to lend his name to suspenders, belts, cravats, overalls, and what not!

He needed police escorts. He couldn't push his way through mobs that wanted to get a fleeting glance at him.

That was in the fall of 1931. Now the curtain is up on another act. It is the fall of 1934, and for the past few months I have wondered whether or not Pepper is still in baseball. Until I heard a few rumors about him several weeks ago, I would not have been sure that he was a member of Frankie Frisch's pennant-chasing Redbirds.

Now I have heard that Martin has sulked on the job, that he has had several serious run-ins with Frisch, and that he requested the club to trade him.

I went out to run down these rumors. The Pepper Kid said he would be pleased to see me, so I called on him yesterday at the Forest Park Hotel.

I started by referring to the 1931 World Series.

"We had a great time then, didn't we?" he said. "Gee, but the folks were fine to me. Lawdy, I didn't know how to act. It sorta flustered me. All I could do was bow, thank 'em, and say, 'That's fine.'"

I wanted Pepper to feel at ease before I put over the big wallop. He reached for his cigarettes and lit one.

"I'm going to be candid, Pep," I started. "Perhaps you haven't heard the gossip going around about you."

"I ain't heard nothin' special about me," he came back.

"Well, I have," I went on. "The boys on the street have accused you of loafing. They say you've had several rows with Frisch, that you won't play any more with the Cardinals if Frankie remains as manager, and in plain words, Pep, if the club loses the pennant they're putting you on the spot."

Martin leaped to his feet, walked around the room, stood before a mirror several moments, and then went back to his chair.

"That's a lie, a gosh-darned lie," he shouted. "Who's sayin' all those things? Pepper Martin ain't never laid down. Looka here, I'll show you something that everybody don't know about."

He rolled up his sleeves.

"Feel this bump here," he said as he grabbed my hand and rubbed it over the elbow of his left arm. I felt a knot the size of an egg.

"This is what's kept me out of so many games," he said. "I twisted it early in the season and was playing when I didn't know what was the matter. I thought it was one of these 'charley horse' things and tried to shake it off. I kept on playing, and one day I slid into a bag. Gee, how my arm pained!

"The next day I couldn't bend it. It was as straight as a board. I couldn't swing a bat. I had to get out.

"I took a brief rest, and while I wasn't playing I helped the boys by pitchin' to 'em in battin' practice. Then do you know what happened? Looka here."

This time the right arm was brought into the picture. An injured muscle was bulging far out of line.

"So you see," he said, "I got two bum arms, and I've been playing for the last couple weeks because I thought I could help out toward the pennant."

Pep pulled a fresh cigarette out of the pack and walked to the corner of the room for a match. He started mumbling to himself.

"Gosh darn it, what gets into these fans when they get to talkin' like that about me?" he resumed. "I've had some hard knocks when I was a kid and before I was a ball player, and I had to fight my way to get in the big leagues, and now somebody says that Pepper didn't do his best this season."

"How about you and Frisch?" I asked. "You two haven't looked very chummy on the field."

"Me and Frisch!" came back Pepper. "It's this away with me and my managers. I've played for a lot of 'em, and it don't make no difference who's managin'. I get out there and play.

"Wouldn't I be a sap to sulk on this job? Who am I a-hurtin'? Nobody but me 'en the missus and my two little girls. If I have a bum year I don't get much money, and I'm out to get all I can because I figure I ain't gonna be playin' ball all my life."

"How does it look for the Cardinals?" I asked.

"We're out to win," he responded, "and if we take the World Series, there ain't gonna be no stage stuff for Pepper. No, sir, he's going back to God's country where they don't say he's been loafing. He's going down to south Texas to shoot deer, doves, and stone hawks and forget about baseball."

One fling at that whoopla stuff was enough for Pepper Martin. He is smart enough to realize that the fickle fans soon forget their heroes.

Sid Keener, St. Louis *Star-Times*

∘ *Saturday, September 29* ∘

[*On September 28, in St. Louis, the Cardinals defeated Cincinnati, 4–0. Winning pitcher, Dizzy Dean; losing pitcher, Benny Frey. The Cardinals were now tied with the Giants, with 93 wins, 58 losses.*]

St. Louis may be celebrating within 48 hours. The coveted National League championship became a possibility yesterday when Dizzy Dean shut out Cincinnati to send the rampant Redbirds into a deadlock for first place with the New York Giants.

The courageous Cards rubbed out the last half game separating them from the Giants as Dizzy Dean's illustrious right arm elevated his total of victories for the season to 29, giving the colorful firm of Dean and Dean 47 decisions.

Diz had only two days between starts when he worked yesterday, but the big fellow was in top form. He limited the Reds to 7 hits and struck out 7, boosting his total of strikeouts to 188, in his hot race for the strikeout crown with Brooklyn's Van Mungo.

No Cincinnati player reached third base, and not once were the Reds able to get more than one hit per inning.

While Dizzy was pitching his sixth shutout of the season, the Cardinals rolled up 12 hits. Medwick was the big gunner with a triple and two singles.

Martin J. Haley, St. Louis *Globe-Democrat*

DODGERS SET TO KICK
GIANTS OUT OF RACE AT
POLO GROUNDS TODAY

Front-page headline, Brooklyn *Eagle*

Paradoxical though it may sound, the outcome of the World Series seems far less in doubt than the result of the National League pennant race. In the series, Detroit looks like the nearest thing to a sure bet since Primo Carnera waved "Yoo, hoo!" to Big Boy Peterson. [*In January 1930, Primo Carnera arrived in New York to begin a campaign which would lead to his fighting for the heavyweight championship. During 1930, he had twenty-three matches, every one of which he won with an early knockout. Carnera's opponent in the first of these setups was someone named Big Boy Peterson, who on January 24 in Madison Square Garden was eliminated in the first minute of the first round.*]

While the Giants and Cards have worn their nerves to a frazzle in the strength-sapping struggle down the home stretch, the Tigers have been "in" since last Monday and have been able to relax and store up energy for the big task ahead. And so Detroit should be an almost prohibitive choice for the series.

For the Giants and Cards there will be no letup. As soon as the National League race is decided the badly used-up winner will have to run another lap around the track with a thoroughly refreshed Tiger.

It will be a bit tragic, at least on the western side of the Brooklyn Bridge, if the Giants are put out of the series by another Greater New York club. Brooklyn already has wrought havoc with its interborough rival by dropping two games to the Cardinals a week ago. If the Dodgers now bump off the Giants, a monument to Casey Stengel should be erected in the Plaza, out in dear old St. Looey. He's a Kansas City boy, anyway, and it wouldn't be out of place. The slogan at the bottom of such a granite shaft might well be: "Pardon my Brooklyn axes." The ax-grinding will start at three o'clock today, and you can bet all the kreplach in Canarsie that them there Dodgers will be bearing down.

Out in St. Louis, the Cardinals suddenly have discovered that the Dean boys are an important asset. Frankie Frisch says he will pitch no one but Dizzy and Daffy until the flag is either clinched or lost. If they win the pennant for St. Louis, the Dean boys, you may be sure, will be handsomely rewarded. Sam Breadon probably will give them a day's rest before the World Series, a pat on the back and two of the best five-cent cigars that can be bought in St. Louis.

Dan Parker, New York Daily Mirror

BALLAD OF BITTER WORDS

Why, Mister Terry, oh! why did you ever
Chortle the query that made Brooklyn hot?
Just for the crack that you thought was so clever,

Now you stand teetering right on the spot!
Vain was your hope they forgave or forgot;
Now that you're weary and bowed with fatigue,
Here is the drama and this is the plot:
Brooklyn, dear fellow, is still in the league.

Sir, if they can they will blithely dissever
Giants in segments unequal or not.
Homicide, Bill, is their plan and endeavor;
Starting on Ryan and Jackson and Ott,
You they expect to reduce to a blot.
La guerre a la mort! (Or in German *"Der Krieg!"*)
Vengeance they want to the ultimate jot:
Brooklyn, dear fellow, is still in the league.

Detroit awaits you? Says Lopez: "Ah, never!"
Pennant for Terry? Says Casey: "What rot!"
Using your scorn as a club or a lever,
Brooklyn will labor and chisel and swat.
Prize in the bag—now it may go to pot!
(Furnish sad music by Haydn or Grieg),
Bill, you won't like it a bit or a lot;
Brooklyn, dear fellow, is still in the league.

L'ENVOI

Bill, get out the bandages; set up the cot;
Trouble looms up in this bitter intrigue.
Stengel is handing out powder and shot:
Brooklyn, dear fellow, is still in the league.

By this time Bill Terry may have some vague idea that the hand of fate is clutching at his epiglottis. His temperature is high; his pulse is low. He spoke some words in jest early last spring, and now they will be flung in his teeth in wrath. The Brooklyn cry is: "Revenge, doubled in spades!"

The Giants have defeated the rollicking Dodgers 14 times in 20 combats this season. Ordinarily they would like nothing better than a short, merry series with Casey's clan. But it's different now. In fact, it's dismal. The Giants have been jittery for a week or more. The way they were playing when last seen in action, they couldn't catch a sofa pillow thrown from a height of six feet, especially if someone said "Boo!" as the pillow was tossed.

They had the prize package in their hands and they dropped it. In trying to pick it up, they have merely been kicking it around. They might have done better in some recent games if they had worn their gloves on their feet. They clattered apart like the old deacon's Wonderful One-Hoss Shay. They couldn't hit. They couldn't field. They didn't run the bases. [*In Oliver Wendell Holmes's "The Deacon's Masterpiece," he described a shay that had lasted for a hundred years, and then,*

> *You see, of course, if you're not a dunce*
> *How it went to pieces all at once,*
> *All at once and nothing first,*
> *Just as bubbles do when they burst,*
> *End of the wonderful one-hoss shay,*
> *Logic is logic. That's all I say.]*

Now the delightful Dodgers are about to open fire with malice propense, compounded quarterly since last February when Bill Terry attempted to rub out Brooklyn with a devastating phrase.

This is bound to be a hard series for the Giants, because each time a fielder reaches for a bounder or tries to peer at a curve he will have spots before his eyes—large spots, like five-dollar bills in packages. An infielder is bound to say to himself, "If I miss this, I'm missing four thousand in cash."

But the delightful Dodgers have nothing to worry about, nothing to do except haul off and take swats at the man who insulted them. Their slogan is, "One for all and all for fun!" Stand clear of the firing.

John Kieran, *The New York Times*

It is amazing—the attitude New York City has taken toward the Giants' desperate battle to save the pennant. Instead of rooting for them, three-fourths of the fans are laughing at them. I can't understand it.

Admitting that Bill Terry is not the most popular pilot in baseball, that he has been guilty of a lack of tact, this still is your town and my town, and the Giants are your ball team and my ball team.

These are the New York Giants, who have been through the years a terrific advertisement for the City of New York.

Say "Giants" to the average American citizen, and the first thing he thinks of is New York. Say "New York Giants," and he is quite likely to murmur "and John McGraw." Like 'em or despise 'em, it was hard to ignore the Giants when McGraw was the man.

Are there no Giant rooters left? Have we grown too metropolitan to pull for our town? Has the Old Guard surrendered, or is it dead? Where are you, George M. Cohan? Where are you, Jack White? Where are you, Billy Moore? Where are you, Snuffy the Cab Driver? [*These were New York "men about town," who were well-known Giant rooters.*]

Those are the Giants out there in the darkening shadows of your own Coogan's Bluff.

Come on! Come on!

Bill Corum, New York *Evening Journal*

◦ *Sunday, September 30* ◦

[*On September 29, in St. Louis, the Cardinals defeated Cincinnati, 6–1. Winning pitcher, Paul Dean; losing pitcher, Paul Derringer. In New York, Brooklyn defeated New York, 5–1. St. Louis thus took over first place for the first time since June 5.*]

BROOKLYN DODGERS 5; NEW YORK GIANTS 1
ST. LOUIS CARDINALS 6; CINCINNATI 1
YES, INDEED, MR. TERRY, THE DODGERS STILL ARE IN THE LEAGUE.

front page headline, Brooklyn *Times-Union*

Those amazing Cardinals have done it. They are in first place alone, a game ahead of the Giants, and Frankie Frisch's men need only one more victory to clinch the championship.

Paul Dean, working with only two days' rest, scattered 11 hits so effectively that the Reds manufactured only one run.

Cheered by a ladies' day crowd of 23,041, Paul Dean hurled brilliantly as he racked up his nineteenth triumph of the season, but it was a team victory. The Cardinals played as a team inspired. Frankie Frisch made seemingly impossible stops, Martin was a stone wall at third base, and Leo Durocher a nimble cat at short, pouncing on everything.

J. Roy Stockton, *St. Louis Post-Dispatch*

They take things very matter-of-fact, these Cardinals. It might be assumed that after their victory, with the knowledge that the Giants had been defeated, there would be wild scenes of joy in the clubhouse. There was nothing of the sort. When Paul Dean walked in, many players shook hands with him and said, "Nice work, Paul." Manager Frisch entered and went through the same ceremony, even pronouncing the same words. Paul, in turn, thanked each of the men who congratulated him and said, "Nice work."

In one corner, Pop Haines expressed his satisfaction by repeating the phrase, "Whatta nine, whatta nine." Pepper Martin said nothing, but his grin was face wide as he prepared for his shower. Dizzy Dean contented himself with patting brother Paul on the back and then opined confidently that if the Cards "gimme a couple or three runs, there ain't goin' to be any play-off."

Manager Frisch was very quiet. In a few words he thanked everybody for their efforts.

There was no cheering, no jumping about, no horseplay. There still remained another game, and the boys were still serious. Not a mention was made of what the World Series might mean; everyone concentrated on the final game of the season.

It was a surprising demonstration or, rather, lack of one.

James M. Gould, *St. Louis Post-Dispatch*

In baseball history, the 1934 season probably will go down as the year in which Bill Terry asked if Brooklyn still was in the National League.

Hugh S. Fullerton, Jr., New York *American*

∘ *Monday, October 1* ∘

[*On September 30, in St. Louis, the Cardinals won the pennant by defeating Cincinnati, 9–0. Winning pitcher, Dizzy Dean; losing pitcher, Si Johnson. In New York, Brooklyn won again.*]

St. Louis is supreme in National League baseball, thanks to the most spectacular drive in the game's long history. This sensational charge ended in a delirium of joy before 37,402 shrieking fans at Sportsman's Park at 4:41 yesterday afternoon, when Jerome Herman Dean won his thirtieth game of the season. The Cardinals finished two full games in front of New York. This year's race was the hottest right down to the wire since 1908, when the Cubs won a protested game from the Giants to decide that year's marathon, and strangely enough the Cardinals will clash with Detroit in the World Series, just as the Cubs of 1908 fought out the fall classic with the Bengals.

'Twas altogether fitting that Dizzy Dean should pitch the Cardinals to their decisive conquest on the final day, the same Diz who launched the campaign in April with a win over Pittsburgh. Dean became the first National League pitcher to win 30 games in one season since Grover Cleveland Alexander won 30 in 1917. [*No National League pitcher has won thirty games in one season since 1934. In the American League, Denny McLain won thirty-one games in 1968.*]

Martin J. Haley, St. Louis Globe-Democrat

Dizzy Dean became King of St. Louis yesterday.

His citadel was the spike-scarred mound of the diamond, his scepter was the blinding streaks of white fire issuing from his right hand, his populace a roaring throng of 37,402 persons filling every seat at Sportsman's Park and overflowing into aisles and ramps.

Never did King Arthur and his knights of the round table, even in their quests for the Grail, bring forth the popular acclaim that befell King Dizzy and his eight colleagues.

As the shadows lengthened and the game drew to a close, the Cardinals were accomplishing "the impossible." Attention was focused on the solidly built young Oklahoman, whose brilliant denouement of a brilliant season lacked only the factor of suspense to complete an Horatio Alger story. [*A popular late-nineteenth-century writer, Horatio Alger wrote many stories about poor boys and young men who overcame impossible odds to achieve spectacular success.*]

Inning after inning passed, the St. Louisans building up a substantial score, the Reds hanging up a row of goose eggs [*scoreless innings*]. The crowd felt that victory would be incomplete without a shutout for Dizzy.

Periods of spasmodic cheering were followed by what might be regarded as near silence. Finally, with the score 9–0, the ninth inning was at hand. The first three Cincinnati men got on base—the crowd and Dizzy got their dander up. A tremendous roar went up as the next man fanned. With two strikes on the following batter, and with the crowd roaring its heart out, attention went to the scoreboard. New York had lost! Now even a louder roar. Still a much louder roar came when Dizzy the King put a third strike against the batter. A pop-up and the game was over.

Many in the crowd found their eyes moist at the end. Many voices were hoarse. The crowd stood at attention, few of its members turning immediately toward the exit. Cowbells, whistles, and shouts set up a terrific bedlam. Outside, bells and automobile horns were heard.

Meanwhile, King Dizzy was besieged by teammates, six or seven trying to shake his hand at the same time. A group of policemen and firemen rushed out and formed a cordon about him and hustled him away to the showers.

Thousands of people surged out onto the field, many seeking autographs from players who straggled in late. Others went to the mound and rubbed their feet on the rubber from which Dizzy pitched.

A small boy in a green sweater brought out a four-pound cake of ice and placed it on the strip of rubber.

"Dizzy told me this morning to put it there after the game," he said. "Said it would be burning up if I didn't. Go ahead and feel it. Even the ice hasn't gotten it cooled down yet."

[*It should be remembered that Dizzy Dean's total of thirty victories was aided by two scorers' decisions, one of which was highly questionable. There was the game against Brooklyn on June 23, when the win was awarded to Hallahan and, several days later, transferred to Dean. And on June 27 there was the patently illegal decision to credit a victory over the Giants to Dean instead of Mooney. Dean actually should be regarded as a twenty-nine-game winner.*]

St. Louis *Globe-Democrat*

"We're in the mon—ey! We're in the mon—ey!" sang James "the Ripper" Collins when he charged into the clubhouse a few seconds after a pop foul from Sparky Adams' bat landed in Billy DeLancey's catcher's mitt to end the Cardinals' nerve-racking National League season. Jim's song may have been off key, but it sounded the Cardinals' keynote of victory. [*"We're in the Money" was a very popular song from the Busby Berkeley musical film* Gold Diggers *of 1933.*]

In they filed through the clubhouse door, a shouting, happy gang, these new league champions. Yelling? Yes—but wait, one among them did not add his voice to the pandemonium. That man was—

Frank Francis Frisch, who dropped astride a bench and sat with the look of a man off whose head an anvil had just bounced. He was bowed down.

The let-down from the strain of the pennant race had him on the ropes.

"Butch [*Yatkeman*], a Coke!" he finally called to the clubhouse boy, and thus fortified, he came to life and, while taking off his uniform, began accepting congratulations.

Dizzy Dean was among the first to grab the manager's hand, and, boys and girls, there was nothing dizzy about the greeting. They shook hands quietly, and Frank moved over to make room for Jerome Herman, and they sat talking until interrupted by photographers.

In the meantime other Cardinals shed their uniforms and hopped into the showers in the adjoining room, where songs were added to the swish of water to increase the happy hubbub. Martin, Buzzy Wares, and Medwick collaborated in the barbershop strains of "I want a girl, just like the girl that married dear old dad," with Martin taking the lead, Wares the barry, and Medwick, of all guys, the tenor!

Bronzed Mike Gonzalez was showing his teeth in a wide grin that wouldn't come off. Also beaming was big Dazzy Vance, who, in the evening of a brilliant career, was for the first time on a pennant winning club.

Jess Haines, oldest Cardinal in point of service [*in age, the oldest was Vance*], puffed a cigar. More subdued than some of the younger players, he may have been thinking of Cardinal triumphs of the past in which he played a more active role.

The noises died down when the Cardinals, in various stages of dress and undress, went into action over a national radio network, their voices going out through some 90 stations to every section of the United States.

Frisch was given an elaborate introduction, in which he was hailed as "The Man of the Hour," and then, clothed only in sincerity and an undershirt, he stood before the mike, thanked the players for their support, congratulated Mickey Cochrane of the Tigers, and concluded, "May the best team win."

Damon Kerby, *St. Louis Post-Dispatch*

A little wooden table, usually reserved for jovial after-game beer parties, is in the center of the bare plank floor of the Giant clubhouse. Manager Bill Terry sat on its edge yesterday. The clubhouse window was open, and his brooding eyes looked at the crowd, a slow tide of soggy felt hats that drained out through the passage beneath his spiked feet.

"I don't know what happened," he said. "I guess the best team won. I hope the Cardinals beat Detroit. I'm pulling for them."

He spoke in a dejected mumble. The words came haltingly. A reporter tried to feed the interview by suggesting that he give a farewell message to the fans.

"Nope," he said. His lips tightened. "You can thank them if you want— not me. In the tenth inning with everything lost they booed me. I thought I was in St. Louis."

You felt sorry for him then. You excused his bitterness.

Someone mentioned Brooklyn. Bill's eyes mirrored his anger as he said, "If Stengel's team had played as hard all year as it did the last two days, it would not be in sixth place."

Terry was asked if he would go to Detroit.

"Nope," he said. "It would be humiliating."

In the Dodger clubhouse the din was deafening. Casey Stengel, clad in a bath towel draped diaper-fashion about his hips, was delivering the general's farewell to his troops. His voice was hoarse from its duties in the coaching box. [*In the thirties, and for some time thereafter, nearly every non-playing manager was also his team's third-base coach.*] His arms threshed wildly.

"Farewell, my bonny men. Some of you are off to maim the gentle rabbit. Some of you will shoot the carefree deer. I bid you Godspeed, my lamby-pies, my brave young soldiers. Go with Casey's blessing upon your sweet heads."

Someone interrupted to report Terry's remarks. Stengel grinned. "So he feels bad, eh? How do you think I felt when he made fun of my ball club last spring?"

Casey hooked his finger into the air in the fashion of Demosthenes delivering a phillipic. "So he says if we had played hard we wouldn't finish in sixth place? Well, if the season lasted another month and we kept playing him he'd finish in last place!"

The Dodgers cheered to the echo.

Casey continued: "He's feeling bad, eh? Well, I'm feeling bad, too. I didn't get any World Series pay check, either. I wish I had his money. They could boo the ears off me. You've got to learn to take it in this business."

Casey held up his hand for attention.

"Just a minute, gentlemen of the press," he said. "Those were Brooklyn fans who did the booing. There isn't a finer, sweeter, better gentleman or lady on God's green footstool than a Brooklyn fan. Three cheers for the Brooklyn fans, my hearties, and"—he turned to glower savagely—"the first mug that doesn't cheer gets a kick in the shins." The entire company cheered.

Jimmy Powers, New York *Daily News*

Said Casey Stengel, "The Giants thought we gave 'em a beating Saturday and yesterday. Well, they were right. But I'm sorry for them when I think of the beating they still have to take. Wait until their wives realize they're not going to get those new fur coats. I've been through it, and I know."

Tommy Holmes, Brooklyn *Eagle*

FINAL NATIONAL LEAGUE STANDINGS

	W	L	PCT	GB		W	L	PCT	GB
St. Louis	95	58	.621	—	Pittsburgh	74	76	.493	19½
New York	93	60	.608	2	Brooklyn	71	81	.467	23½
Chicago	86	65	.570	8	Philadelphia	56	93	.376	37
Boston	78	73	.517	16	Cincinnati	52	99	.344	42

[*In the second entry for March 14, Dizzy Dean was quoted as saying, "It will require about 95 games to win the pennant, and the Giants can't take that many. That's why we will win." At that time Dizzy also said that he and his brother together would win between forty-five and fifty games. In fact they won 49. Dizzy Dean, incidentally, was tops among pitchers in strikeouts for the year with 195, while Paul Dean, with 150, finished in third place behind Brooklyn's Van Mungo. As for the other Cardinals, Rip Collins batted out 35 home runs to tie Mel Ott for the league lead in that category; Joe Medwick hit the most triples, 18; and Pepper Martin led all base stealers with 23 thefts.*]

∘ *Tuesday, October 2* ∘

"We're gonna win," shouted Dizzy Dean, as he playfully pummeled brother Paul on the rear platform of the Cardinal special just before it left Union Station last night bound for Detroit.

Long before the time of departure, 7:30, the midway around the entrance to the train shed was jammed with people trying to get a glimpse of the Redbirds.

The players, some accompanied by wives, arrived singly and in twos and threes. Dizzy, Mrs. Dean, and Paul arrived about 7 o'clock, but Dizzy had to dash out to a restaurant for something to eat. He appeared in excellent spirits, posed for photographers after he had a sandwich, and kidded Paul when the youngster was hauled out from a car to pose.

Joe Medwick, with his bull dog pipe, Chick Fullis, Ernie Orsatti, Leo Durocher and Mrs. Durocher, and Virgil Davis stood around outside the train until the last minute.

Bill Hallahan, of the pugnacious chin, was quiet, as usual. Asked how he felt, Bill replied, "Swell. My left arm feels great, and you can bet if I get in there I'll bear down with every pitch."

Frank Frisch showed the effect of the strain he has been under. He appeared tired, and his face was haggard. But a couple of nights' rest, and Frisch will be ready to do.

W. J. McGoogan, *St. Louis Post-Dispatch*

Detroit—Frank Frisch, cold to this whoop-de-do stuff, slumped in his Pullman seat riding over from St. Louis. Others were singing and shouting—cutting up like a bunch of young college boys. Frisch grunted.

I asked the Fordham Flash, "How did the Cardinals put this over?"

"I'm glad you asked," he replied. "Sit down. I'll give you some inside stuff. We won this pennant because I wouldn't let the fellows give up. There are times during a season when a player loses his fighting spirit. That's when the manager enters the scene."

Dizzy Dean strutted down the aisle and gave Frisch a friendly jolt against the ribs.

"Look at Frankie, boys," shouted Diz. "Deep in thought again. Don't worry, Frank, we'll win the Series for you."

Frisch gave Diz a short nod and advised him to "keep moving."

"Where were we before Diz interrupted us?" picked up Frankie. "Oh, yes, about managing the club. I kept after them day after day. I guess they thought I was pretty tough. Well, I was.

"I couldn't afford to let them go into a tail-spin. My job was to keep the fellows moving. I had to jack them up. I had to keep after Joe Medwick about playing in certain spots in left field. I had to keep talking to Jimmy Collins. I had to do this and that.

"When we'd lose, they'd come into the clubhouse filled with gloom. They'd moan in the hotel lobby that night. They'd come to the park the next day cussing about the line drive that was caught. They'd be ready to sag. I had to hold 'em up.

"'We ain't going to win the pennant if we continue beefing about bad luck' is the way I'd talk to the boys.

"In the first week of September we lost a double-header to the Pirates. That was the end of the pennant boom, most everyone believed. The players were ready to give up. I never saw such a dejected bunch of athletes as my boys riding into New York. I sat alone. I was hot—I was boiling. I realized that this wasn't the time to chuck it up."

Frisch pounded his fist on the window to emphasize his words.

"I sent orders to the players that we would hold our meeting [*on September 5*] in the Brooklyn clubhouse one hour earlier than usual," said Frankie. "I burned them like they'd never been burned before. 'Are you fellows going to quit?' I shouted. 'It ain't over. If you fight to the finish, we won't be beaten.'

"The change was remarkable. They started kicking the benches. They dressed with fire in their eyes.

" 'We ain't givin' up, Frankie,' growled Dizzy. 'I'm pitchin' today and I'll show you we ain't beat.'

"I can hardly describe the change in my club. From then on they were a great club. There you have the Cardinals. They tried to count us out when we were seven games behind the Giants on September 6. We wouldn't be counted out.

"That's why we won the pennant."

Sid Keener, St. Louis *Star-Times*

∘ *Wednesday, October 3* ∘

Detroit, Oct. 2—All the old-time glory of the World Series blazes again.

All the old-time romance and color and tradition have suddenly been revived after a long stretch of pallid, perfunctory presentations of baseball's biggest event.

A new, livelier background of action, with new characters spreading over the scene with grandiloquent words and gestures, has brought back to America's national pastime, and its autumnal struggle, all the ancient splendor and excitement of bygone years when no other sport greatly concerned the nation.

Here in Detroit is the World Series as it ought to be.

Here, on the evening before the opening game, crowds wait at the ball yard gates, crowds hang around the hotel entrances and jam the lobbies, arguing baseball to the point of acrimony. The whole city is alive, personally interested, boiling with civic pride, hoping for a massacre of the St. Louis Cardinals.

And this is the way it ought to be.

Damon Runyon, New York *American*

Detroit, Oct. 2—Like the Brothers Romulus and Remus, who drank a breakfast of wolf milk on the banks of the Tiber and proceeded to go

places and do things, the Brothers Jerome and Paul Dean early this morning detrained, sipped orange juice in a hostelry on the Detroit River, and
then proceeded to take charge of this bunting-draped, horn-blowing, fan-
infested Mecca.

The two brothers, the most sensational adolescents to bounce into baseball headlines in this generation, literally held the sole attention of this
cock-eyed village. Schoolboy Rowe? [*Detroit's leading pitcher, Lynwood
Thomas Rowe, had 24 victories, including 16 in succession, tying an American League record. He was known as "Schoolboy" because he had signed his
first professional baseball contract while he was still a high school student.*]
Frankie Frisch? Mickey Cochrane? You ceased to think or hear of them.
The Deans were the story. Whither they went there immediately followed a
siren-shrieking squad of police cars, a clattering escort of stick-swinging
mounted patrolmen, and a surging, ogling crowd of fans.

Out to the ball park for practice. Back to the hotel for food. Through
the streets, bucking in and out of taxis, popping up and down elevator
shafts, the two brothers went, mutually advising, congratulating, and supporting each other.

Both have rich, deep voices. Simultaneously they rear back their heads
as some happy thought strikes them and their hearty laughter echoes in the
frosty air that blows off Lake St. Clair.

The sky darkens. The street lights bloom. Calliopes parade the downtown district playing "The St. Louis Blues." The Deans lean out of the
window to jeer, and instantly traffic below snarls so tightly a call goes to
the harried neighborhood precinct captain for more reserves.

Mob hysteria is so great the very window panes rattle as one sits and
watches while the teeming sidewalk procession, with hallowe'en fanfare
and horns, passes in raucous review. Scalpers are reaping fortunes, hotels
are bedlam, highways are thronged, trains disgorge an increasing stream of
soot-dusted fanatics.

The Deans are on every lip. Vaudeville actors insert allusions to them in
impromptu acts, movie organists compose parodies of popular songs in
their honor. The papers carry headlines of the size usually employed to
announce a declaration of war. They tell hourly bulletin movements of the
two grinning, roistering, record-breaking farmer boys.

Dizzy didn't put on a uniform today. At the ball park he picked up a
bat, walked to the plate, and hit a couple. He removed his coat and hit a
few more. He took off his vest after that and continued hitting. Then he
picked up his garments and walked away as if he was just having a good
time. Because he didn't put on a uniform proved to the experts that Frisch
had told him to get all the rest possible before tomorrow afternoon. How-

ever, the effervescent Dizzy was a great lobbyist during the day. He made predictions and autographed everything but the paintings on the wall of his hotel.

Jimmy Powers, New York Daily News

Grace, beautiful blond bride of a week of Leo Durocher, has already taken charge of the family pocketbook.

Leo, with his smiling bride always at his elbow, was going through the hotel lobby promising to buy every friend he met a hat if the Cards didn't win the Series.

Finally the little bride whispered, "Listen, honey, don't you think you'd better go slow on those hats? Hats cost money and it's a long winter, and you know, darling, you might lose."

Leo sheepishly agreed to forego the promises.

St. Louis Post-Dispatch

An army of dyed in the wool fans from Maine to California laid siege to Navin Field Tuesday night.

Three thousand bivouacked around the four walls of the baseball arena in preparedness for the onslaught on the ticket windows, from which 20,000 bleacher seats will be sold Wednesday morning for the first World Series game.

They came with box lunches, camping equipment, blankets, riding breeches, boxes, crates, and folding beds.

Cribbage, pinochle, poker, and even bridge were played to while away the time until finally they spread blankets on the damp, grassless ground and lay in fitful sleep.

Hawkers yelled their wares, sandwiches, coffee, peanuts, candy bars, and box lunches.

Crude chairs made of four sticks were sold for 25 cents each. Bushel baskets, vegetable crates, pop and beer bottle cases, and boxes of every make and description were sold for 15 to 25 cents for use as seats.

Pictures of the Tigers, ready for framing, were retailed at five cents each, while two intrepid fans, the first to be in line, were selling their own photographs for a thin dime.

Women were among the fans in the ticket line. They laughed, played cards, asked to have their pictures taken, and then powdered their noses.

Because of the temperate weather many did not bother to bring blankets. In fact some preferred to spread the blankets on the ground and catch a few hours of rest rather than use them for warmth.

Throughout the night the badges of Detroit's police glistened as they kept watch. The officers paced back and forth and protected the walls so none could climb them before the ticket windows opened.

John Wagner, Detroit *Free Press*

° *Thursday, October 4* °

[*On October 3, in Detroit, the Cardinals won Game 1 of the World Series, 8–3. Winning pitcher, Dizzy Dean; losing pitcher, General Crowder.*]

The magic name of Dean, rather than any magic exhibited by Dizzy, beat the Detroit Tigers in the first game of the World Series. Dizzy pitched a fair game of ball. The Tigers played an atrocious game of ball. Dizzy tossed his glove on the mound, as the saying is, and the Tigers were licked. Awed by his presence, they went to pieces early in the game, committed five costly errors, and gave the Cards such a commanding lead that when they began to find themselves it was too late.

If the strategy was to concede the first game because Dizzy's name was at the bottom of the lineup, Cochrane and the boys made a complete job of it. But Mickey was wrong in assuming there was no chance of beating Dean. [*The allusion here is to Cochrane's curious decision to select Alvin "General" Crowder as his starting pitcher. Crowder had won only 9 games against 10 losses, whereas four other Tiger pitchers had 15 or more victories each, including Rowe with 24 and Bridges with 22.*] Had he started Schoolboy Rowe, he might have started off on the right foot. To be truthful, no Schoolboy Rowe was needed today. General Crowder might have done it with the same support Dizzy received. When the General went out of the game in the fifth for a pinch-hitter, he had allowed only one earned run.

The ball game was booted away in the second and third innings when the Tiger infield became so panicky they muffed easy tosses, gummed up ground balls they would ordinarily catch in their hip pockets, and made wild tosses when there was no occasion for hurrying throws. Marvin Owen, the young third sacker, started the fumbling, and soon the whole infield was seized with an attack. Gehringer dropped an easy underhand toss for a force-out. Owen made a wide toss to first. Shortstop Billy Rogell foozled an easy grounder. Then first baseman Hank Greenberg, to make it unanimous, let a grounder go through his legs.

Baseball experts agreed that Gehringer's error was the crudest misplay ever made in a World Series. Rogell, standing a few yards back of second, tossed the ball to him, underhand, for an easy force-out. Gehringer caught the ball, touched the bag, then suddenly grew panic-stricken and started to juggle the ball. Finally it dropped from his hands, and Orsatti, who had been called out, was now declared safe. This misplay sent the whole infield into the jitters. [*Ironically, Hall of Famer Gehringer is generally regarded as one of the two or three best second basemen of all time.*]

So jittery were the Tigers, they couldn't see that Dizzy wasn't at his best. Not till late in the game did it occur to them that he was in the hole with almost every other batter. He had a three-and-two count at least a dozen times. Altogether, Dean allowed eight hits and walked two. Several times Dizzy showed that his overworked arm is both tired and sore. His teammates crowded around him often in the late stages of the game, plainly worried lest he blow up.

Joe Medwick's four hits, one of them a homer, made him the batting hero. His homer was the only earned run Crowder allowed.

Frankie Frisch handled his club faultlessly. There is a vast difference in temperament between the two teams, by the way. The Tigers are high strung; the Cards, phelgmatic. Like Dean, who hasn't a nerve, even in his wisdom teeth (if any), his mates seem to regard every game as just another contest, nothing over which to get unduly excited.

Dan Parker, New York Daily Mirror

Even if Jerome Herman Dean didn't come up to expectations yesterday, he doubtless satisfied himself last night in his role of radio broadcaster to the Antarctic expedition of Rear Admiral Richard Evelyn Byrd.

"Howdy there, Dick Byrd, down at the South Pole," Dean began after a Columbia network announcer made an introduction and explained that Dizzy would give "the inside story of today's game."

Dean spoke as though addressing an old Yell County, Ark., friend of boyhood days instead of a Rear Admiral with as many decorations as he had winning games this year.

"Well, it was a hard-pitched game," Dizzy said. "I didn't have anything on my ball. That's why I had to work so hard. I finally staggered through. But it was a lousy, tick-flea-and-chigre-bit ball game.

"Them Tigers wasn't so good as I figured they belonged to be. Why, I could take any of four National League teams and beat 'em for a World Series—if I pitched."

Asked about Mickey Cochrane's judgment on his pitching selection, the irrepressible Dean replied, "Mickey used good gumption. You see, he knew if I was at my best, nobody could beat me. So he saved Schoolboy Rowe for another game instead of puttin' him against me like I would have admired to have him done.

"But I'd be tickled plumb pink to pitch tomorrow again. I'd have my stuff I know and I'd shut Detroit out. If they'd let me pitch all the games, I think I could probably win all four."

St. Louis Post-Dispatch

Detroit, Oct. 4—Dizzy Dean is beyond doubt the most entertaining character baseball has seen since the mighty Ruth came tramping up the road to fame.

Which reminds me that he telephoned Ruth yesterday morning, and here is a rough transcript of their conversation.

"Hello, is this Mr. Ruth?"

"Yes, this is Babe."

"Say, Mr. Ruth, this is Dizzy Dean. I just called up to say hello and to thank you for putting me on your All-American team this year. I sure was proud of that, and I don't know how to thank you enough, Mr. Ruth."

"Aw, that's all right, kid, you deserved to be there. What the hell, you deserved to be on there, kid."

"Well, thank you. I just wanted to say hello, Mr. Ruth, and thank you."

"That's all right, kid, I'll see you at the game."

"You mean you'll come in the clubhouse. Gee—"

"No, I won't be in the clubhouse, but I'll see you on the field."

"That'll be swell, Mr. Ruth, but I wish you'd come in the clubhouse if you get a chance."

"I'll be seeing you, anyhow, kid, and though I'm an American Leaguer, good luck."

"Gee, Mr. Ruth, that's swell. I'll be seeing you out there."

Babe was much surprised at Dizzy's calling him Mr. Ruth, and I print this conversation to try and give you a little clearer idea of what Jerome Herman really is like. So many people have him wrong.

His boastfulness is not annoying. But he does talk freely, and if he thinks he can win 30 games or that he and Paul together can win 45, or that he could pitch 4 straight games in this series, well, then, he just pops up and says so.

Bill Corum, New York *Evening Journal*

Dizzy Dean pulled a couple of his pet tricks yesterday. One was winning a ball game. Another was sending a telegram—collect.

Branch Rickey, kept in St. Louis by business, wired Dizzy his congratulations. He also invited the Deans to be his guests at a party Friday night along with other notables. Here's Dizzy's reply:

"Many, many thanks. This American League is a pushover. Breezed through today with nothing but my glove. If possible, have Dad on airplane in time for game tomorrow. Wire time of arrival. Tell everybody hello. Henry Ford will be my guest in St. Louis Friday. Cook a good meal for all of us—sandwiches and everything. Will Rogers and Joey Brown [*the film actor, Joe E. Brown*] coming, too. Thanks again."

Dizzy's father, en route to St. Louis by bus, was reported crossing Texas last night, so there is no likelihood of his seeing today's game.

St. Louis *Globe-Democrat*

To a stranger unaware of what was going on Wednesday, the downtown area of Detroit was not Detroit the Dynamic, but the Deserted Village.

For three hours—between one and four o'clock—the business district resembled siesta-hour in a Central American town. Nobody worked. Doormen stood in front of theaters trying to look as important as their uniforms indicated. [*At that time, uniformed doormen stood before all downtown motion picture houses.*]

Almost the sole center of humanity was the parkway in Washington Blvd., where some 4,000 fans watched an electrical scoreboard portray bad news. The only time that sea of sad faces was rippled with a wave of laughter was in the third inning when it appeared that the Tigers might stage a rally. At that point, women hugged one another and danced in the street, and men clapped one another on the back. By the curb, four Negro boys, equipped with one guitar and four excellent voices, broke into white-toothed grins and slid into an enthusiastic rendition of "Tiger Rag" in the manner of the Mills Brothers. The crowd joined the quartet, but the enthusiasm was soon doused, and the pall of gloom again descended.

[*The Mills Brothers began to sing professionally in 1922, when they were still children. Their first hit record was "Tiger Rag."*]

Shoe shining establishments were exceptionally popular. The reason was twofold. Every bootblack is an ardent Tiger supporter who follows the proceedings via the radio. When the "breaks" went against the favorites, the "Nicks" and "Georges" worked out their anger on the customers' shoes, and there were plenty of deluxe shines given out.

The consensus of sidewalk fans was, "Now that the fearsome 'Diz' has done his stuff, the Tigers will get down to baseball as usual."

Detroit *Free Press*

Detroit, Oct. 4—Mrs. Patricia Dean, wife of the Cardinals' pitching wonder, curled up in pajamas in her hotel suite and talked about the most talked-about man in baseball.

"I wish you could know Dizzy as I do! He's the sweetest kid in the world. Only when he gets home does he let down. When he comes to the door I get him right to bed. In one game this summer he lost 12 pounds. Whenever he pitches, I make him rest at least an hour before he has supper.

"I have to watch every mouthful he takes and make him eat. I sit over him at breakfast until he has cleaned up his plate, and I feed him cod liver oil all the time. I sometimes wonder if fans realize what pitching a game means to a pitcher.

"Yes, Dizzy's wonderful. We've been married four years. I'm two years older than he, and to me he seems like a little boy. His mother died when he was four. His family was terribly poor, lived on a farm, near Holdenville, Ark. Many a time they did not have enough to eat. And he didn't have any clothes except a pair of overalls. He never went beyond the fourth grade.

"His dad has often told me about the baseballs Dizzy made when he was a kid. He used a stone for the center and wound it with a string or unraveled an old sock to wrap the stone. That's the kind of childhood Dizzy had—no money for such things as baseballs. The bat was a stick he cut himself in the woods and whittled down smooth.

"I've been pretty close to tears when I think of that little gawky boy throwing homemade baseballs at his baby brother. He was just a gangling youngster. When he was 15 he lied about his age and got in the army down in San Antonio. A lot of the boys he soldiered with told me about him.

"The orneriest, laziest kid in the outfit, they said—and then they put him to playing baseball. That was his first competitive game, in the army. He took to it like a duck to water. The rest you know. Farmed out by the Cardinals—and then this sudden fame. Now you understand why I could never let anything happen to Dizzy. He's got to have some happiness, some security."

Mrs. Dean turned a new carat and a half diamond on her finger.

"It's my 'pennant trophy,'" she said. "Dizzy got it last week, and it celebrates a lot of things besides the victory. In the first place, we just paid off the last of the mortgage on our home in Bradenton, Fla. It is free and clear. That is one thing we've worked for. We have annuities and government bonds! Dizzy is never going to be a 'has-been' pushed about as a down-and-outer!

"I wouldn't let Dizzy buy me a ring when we were married—I said no ring until our home is paid for. And here's the ring. Isn't it beautiful?

"When we were first married, Dizzy got $3,000 a year and we saved $1,800. I did my own washing and cleaning, and was glad to do it. Now we have our home! That means as much as the pennant to us. It's been a hard road up for Dizzy. Just look at his hair some time. He's only 23, and he is almost white. He won't last more than five years at the rate he's going, and I want to make those five years glorious.

"Sometimes, if Diz gets a little obstreperous, I just say, 'Diz, you're the world's greatest pitcher on the diamond, but here at home you're just a husband.' Then he laughs and says, 'O.K.'"

Vera Brown, St. Louis *Star-Times*

◦ *Friday, October 5* ◦

[*On October 4, in Detroit, the Cardinals, in 12 innings, lost Game 2 of the World Series, 3–2. Winning pitcher, Schoolboy Rowe; losing pitcher, Bill Walker.*]

A long, lean lad from the little town of El Dorado, Ark., with fire and magic in his pitching arm, hamstrings the wild dash of the St. Louis Cardinals. Lynwood C. Rowe, called "Schoolboy," six feet four inches from head to heel and weighing 205 pounds, blinds the batting eyes of the sluggers of the Mound City after getting away to a bad start, holding them helpless until his teammates can claw their way to a tie in the ninth inning and finally to victory in the twelfth.

In the first three innings, the boy who just four years ago was pitching in a Sunday school league in Arkansas, is rather nervous, and the cocky Cardinals hammer his right-handed delivery for six hits and two runs. Then "Schoolboy" hitches up his pants, pulls the peak of his cap, and settles down.

From the fourth inning until one man is down in the eleventh, and Pepper Martin hits a double, Rowe beats back the Cardinals in amazing fashion, with Martin the only man to get on base.

In the ninth, with one out and Detroit hope at low ebb, Gerald Walker, pinch-hitting for Jo-Jo White, drives in the tying run, and in the twelfth, with Schoolboy still holding the Cardinals at bay, the veteran Goose Goslin pounds in the winning tally on the heels of bases on balls handed to

Charley Gehringer and Hank Greenberg by Bill Walker, who had succeeded Wild Bill Hallahan. Gehringer carried the mail over the pan, and Detroit went daffy.

The story of the game, despite the mighty pitching by Schoolboy after the third, should be the story of a victory for Hallahan and the Cards by a score of 2 to 0. Wild Bill allows the Tigers six hits in 8⅓ innings, then is victim of a curious happenstance.

With one out and a runner on second in the Tigers' half of the ninth, Walker bumps a foul into the air toward first, apparently an easy catch for Ripper Collins.

As DeLancey, the catcher, and Hallahan start in the direction of the ball, Collins nonchalantly waves them away. The wind takes hold of the ball and drifts it back toward DeLancey, but Collins keeps running and waving to indicate that he is in charge. Then, apparently, he takes his eye off the ball, and it drifts out of his reach to fall in foul territory. On the next pitch the pinch-hitter drives in the tying run.

Before this Rogell hits a fly to center and Orsatti misjudges the ball, a drive that Orsatti would pocket 99 times out of 100.

The luckless "Wild Bill" is long since forgotten in the wave of exciting events that follow one of the biggest baseball demonstrations in history in the ninth, when the air seems to be filled with gigantic snowflakes, appropriate enough in the temperature, as the crowd tears up newspapers and throws the pieces to the breeze—and a man collapses and has to be carried out by police—and several women faint and others are rendered hysterical—and even blasé baseball writers run the risk of tumbling off their precarious perches on the roof of the stand as they peer down into the field.

The song must be of Lynwood "Schoolboy" Rowe, not of Wild Bill Hallahan, for the world does not ask you how you won—but did you win? It cannot pause to listen to the sad, sad tale of a loser.

                                        Damon Runyon, New York *American*

Detroit, Oct. 4 (AP)—Tigertown quaked with the roar of the victors tonight. Twenty-five years of baseball emotion, checked and suppressed by the lacklustre years that followed the Ty Cobb era, exploded in grand blast as Goose Goslin rapped out the tell-tale single and Charley Gehringer came pounding home with the winning run. [*This was only the second time the Tigers had won a World Series game, and the first time they had won at home. Their other victory had been in Chicago on October 12, 1908, a Series which Detroit lost four games to one.*]

The last hit sent thousands swarming to the streets. The business life of the city stopped cold. The open windows of skyscrapers let loose a shower of ticker tape and paper scraps. Bells, whistles, horns took up the deafening refrain.

Traffic wheeled to a stop, snarled in a mass of confusion. The doors of stores, shops, and offices flew open to disgorge a swirling mass of men and women, yelling, singing, dancing in the streets.

Tiger fans at Navin Field who waited for 21 innings of play to see the Tigers out in front in the scoring, hurled everything they could lay their hands on—hats, bottles, cushions, and papers. They swarmed across the field and out through the exits to join the roaring crowd in the streets.

The New York Times

Albert M. Dean, 62-year-old father of the illustrious Dizzy and Paul, is in St. Louis for the World Series and is taking, in stride and with poise, the honors that go with being the father of the most famous brother combination in these United States.

Since you have read many humorous stories from the sticks, you are prepared for anything when you meet Mr. Dean. You are looking for an eccentric. But the Dean boys' father is a quiet-spoken, retired cotton picker and farm hand who is no more flustered by questions than is Will Rogers. Rawboned with the facial features of Dizzy, he shows in his gnarled hands that he has gone through the mill of hard work. But he is still erect. He has gray hair, blue eyes, and a deeply lined face. He wore a dark blue suit, a deep blue shirt, and a neat bow tie.

Had his sons been "good boys?"

"No man could ask for better sons," he replied.

"Dizzy was always a little stubborn, but if you could brag on him he would work his head off. You couldn't, however, get anywhere with severe methods. When he was a youngster I'd tan him until his back was on fire, but he would just get white mouthed and wouldn't budge. He had to be smoothed down.

"Paul"—and "Pa" Dean smiled. "Shucks, Paul never gave anyone any trouble. He was always agreeable.

"I had my hands full, trying to raise my three boys, but I always tried to do what I could for them. They went to Sunday school regularly—and stayed for preachin', too."

Had the two boys remembered their father since they had become prominent? Since a lame back had forced him to quit work four years ago?

"I've never wanted for anything," he replied. "They've sent money promptly when I asked for it, when I've run a little short. Remember, they haven't got a lot yet in spite of their fame. Next year, however, will be different."

What did he think they would be worth next year to the Cardinals?

"That's a question for them to settle," he answered. "As a baseball fan, and not a father, I would say that Dizzy would be worth $15,000 and Paul $10,000."

Wasn't a man who could win 30 games and had the drawing power of Dizzy worth more than $15,000?

"No," he answered. "I believe in doing the right thing. Fifteen thousand dollars seems to be a reasonable figure."

And come to think of it, $15,000 a year is not bad money for a man of 24.

Damon Kerby, *St. Louis Post-Dispatch*

∘ *Saturday, October 6* ∘

[*On October 5, in St. Louis, the Cardinals won Game 3 of the World Series, 4–1. Winning pitcher, Paul Dean; losing pitcher, Tom Bridges.*]

They moved the World Series to St. Louis, and the show went on in an atmosphere unlike that of any other city in the major leagues.

When the World Series comes to town there is a stirring and churning through the cotton belt and the southwest, and up they come, the nuts from the true baseball country where the ball players are raised for the big-city trade and acquire early schooling in the minor leagues. [*Until 1958, St. Louis was the southernmost and westernmost city with a major league baseball team.*]

Up they came to St. Louis and watched Daffy Dean, one of their own, lick the Tigers.

There were wide hats in the audience, and the high and whiny voice of the Texas and Oklahoma trade was heard in the uproar. A fat squaw in a green dress looked down from a seat near the press coop in the upper deck.

The World Series crowd was drawn from Arkansas, too, and rural Missouri and little towns in Tennessee and Mississippi, where nothing much happens and a World Series within driving distance is not to be missed. They know their baseball better because they have more weather for it than northerners. And there is a long spell between planting and picking when there isn't much to do but play ball or go to minor league games. You can't hurry cotton.

They had sent up the Dean boys and Schoolboy Rowe and Pepper Martin and a lot of others who worked in yesterday's entertainment. They knew them intimately way back when.

It was a curious demonstration of baseball, performed before the knowing, critical gaze of the most expert class of customers in the country. The Tigers avoided victory as though it were something dead, and continued to shy away from opportunities until Brother Daffy Dean realized that here was an unclaimed World Series game lying around and walked off with it himself. Brother Daffy could hardly help winning from a ball club which had 14 runners on base and twice had the bases full but scored only one run.

Brother Daffy didn't pitch much better than Tom Bridges, the unfortunate victim of the Tigers' indifference in the pinches, and Elon Hogsett, the Indian, who finished after Bridges lost heart in the fifth inning.

Daffy gave 8 hits, including a double and 2 triples, and walked 5 men and hit another. No pitcher who permits 14 men to get on base has any right to stand and acknowledge his own magnificence with any low sweeping bows, although Brother Daffy will do so, nevertheless.

The Dean boys live within Huey P. Long's zone of influence, and modesty is not among their vices. They admit that they are very good, and they have an exasperating knack of winning even when they aren't. They deride their enemies with scornful banter, and predict how badly they are going to lick them and then, like Huey, they do.

Brother Dizzy was down in the bullpen warming up just for exercise during the eighth and ninth innings. As the game ended, Brother Dizzy slung his sweater over his shoulder and walked up fast, shouldering ball players, customers, and policemen aside to intercept Daffy at the lip of the Cardinals' dugout. He placed his left hand on Daffy's shoulder, looked him dead in the eye, and solemnly acknowledged that next to his older brother, Daffy was the best pitcher in the world.

Yet neither of them pitched so well in winning the Cardinals' two games to date but that a little better attack would have beaten them. The Tigers this time were so bashful in emergencies that ball players in the stands could recognize them only by their uniforms. They were always on base, and the statistics favor them in all columns except the score. Hitters on both sides took toe holds and slammed long flies to the outfield which just barely weren't the material which runs are made of. Daffy wasn't much better than the humble journeymen he licked.

The Cardinals had made only two runs when they came to bat in the fifth, but Bridges seemed discouraged, since his teammates had left 11 men on base and couldn't give him even one run. Pepper Martin, a triple and a run to his credit already, led off with a double against the chicken wire in right field. He scored when Rothrock drove a long triple to the extreme left corner of the outfield. Frisch singled, scoring Rothrock, and Bridges was excused.

Hogsett walked slowly into the box, surveyed a gloomy situation calmly, and flexed his left arm with a few practice shots at Cochrane's mitt. He took firm control as Medwick hit into the first double play of the Series. Rip Collins then should have been out, but shortstop Rogell made a bad throw to first. Cochrane then caught him stealing.

The Tigers have been that way all through the Series. They kick the ball and have to fight their way out of trouble. They wait until two are out to start hitting.

They have the look of losers, whereas the Deans are overbearing even when mediocre.

Westbrook Pegler, Chicago *Daily News*

When the Cardinals reached their dressing room, they swarmed around Paul Dean, yelling and slapping him on the back. Dean sat in front of his locker, declaring he never was so tired in his life. He was dripping perspiration and puffing like a racehorse.

"They didn't give me much trouble," he said. "I was faster the last two innings than at any time during the game. I don't hold no ball club cheap, and that's the reason I beared down."

Someone asked if he was nervous pitching his first World Series game.

"Me nervous? Not me," he said. "There wasn't nothing to get nervous about. I wasn't right during the first part of the game. I had the lousiest curve today I ever had in my life."

Pepper Martin heard that remark and yelled, "Boy, but you certainly had a fast one."

Dean continued: "I guess the reason I wasn't working so good is because I've had too much rest. I ain't pitched in six days."

Charles Dunkley, St. Louis *Globe-Democrat*

∘ *Sunday, October 7* ∘

[*On October 6, in St. Louis, the Cardinals lost Game 4 of the World Series 10–4. Winning pitcher, Eldon Auker; losing pitcher, Bill Walker.*]

The shadow of a national sporting tragedy missed Sportsman's Park by the breath of the gods yesterday as the Tigers clawed and maimed five pitchers to trim the Cardinals.

The near tragedy of the wild and woolly afternoon came in the fourth inning when Frank Frisch took a monumental gamble by sending Dizzy Dean to run for Virgil Davis at first.

A moment later the wild roar of the big crowd faded to a stunning stillness as Dizzy lay unconscious on the field. On this startling play Pepper Martin rapped one to Gehringer. Gehringer tossed the ball to Bill Rogell, the Tiger shortstop, forcing Dean at second. Dean was still plowing at top speed on his way to the bag, just three feet away, with his head in the road, six feet three inches above the infield clay as Rogell attempted to complete the double play by whipping a fast one to Greenberg at first.

The speeding ball never found its first target. It struck Dizzy Dean squarely on the head with such terrific force that it bounded 30 feet into the air and more than 100 feet away into Hank Greenberg's glove in short right field. The impact of the ball and glove sounded like the backfire of an automobile. Rogell crowded everything he had into a fast throw, and when the leather struck Dean's skull the great Dizzy crumpled and fell like a marionette whose string had snapped.

A swarming rush of players surrounded the stricken star in less than two seconds, as a hush descended on 36,000 spectators who feared the worst.

Dean was carried half unconscious to the bench and put under a doctor's care, with a later announcement that he would be in shape again to carry on his Tiger hunt with an unfractured skull. The blow that floored Dizzy would have knocked down two elephants. The wonder is that the entire top of his head was not shot away at such close range.

This near-tragic episode was only one of a series of events that made this game one of the most ragged that ever crowded its way into a post-season championship.

It fell to the lot of Eldon Auker, a Jayhawker from Kansas, a football player under Bo McMillan at Kansas State, to face Tex Carleton, the football entry from Comanche, Tex.

Carleton once played for T.C.U. This was baffling for a moment. Here were two ex-collegians trying to steal the show from the brush and the sage—from the boys of the open road and the school of the harder way.

Auker deserved to win by a mile. He allowed only one earned run as three Cardinal tallies were kicked over the plate when Rogell lost a ground ball in the sun, hit Dean on the bean, and even Gehringer let Ernie Orsatti wreck a double play by pulling a Marty Brill blocking act by jolting the ball from Gehringer's grip. [*Marty Brill had been a great blocking back at Notre Dame and had played on Knute Rockne's last team, in 1930.*]

It was that type of game—crash and crack—dive and scramble—shoulder and spikes for those in the road.

The Cardinals got the jump in the second on Medwick's single and Collins' double. The Tigers came back for three in the third on Cochrane's double, passes to Gehringer and Goslin, and a rataplan of singles from Rogell, Greenberg, and Owen—three runs.

It might be mentioned that Rogell drove in four runs and Greenberg slapped in three for the largest hitting day of the Series. They were the pair that hacked and hammered at five Cardinal moundsmen—Carleton, Dazzy Vance, Bill Walker, Jess Haines, and Jim Mooney. This was the first shot Vance ever drew in a World Series since the Dazzler began with Red Cloud, Neb., back in 1912.

The old Dazzler allowed only one clean hit, and did well enough before Virgil Davis took his place at bat to make way for the play that came near costing Dizzy Dean his cupola or his conk.

The Tigers were leading, 5 to 4, when the Simoon blew in from Lake Michigan in the eighth. This was the big inning of the Series—five runs scored, giving a crushing lead to Auker still bearing down, his underhand delivery rolling back every attack in a game he might have won in a breeze if his infield had not handed the Cardinals three runs just when the going was rough.

While all this was taking place the redoubtable Pepper Martin was in the throes of an off day. Pepper purchased a quart of ice cream the night before, which he inhaled on the spot. In this game he blew himself to three errors and a high throw to first which might have been scored either way. [*Martin still holds the World Series record for the most errors by a third baseman in one game.*]

This is the sort of Series you won't forget. It carries all the elements and colors except lavender and old lace.

Grantland Rice, New York *Sun*

Yesterday we saw what was probably the greatest managerial World Series boner in the history of baseball. Frankie Frisch took a million dollar asset and used him on a ten cent job.

In the fourth inning, Virgil Davis, batting for Dazzy Vance, singled to right, scoring Orsatti from second. And then the crowd suddenly let out a loud yell. Here is what they saw. Dizzy Dean, grinning and spotless in his uniform. Dean, the pitcher who had won 30 games and pitched the Cardinals into the pennant, who had won his first Series game with but two days' rest, Dean who was sheer poison to the Tigers and probably the most valuable pitching asset a ball club ever had, was going in to run for Davis. The crowd thought it a great lark and yelled and cheered, and Dizzy roosted on the base with his features torn apart with a wide grin.

In the press box reporters looked at one another, puzzled. Dean to run? What for? The bat boy can run. Or any utility player or pinch hitter or pitcher. But Dean—the man on whom the Cardinals were depending to win the Series for them—in Heaven's name, why? A slide into second, a wrenched ankle, a spike cut, a bruised arm or torn ligament, or hurt shoulder, and there goes your star pitcher. Dean was worth fifty or sixty thousand dollars to the Cards on their Series cut alone. Frisch was wasting that money on a job that could have been filled by a $500 rookie. Why? No one will ever know. We all waited a little breathless, to see what would happen. Disaster struck like forked lightning and in a totally unexpected manner.

Incidentally, after Dean had been carried to the dressing room, his first question was, "Did they get Martin at first?"

Paul Gallico, New York *Daily News*

Frankie Frisch explained why he had used Dizzy Dean as a pinch runner.

"Dean kept pulling my sleeve and begging me to use him," Frisch said. "I knew that he was a fine runner and that I had used him as such before. I did not think it even remotely possible that he could be injured in such a role, so I consented and let him go." [*Once before during the 1934 season, Dean had been used as a pinch runner, on August 26, when, as on October 6, he ran for Virgil Davis.*]

Dizzy, apparently intoxicated with fame, saw another chance to get before his public, and he teased Frisch into letting him run. And that probably is the fundamental reason why he got into the game—and into trouble.

John E. Wray, *St. Louis Post-Dispatch*

St. Louis, Oct. 6 (AP)—The Dean brothers have now suffered the penalty of greatness—a police guard.

It came about because of Dizzy's indiscretion when he was leaving Sportsman's Park after the game yesterday. [*Friday, October 5*]. Two

smartly dressed young men offered him a lift to his hotel in their automobile, which bore New York license plates. Dizzy hopped in.

Sam Breadon, president of the Cardinals, witnessed the incident and
sent a frantic messenger after his pitching ace.

"Do you know these men?" demanded Breadon when the messenger
returned, Dizzy in tow.

"No, they're just fans," Dizzy replied.

Maybe that is all they were, but Breadon lectured the pitcher about
gamblers and kidnappers, and sent him to the hotel in a cab. After that he
called police and arranged for a guard.

The great Dizzy was proud of his escort and introduced the policeman
by name to all he met. Each introduction was followed by a gesture of the
thumb, and a whisper, "He's guarding me."

The New York Times

° *Monday, October 8* °

[*On October 7, in St. Louis, the Cardinals lost Game 5 of the World Series,
3–1. Winning pitcher, Tom Bridges; losing pitcher, Dizzy Dean.*]

The fifth game of the World Series was a grand clash of theories, some of
which were knocked down and trampled on before the afternoon was over.

Manager Frank Frisch sent the eminent Dizzy Dean to the mound. Dizzy
had been hit on the head with a thrown ball and had spent the night in a
hospital. With no hands to shake, no score cards to autograph, no speeches
to make, and no visitors allowed. It was the quietest night that the great
Jerome Herman had enjoyed in a month. And the longest sleep. He reported that he was bubbling over with good health, and Manager Frisch
tossed him into the fray, confident that, sick or well, Dizzy could beat any
team. Manager Frisch had the further theory that if by accident the Series
went to seven games Jerome Herman could come strutting back after one
day's rest and blow down the Tigers.

That was the Frisch plan of battle. The first theory of Gordon Stanley
Cochrane was a negative one. He refused to send Schoolboy Rowe against
the Cardinal ace. His next theory was positive. He sent Tommy Bridges of
Tennessee back against the Cardinals on the theory that when Tom was
chased by a ball club he nursed a deep grudge and regularly got revenge by
coming back off the ropes and giving them a dreadful dusting.

Manager Frisch had still another theory under his cap. He had noticed that Ernie Orsatti in the outfield didn't know what to do in a 12-mile breeze. When fly balls were hit his way, Ernie was tacking to starboard when he should have gone to port. Manager Frisch had the theory that Chick Fullis would be a safer man in a strong breeze or even light airs, and Chick accordingly took a station in center field.

Of these theories, Cochrane's stood up, and Frisch's were knocked out of shape, if not actually flattened. The great Jerome Herman was not good enough to hold the aroused Tigers in check and did not even finish. Still, he didn't go down under a heavy fire or hoist the white flag of surrender. He was withdrawn to let Pat Crawford swing for him in the eighth round of a close but losing battle.

Manager Frisch's theory on the replacement of Ernie Orsatti by Chick Fullis proved to be half right, which wasn't enough. Chick was better out there on fly balls, but Manager Frisch's theory didn't cover ground balls. Neither did Fullis. Chick let one drift by in the second inning, and it helped the Detroiters get their first run. He let another go right through him in the sixth, and this was directly responsible for the third Tiger run.

This second or subordinate theory of Frank Frisch upset his No. 1 or main theory. If Fullis hadn't shown his fancy footwork in center field, the teams might have played right into the dark of an October night dead-locked at 1–1.

Charley Gehringer had hoisted a homer to the right field pavilion roof in the sixth inning. Bill DeLancey hit a duplicate of that blow in the seventh. There was no way of charging off those runs. They could be put down in red ink and debited to the rival pitchers.

But Fullis should have held Pete Fox's blow in the second inning to a single. He couldn't pick it up, and it went for a double, allowing Greenberg to score from first base. Two were out at the time, and the next batter was Bridges, who was up to his regular batting form and struck out.

In the sixth inning Rogell singled straight over second base, and Fullis came dashing in to meet the ball. Somehow they never met. The ball hopped by and went to the flagpole against the center field bleachers. Rogell reached third and trotted home on Greenberg's fly to right.

It can't be that the knock on his head hurt the great Jerome Herman to any extent. He was good, but Tom Bridges was just a bit better and de-served to win, with or without Chick Fullis' assistance.

Tennessee Tom scattered seven hits. Only in the ninth did two of them come in one inning. He didn't give a base on balls all afternoon. Tom had them popping up or grounding out most of the time. He was ahead of the hitters all the way and was ahead of Dizzy Dean when the great one was called off in favor of a pinch-hitter. Mickey Cochrane guessed right on Tennessee Tom, and now he is confident that nothing can halt the Tigers today except rain.

John Kieran, *The New York Times*

Bill DeLancey last night was reported fined $200 by Umpire Brick Owens for uncomplimentary remarks in yesterday's game, but Commissioner Landis said he alone could assess a fine and knew nothing of the matter.

Announcement of the fine was made by Mickey Cochrane, who said it was inflicted while DeLancey was fanning on three called strikes in the ninth.

When Owens called the first strike on DeLancey, according to Cochrane, the Redbird catcher snapped out a few short cuss words, and Owens told him it would cost him a $50 fine.

"Why don't you make it $100, you thievin' bum," DeLancey yelled back.

"A hundred it is," Owens retorted.

"Make it two," DeLancey screamed.

"Two it is," came back Owens.

Cochrane ended the argument by reminding DeLancey he'd better keep his mouth shut or he wouldn't have any World Series check coming. [*Since Landis did not levy a fine against him, and since the umpire had no right to do this, Bill DeLancey did not lose any money because of this incident.*]

St. Louis *Globe-Democrat*

∘ *Tuesday, October 9* ∘

[*On October 8, in Detroit, the Cardinals won Game 6, 4–3. Winning pitcher, Paul Dean; losing pitcher, Schoolboy Rowe.*]

The Schoolboy flunked his homework, and the big baseball debate will go into the final clinch. Oklahoma won out over Arkansas when Daffy of the Deans outpitched the El Dorado scholar and tied up the Series in a bitter battle.

What hurt Lynwood T. Rowe was that he could not suppress Lippy Leo Durocher, whose batting record long ago earned him the sobriquet of

"The All-American Out." Through the early games of this Series there were some queries as to why Lippy Leo carried all that lumber when he went up to the plate. It was a weight on his shoulders. He is none too strong. He could have done just as well bare-handed. [*In the first four games of the World Series, Durocher had one hit, a single, in sixteen times at bat. The jeering remarks concerning Durocher, the weakest hitting regular on the St. Louis team, might be contrasted with the relatively mild tone of the press and television response to Mike Schmidt, the Philadelphia Phillies' most powerful hitter—who earns an annual salary of $900,000—after he had completed the 1983 World Series with one bloop single and no RBI's in twenty times at bat.*]

Then Lippy Leo came up with a good hit on Sunday, and yesterday he really got into the spirit of things. He went up there as though he meant to hit. He didn't hem and haw or pull down his cap or scratch the dirt from his cleats. He took a toe-hold like a determined hitter and pounded the ball solidly for three hits. He scored two runs and paved the way for another. Now he has something to talk about, not that it makes any difference to Lippy Leo. At all times he talks fluently with or without cause or reason. Lippy Leo will never be crippled until his voice gives out.

Gordon Stanley (Mickey himself) Cochrane was sitting in the driver's seat. Now he is in a depression, if not a deep hole. Coming back to the jubilant home city of the Tigers, he figured to shoot the Schoolboy at the Cardinals and cinch the Series. Well, the Schoolboy didn't pass his test, and the seesaw Series goes into the final game with the Cardinals holding an edge in the eyes of most observers.

When Rowe wavered, Manager Mike did his best to win the game single-handed. He was all alone in his early attack on Daffy of the Deans. He singled in the first, singled in the third, and singled again in the sixth. Up to that time he was the only Detroit batter to hit safely. They were hot smashes that burned the fingers of the Cardinals' infielders.

The Cardinals teed up on Rowe in the very first inning and scored a quick run on Rothrock's double and Medwick's single. The Tigers evened the score in the third when Daffy walked Jo-Jo White with two out. It's always a mistake to walk White because as soon as somebody walks him he starts running.

Jo-Jo tore down toward second in an attempt to steal. Finding Frank Frisch there waiting for him with the ball, Jo-Jo took out the old Fordham Flash with a rolling block. Those Tigers have been hitting the bases and the basemen hard since Manager Mike spoke to them about their ladylike sauntering in the first three games.

So Jo-Jo White knocked Frisch for a row of revolving samovars and continued to third base when the ball dribbled away from the scene of the crime. It was easy for him to score on Cochrane's smash to Rip Collins that went for a hit.

That run tied the score, but it may have cost the Tigers ultimate victory because Manager Mike crashed heavily into first base running out his hit and was spiked on the knee by Daffy Dean, who had run over to cover.

There was some fear that they would have to gather up Mickey and trundle him off in a barrow, but the injured leg was the same one that Muscles Medwick had battered earlier in the Series. Mike still had one leg left. He was determined to hobble along on that one.

Where it really hurt was in the sixth inning. The Cards jumped on Rowe again in the fifth, led by Lippy Leo Durocher. On hits by Durocher and Pepper Martin and a bad throw by Goslin, they had scored two runs and were leading, 3–1.

In the Tiger sixth, White was first man up, and Daffy of the Deans presented him with another free ticket to first, despite the foolishness of such a procedure as proved in the third inning. Cochrane nearly tore the glove off the hand of Ripper Collins with a wicked smash for a single, and White waltzed around to third. Gehringer dribbled a grounder through the box that Daffy muffed, and the Tiger rooters were in a frenzy of delight. White had scored, Cochrane was on second, Gehringer on first, and none out.

A sacrifice bunt was the play, and Goslin tried it. But limping Mike with the game leg couldn't get down to third before Catcher DeLancey had picked up the bunt and ferried it to Pepper Martin for a force play. Hank Greenberg's smashing single sent Gehringer home to tie the score, but Cochrane's lameness spoiled a great chance for the Tigers to clinch the Series then and there.

The Cardinals came right back and added a run in their half of the seventh. With one out, Durocher banged a rousing double to deep right-center and rode home in style when Daffy either accidentally or on purpose singled to right. In any event, he did single, and the boys might as well have gone to the showers right there. The game was over.

It was an exciting festival for Dean the Younger, and he had himself to blame for the hot spots. He gave two bases on balls that were turned into runs. But he came through right side up with a wide grin. He had beaten Schoolboy Rowe, he had tied up the Series, and he had won his own game with a hit to right that drove in the deciding marker.

Seeing that the Deans have accounted for the three Cardinals' victories,

Dizzy and Daffy are trying to talk Manager Frisch into letting them pitch the seventh game, separately or together. As Dizzy remarked, "This is a family matter."

John Kieran, *The New York Times*

Kids out of school, a torrent rushing over a dam, madmen on the loose, that's how the Cardinals stormed into the dressing room. Uniforms were all but torn off, sweaty bodies engaged in bumping matches that threatened the permanency of the very walls.

"You can have anything I got," screamed Dizzy Dean. He hurled himself on his brother, and wrestled him to the floor. "Oh, baby, what a guy you are! What a guy, what a pitcher!"

Arms wrenched "Diz" free from Paul's body, not to let the youngster rise but to serve as a fresh outlet for a frenzy of emotions. Orsatti, Martin, Collins flung themselves on the younger Dean to pound home their congratulations. Ol' Mike Gonzalez, his gold teeth outglaring the blinding flashlights, stood in the center of the rom, repeating, "Who says we're dead?"

Frankie Frisch sat in sodden fatigue, his shirt half off, his locks matted into porcupine quills. He was too tired even to breathe, but a wan little smile testified to his joy over Paul's victory that may save the world's title for the Cardinals.

"Dean tomorrow, the other Dean?" we asked.

"If I last till tomorrow, maybe," he said. "Dean or Hallahan. I don't know yet."

Dean or Hallahan, but it will be "Dizzy" you can bet all the tea in China. Wild horses won't keep him on the bench. In the end Frisch will say yes because he can't say no. It's his best bet, and after tomorrow there is no tomorrow at all. Under a sputtering shower the "Dizzy" one washed soap from his eyes and hollered, "The greatest pitcher the Dean family ever had, that kid brother of mine. Didn't he prove it? Didn't he?"

Over in a corner, "Rip" Collins sat, opening a letter. It was an anniversary card. "Married 12 years ago today," he smiled. "I couldn't give my wife a better present."

John P. Carmichael, Chicago *Daily News*

In the Tiger clubhouse the ludicrous expressions on the faces of Graham McNamee and the moving picture men was worth a stiff admission price. [*Graham McNamee was the first nationally known sports broadcaster. He was*

behind the microphone in Yankee Stadium in the first month of its first season,
April 1923, for the initial broadcast of a major league baseball game, and
later in the same year he was the announcer for the first World Series broad-
cast.] They had a setup worthy of a Belasco. [*David Belasco was a theatrical*
producer who had died in 1931.] Kleig lights, wires, huge cameras, and
other paraphernalia were scattered all over the place, waiting to have
Mickey Cochrane say for posterity just how he won the World Series.

Instead, there was poor Mickey lying on a table with a doctor and trainer
working over the long cut on his kneecap inflicted by Daffy Dean's spikes.

St. Louis Post-Dispatch

∘ *Wednesday, October 10* ∘

[*On October 9, in Detroit, the Cardinals won the baseball world's champion-*
ship by beating the Tigers, 11–0. Winning pitcher, Dizzy Dean; losing pitcher,
Eldon Auker.]

The dizziest, maddest, wildest, and most exciting World Series game
played in recent years began with a seven-run batting rally in the third
inning that gave the Cardinals the championship of the world for 1934,
was interrupted by one of the wildest riots ever seen in a ball park in the
sixth inning, and wound up, of all things, with the spectators engaging in
an old-fashioned pillow fight in which for a half an hour the populace
stood around and hurled seat cushions at one another. For the first time
that I know of, the crowd forced a manager to remove a player from the
field. Twenty thousand people massed a-slant in the left field bleachers
turned into a deadly and vicious mob. Only the barrier of a steel screen
and locked gates prevented them from pouring into the field and mobbing
Outfielder Joe Medwick, who bears the incongruous nickname of Ducky
Wucky.

In the sixth inning, with Pepper Martin on second and two out, Medwick hit a triple against the center field fence and slid into third base.
Marvin Owen stepped on him, but whether by intent or accident, no one
could tell. But there was no mistaking Medwick's ideas as he lay on the
ground on his back and suddenly began lashing out at Owen's legs with his
spiked feet. One-two-three, his feet flashed, and then he kicked with both
together like Joe Savoldi. [*A former Notre Dame fullback, "Jumping Joe"*

Savoldi was then a professional wrestler, noted for his "flying drop-kick," in which he hurled himself feet-first at his opponent.]

Then they were at one another, with Umpire Bill Klem in the middle. The coaches stepped in. The other players ran over, and what is known as "cooler heads" prevailed. The Cardinals swarmed from the dugout, a red mob, but returned immediately. Klem must have seen provocation for Medwick, for neither man was punished. Medwick held out his hand to Owen. The Tiger third baseman refused it petulantly and returned to his station. Medwick remained on third and scored on Collins' single. De-Lancey struck out, ending the inning. The teams changed places, and without the slightest warning the dangerous storm broke.

Medwick began to jog out to his position in left field. In an instant the entire bleacher section, a tall, sloping stand holding 20,000, was on its feet blasting him to a standstill with a wave of booing that broke over his head like a comber curling over a lone swimmer. He came closer, and 40,000 arms were lifted against him, waving him back. Then a single red apple flew from the crowd and rolled at his feet, and Medwick fielded it lazily and gracefully, the way an infielder scoops up an easy grounder, and threw it back to the fence. The next moment the air was full of flying fruit—apples, oranges, bananas—and beer and pop bottles, the fruit squashing and breaking into little bits, the ugly brown and white bottles striking the turf and rolling over and over.

I watched the crowd and Medwick and the pelting missiles through my field glasses, and it was a terrifying sight. Every face in the crowd, women and men, was distorted with rage. Mouths were torn wide, open eyes glistened and shone in the sun. All fists were clenched. Medwick stood grinning with his hands on his hips, just out of range of the bottles. A green apple rolled to his feet, and he fielded that, too. Umpires and attendants rushed out to left field and began picking up the mess. Medwick came back to the diamond. One cameraman ran out and leveled his box at the patch of inflamed and angry people all afire with mob hatred. In a moment cameramen were all over the field. Medwick and Pepper Martin began to play a little game of pop-ball between themselves, Martin making the ball bounce off his biceps into Medwick's hand and Medwick whipping it up behind his back to Martin. The crowd began to chant in a swelling, choleric chorus, "Take him out, take him out!"

For the second time Medwick started for his position, and the storm broke with renewed fury, with more bottles and less fruit. The outfield was covered with attendants with bags picking up the glassware as fast as it landed. One of them narrowly escaped being hit on the head. Someone in the dugout had sense enough to send out a sweater to Dizzy Dean, whose arm was getting cold.

Again Medwick returned to the diamond while the field was cleared, and then for the third time he tried to take his position. And he did a pretty brave thing. He trotted out and turned his back on the stands. Mobs are rank cowards, and the sight of courage inflames them beyond all reason. By far the most dangerous peal of rage broke from them this third time. Heavy milk bottles flew onto the field. The police stood quietly by against the fence along the bottom row and did nothing. "Take him out! Take him out!" The chant echoed and re-echoed like a football yell. Mickey Cochrane ran half way into left field, and with one gesture tried to pacify the mob. It had no more effect than throwing a pebble into the ocean. Cochrane returned to the diamond. The umpires walked around helplessly.

Judge Landis from his box beckoned to Medwick, Frisch, and Owen. They trotted into his box between home and first base. Umpire Klem joined them. There was a short discussion. Landis did the sane and reasonable thing. Flames were creeping near a powder mine. He extinguished that flame by asking Frisch to remove Medwick. Then only did this mad game continue.

During the next inning, Medwick, with a police escort, walked across the field and into the dugout. Once more the boos thundered. One more bottle was hurled at him, and then he vanished and the crowd was satisfied. Unheard-of in the annals of baseball, IT had worked its will, IT had taken an active and potentially terrible part in the game. When the thing was done, the poor Tigers had been soundly whipped by the humiliating score of 11 to 0.

Paul Gallico, *New York Daily News*

In the wake of Western dust, blown up by the two cyclonic Deans, the St. Louis Cardinals take their place today on the top plateau of baseball.

Riding along on the rubbery, loose-jointed arm of the dazzling Dizzy, they cut their way to the front through six Tiger pitchers and a wild and savage barrage of beer bottles, oranges, and other hurtling implements composed of fruit, wood, iron, and glass thrown from the left field bleachers, which turned the game into a woolly riot that looked like the two battles of the Marne, with Verdun and Tannenberg thrown in. [*The reference is to battles waged in World War I.*]

Sling-shot Dizzy slaughtered the Tigers as he held them to six scattered hits, but it remained for Ducky Wucky Medwick to steal a big part of the show and start one of the neatest young riots that any World Series has ever known.

After the riot or whatnot it was the two country kids from Oklahoma who took charge of this show with all the mastery of a Booth or a Barrett, a George M. Cohan or a Walter Huston, a Mansfield or an Arliss. [*Edwin Booth and Laurence Barrett were nineteenth-century actors; Walter Huston and George Arliss were popular actors during the first part of the present century, George M. Cohan was America's most famous song-and-dance man and Richard Mansfield was a noted nineteenth-century English actor.*]

In spite of fines and suspensions and brotherly strikes, they carved their way to 49 victories. On top of this the two kids from the brush and the bush, from the dust and sage of the Southwest, won all 4 Cardinal victories—4 winning charges in 5 starts—for one of the most amazing dramatic drives beneath the great white spotlight that sport has ever known—and you can go back 4,000 years if you have the energy and time.

"I've got to keep up with Paul," Dizzy said before the game. "I'd like to win anyhow—I always like to win—but I can't let Paul down. He carried us to the seventh game. It's my time now, and if I have to I'll just throw my arm off to show the two Deans still move together. I wouldn't let Paul down for the world. A great pitcher? Sure, I know that. But he's a great kid on the side. They don't come along like Paul. He's the finest kid you ever met."

As the bulky figure of Babe Ruth fades out of the picture, an old-fashioned schooner fading into the fog, two kids from the dust of the Western trail take his place as the greatest sensations baseball has known—matching the glamour of Mathewson, Hans Wagner, Ty Cobb, and Babe Ruth.

But these two country kids have come along with a sudden blaze and flame that surpasses in its dramatic flourish the leaders of the old parade. In one brief six months, they have called upon two strong right arms to write one of the greatest of all sporting classics.

And in the midst of the Dean triumph, don't overlook Pepper Martin, who came back with a rushing, rowdy, ripping attack to regain the place he held a few years ago as one of the best ball players that ever carved and slashed and ripped his way from goatdom to the purple toga. Except that the Pepper's interest in a purple toga would be less than nothing with his baggy trousers, open shirt, and a front piece that has only casual interest in a razor.

What a ball player!

And in spite of his banishment I'll say the same for Ducky Wucky Medwick, the Cardinal Cossack, who plays the game up to the hilt of flying spikes. Did Detroit ever see Ty Cobb along the base paths?

The Tigers today know how Bill Terry's Giants and the rest of the National League must have suffered. The twin poisons of sport carried their venom to the final out.

Grantland Rice, New York *Sun*

(AP)—The world champion Cardinals will receive $5,941.19 each as their share of the World Series receipts, while each of the Detroit Tigers will get $4,313.90. The shares include receipts from the radio rights, sold to the Ford Motor Company for $100,000.

The Cardinals split their receipts 25 ways; the Tigers divided theirs into 23 shares. The Cardinals also voted $3,000 in donations to club attendants, cutting their actual shares to $5,821.19 each. [*The twenty-five Cardinal shares included the twenty-three active players and Coaches Gonzalez and Wares.*]

St. Louis *Globe-Democrat*

Frank Frisch: "They sure made it hot for us this year, but the Cardinals came through in great style clear to the end when we needed every ounce of energy to win. We needed it, and we had it. There's the story in a nutshell. It seems as though the team lines up just as well as they do on the ball field. Here's our line-up on smoking: 21 out of 23 Cardinals prefer Camels."

"Rip" Collins: "Poling out home runs takes a lot of energy—a Camel has a way of turning on my energy."

Joe Medwick: "Smoking Camels takes away the tired feeling as soon as I leave the field, and turns on my 'pep' again."

Dizzy Dean: "Smoking a Camel sure brings back your energy after a hard game."

"Pepper" Martin: "I can smoke all the Camels I want without upsetting my nerves."

Paul Dean: "A Camel gives me the feeling of having more energy and never gives me jumpy nerves."

From a full-page newspaper advertisement

○ *Index* ○

Entries of particular significance
are followed by an asterisk (*).

313